_____

By

_____

On the Occasion of

_____

Date

_____

RENEW MY HEART

Daily Devotional Insights from the Writings of John Wesley

COMPILED BY ALICE RUSSIE

BARBOUR
PUBLISHING

ISBN 1-59310-376-X

Published by Barbour Publishing, Inc., P.O. Box 719, Uhrichsville, Ohio 44683, www.barbourbooks.com

Our mission is to publish and distribute inspirational products offering exceptional value and biblical encouragement to the masses.

 Member of the
Evangelical Christian
Publishers Association

Printed in the United States of America.
5 4 3 2

Dedicated to God
in grateful appreciation for
John Wesley and
those ministers of the gospel
"who follow in his train."

About John Wesley

Short though he was, the Reverend John Wesley stands head and shoulders above others of his time. God used John and his hymn-writing brother Charles to shake England with the scriptural, evangelical truths of grace, faith, repentance, justification, and sanctification. A revival of major proportion spilled out of London into thousands of hamlets, towns, and cities throughout the British Isles, even across the Atlantic to the American colonies.

John Wesley was born in 1703 in Epworth, Lincolnshire, into the large family of an Anglican clergyman. He was educated at Oxford and ordained to the Anglican priesthood. On a missionary voyage to Georgia, he met some German Moravians, by whose piety and simple, steadfast faith he was deeply impressed. When he returned to London, he was helped greatly by a Moravian, Peter Böhler, and in 1738 John reported his "heart strangely warmed" while someone was reading from Martin Luther's "Preface to Romans." He said he then knew that God had, for Christ's sake, forgiven his sins.

He immediately began preaching with a new fervor, and soon pulpits of the Church of England began closing to him. Encouraged by the Reverend George Whitefield, he began "field preaching," thus reaching the most neglected classes of English society. His listeners often numbered in the thousands; crowds of 30,000 were reported more than once.

For more than fifty years, Wesley went up and down England and Wales and into Scotland and made numerous voyages across the Irish Sea to Ireland. He preached the gospel unceasingly and wrote voluminously; he also organized believers and inquirers into "societies." These societies were visited in "circuit" by Mr. Wesley, or by those itinerant preachers appointed by and associated with him in the work. Later, after his death, these societies became the backbone of the infant Methodist Church.

The Wesleyan revival drew its power from John's and Charles's emphasis in sermon and song upon an "experimental" (we would say *experiential*) living faith. John repeatedly spoke and wrote of the "faith that worketh by love" which produced a changed heart and life: inward and outward holiness. Although he responded incisively to critics whenever his preaching was attacked in the press, John Wesley did not concern himself with philosophical or speculative theology. He was too busy warning people to "flee from the wrath to come" and urging them to follow after perfect love—loving God with all their heart, mind, soul, and strength.

John Wesley died in London in 1791. Having murmured, "God be merciful to me a sinner," he passed into his Master's presence crying, "Best of all, God is with us."

Preface

From John Wesley's own Preface to
Sermons on Several Occasions, 1746

"I have thought, I am a creature of a day, passing through life as an arrow through the air. I am a spirit come from God, and returning to God: just hovering over the great gulf; till, a few moments hence, I am no more seen; I drop into an unchangeable eternity! I want to know one thing—the way to heaven; how to land safe on that happy shore.

"God Himself has condescended to teach the way; for this very end He came from heaven. He hath written it down in a book. O give me that book! At any price, give me the book of God! I have it: Here is knowledge enough for me. Let me be *homo unius libri* (a man of one book).

"Here then I am, far from the busy ways of men. I sit down alone: Only God is here. In His presence I open, I read His book; for this end, to find the way to heaven. Is there a doubt concerning the meaning of what I read? Does anything appear dark or intricate? I lift up my heart to the Father of Lights: 'Lord, is it not Thy Word, "If any man lack wisdom, let him ask of God?" Thou "givest liberally, and upbraidest not." Thou hast said, "If any be willing to do Thy will, he shall know." I am willing to do, let me know, Thy will.'

"I then search after and consider parallel passages of Scripture, 'comparing spiritual things with spiritual.' I meditate thereon with all the attention and earnestness of which my mind is capable. If any doubt still remains, I consult those who are experienced in the things of God; and then the writings whereby, being dead, they yet speak. And what I thus learn, that I teach.

"(Yet) how far is love, even with many wrong opinions, to be preferred before truth itself without love! We may die without the knowledge of many truths and yet be carried into Abraham's bosom. But, if we die without love, what will knowledge avail? Just as much as it avails the devil and his angels.

"The God of love forbid we should ever make the trial! May He prepare us for the knowledge of all truth, by filling our hearts with all His love, and with all joy and peace in believing!"

NOTE: Within the readings, references in parentheses, same size type, are those appearing in the Reverend Wesley's original sermons. References added by the compiler, for clarification, appear as "see. . .(reference)," also in parentheses, but in smaller size type.

Salvation by Faith

By grace you have been saved through faith.
EPHESIANS 2:8 NASB

All the blessings which God has bestowed upon men and women are of His mere grace, bounty, or favor—His free, undeserved favor, *altogether* undeserved—we have no claim to the least of His mercies.

It was free grace that "formed man of the dust of the ground and breathed into him a living soul," then stamped on that soul the image of God and "put all things under his feet." The same free grace continues to us at this day life and breath and all things. There is nothing we are, or have, or do which can deserve the smallest thing from His hand.

"All our works, You, God, have wrought in us." These, therefore, are so many more instances of free mercy: And whatever righteousness may be found in us, this is also the gift of God.

The *gift of God* is that *you have been saved through faith.* Neither this faith nor this salvation is owing to any works you ever did, will, or can do. *For we are His workmanship* (v. 10) shows that salvation is by faith, and that faith is the gift of God.

Grace is both the beginning and end. This lays the axe to the very root of spiritual pride and all glorying in ourselves. Grace, without any respect to human worthiness, confers the glorious gift. Faith, with an empty hand, without any pretense to personal merit, receives the heavenly blessing.

Grace upon Grace

All have sinned and fall short of the glory of God.

ROMANS 3:23 NASB

How, then, shall a sinful man or woman atone for even the least of their sins? With their own works? No. If their deeds are ever so many or "holy," they are not theirs but God's. But indeed, their works are all unholy and sinful themselves, so that every one of them needs a fresh atonement. Only corrupt fruit grows on a corrupt tree. And their hearts are altogether corrupt and abominable—being short of the glory of God, the glorious righteousness at first impressed on their souls like the image of their great Creator. Therefore, having nothing, neither righteousness nor good works, to plead, their mouths are utterly stopped before God.

So if sinful men and women find favor with God, it is grace upon grace! If God grants still to pour fresh blessings upon us, yes, even the greatest of all blessings, salvation, what can we say to these things, but "Thanks be unto God for His unspeakable gift!"

And so it is. "God commendeth His love toward us, in that, while we were yet sinners, Christ died" to save us. Only by grace, then, are we saved through faith.

Grace is the source, faith the condition, of salvation; and both are gifts of His bountiful love.

Saving Faith: More Than These

That we may be justified by faith.
GALATIANS 3:24 NASB

So that we fall not short of the grace of God, we need carefully to inquire what is that faith through which we are saved; for it is more than (goes beyond) all these:

First, it is not merely the faith of a heathen, whom God requires to believe "that God is; that He is a rewarder of them that diligently seek Him"; and that He is to be sought by glorifying Him as God, by giving Him thanks for all things, and by a careful practice of moral virtue, of justice, mercy, and truth, toward their fellow creatures.

Nor, secondly, is it the faith of a devil, though this goes much farther than that of a heathen. The devil believes not only that there is a wise and powerful God, gracious to reward and just to punish; but also that Jesus is the Son of God, the Christ, the Savior of the world. And he trembles in believing that Christ will tread all enemies under His feet, and that all Scripture is given by inspiration of God.

Thirdly, the faith by which we are saved is not barely that which the apostles themselves had while Christ was yet upon earth. They so believed Him as to leave all and follow Him; being granted power to work miracles and to heal all manner of disease; power and authority over all devils; even being sent by their Master to preach the kingdom of God.

Yet, *saving faith* is more than all these.

Saving Faith

> *You have been saved through faith.*
> EPHESIANS 2:8 NASB

This faith through which we are saved is, first, a faith in Christ. Christ and God through Christ are the proper objects of it, by which it is absolutely distinguished from the faith of ancient or modern heathens.

From the faith of a devil it is fully distinguished by this: It is not a speculative, rational, lifeless assent, a train of ideas in the head; but a disposition of the heart. For the Scripture says, "If you confess with your mouth the Lord Jesus and *believe in your heart* that God has raised Him from the dead, you will be saved" (see Romans 10:9 NKJV).

Saving faith differs also from that faith which the apostles themselves had while our Lord was on earth in that it acknowledges His death as the only sufficient means of redeeming us from death eternal, and His resurrection as our restoration to life and immortality. For He was delivered for our sins and rose again for our justification.

Christian (saving) faith is not only an assent to the whole gospel of Christ, but also a full reliance on the blood of Christ—a trust in the merits of His life, death, and resurrection, a leaning upon Him as our atonement and our life—*as given for us* and *living in us*. And consequently, a closing with Him, and a cleaving to Him as our "wisdom, righteousness, sanctification, and redemption," or in one word, our salvation.

Saved from Sin

For by grace are ye saved through faith;
and that not of yourselves:
it is the gift of God.
EPHESIANS 2:8 KJV

What is the salvation which is through this faith?

First, whatever else it implies, it is a *present* salvation. It is something attainable, yes, actually attained, on earth, by those who are partakers of this faith. Note the words of the apostle to the believers at Ephesus, and in them to the believers of all ages, not *You shall be* (though that also is true), but you *"are saved through faith."*

You *are saved* (to comprise all in one word) from sin. This is the salvation which is through faith. This is that great salvation foretold by the angel, before God brought His First begotten into the world: "You shall call His name JESUS for He shall save His people from their sins." And neither here, nor in other parts of holy writ, is there any limitation or restriction: All His people, or as elsewhere expressed, "all that believe in Him," He saves from all their sins; from original and actual, past and present sin, "of the flesh and of the spirit." Through faith that is in Him, they are saved both from the guilt of sin and from the power of it.

Saved from Guilt

That [faith is] not of yourselves,
it is the gift of God.
EPHESIANS 2:8 NASB

All who are partakers of the salvation which is by this faith are saved from the guilt of all past sin. All the world is guilty before God, so much that should He be extreme to mark what is done amiss, there is none who could stand before Him. For by the law is only knowledge of sin, but no deliverance from it. So that even by fulfilling the deeds of the law no one can be justified in His sight.

Yet now the righteousness of God—which is by faith of Jesus Christ—is revealed unto all who believe. Now they are justified freely by His grace, through the redemption that is in Jesus Christ.

This Jesus has God set forth to be a propitiation, a complete satisfaction for our sins, through faith in His blood, to demonstrate His righteousness by the forgiveness of sins previously committed.

Christ has taken away the curse of the law by being made a curse for us. He wiped out the handwriting that was against us, taking it out of the way, nailing it to His cross.

And so, there is therefore now no condemnation to those who believe in Christ Jesus.

Saved from Fear

In whom we have boldness
and confident access through faith in Him.
EPHESIANS 3:12 NASB

Being saved from guilt, those who are partakers of this salvation by faith are saved from fear. Not, indeed, from a filial fear of offending but from all servile fear: from the fear which has torment, fear of punishment, fear of the wrath of God, whom they no longer regard as a severe Master but as an indulgent Father.

They have not received the spirit of bondage but the Spirit of adoption, whereby they cry *Abba, Father*. The Holy Spirit Himself bears witness with their spirits that they are children of God.

They are also saved from the fear, though not from the possibility, of falling away from the grace of God, and coming short of the great and precious promises. Thus, they have peace with God through our Lord Jesus Christ. They rejoice in hope of the glory of God. And the love of God is poured out in their hearts through the Holy Spirit who is given unto them.

And by this they are persuaded (though perhaps not always with the same fullness of persuasion) that neither death, nor life, nor things present, nor things to come, nor height, nor depth, nor any other thing shall be able to separate them from the love of God, which is in Christ Jesus, our Lord.

Saved from the Power of Sin

We know that anyone born of God
does not continue to sin.
1 JOHN 5:18 NIV

Those who are partakers of this faith, are, through it, saved from the power of sin, as well as from the guilt of it. The apostle declares, "You know that He was manifested to take away our sins, and in Him there is no sin. Whoever abides in Him does not sin" (1 John 3:5–6 NKJV). Again, "Dear children, do not let anyone lead you astray. . . . He who does what is sinful is of the devil. . . . Whoever believes. . .is born of God. . . . And no one who is born of God will continue to sin" (1 John 3:7–9 NIV and 5:1 NASB).

One who is thus born of God does not sin (1) by any habitual sin; for all habitual sin is sin reigning: But sin cannot *reign* in any who believes. Nor (2) by any willful sin: For, while he abides in the faith, his will is utterly set against all sin, and he abhors it as deadly poison. Nor (3) by any sinful desire; for he continually desires the holy and perfect will of God; and any tendency to an unholy desire, he, by the grace of God, stifles in the birth. Nor (4) does he sin by infirmities, whether in act, word, or thought, for his infirmities have no concurrence of his will, and without this they are not properly sins.

Thus, one who is born of God "does not sin": And though one cannot say he has not sinned, yet now he does not sin.

Justified by Faith; Born of the Spirit

A man is not justified by observing the law,
but by faith in Jesus Christ.
GALATIANS 2:16 NIV

This is the salvation which is through faith: a salvation from sin even in this present world, and from the (eternal) consequences of sin, both often expressed in the word *justification*.

Taken in the largest sense, this implies a deliverance from guilt and punishment by the atonement of Christ actually applied to the soul of the sinner who is now believing on Him; and a deliverance from the power of sin through Christ *formed in the heart* (see Galatians 4:19).

So that one who is thus justified, or saved by faith, is indeed *born again*. He or she is *born again of the Spirit* unto a new life (spiritual, heavenly, divine, like its author), which is "hid with Christ in God." And, as a newborn babe, that one gladly receives the "sincere milk of the Word and grows" by it, going on in the might of the Lord God—from faith to faith, from grace to grace, until coming at length unto "a perfect man, unto the measure of the stature of the fulness of Christ" (Ephesians 4:13 KJV).

Faith Establishes the Law

Having been freed from sin,
you became slaves of righteousness.

ROMANS 6:18 NASB

Is the salvation, the justification, that comes by faith *against* holiness and good works?

It would be so, if we spoke, as some do, of a faith separate from these. But we speak of a faith that is *productive* of all good works and of all holiness. This objection is not a new one, however, but one as old as St. Paul's time. Even then it was asked, "Do we then make void the law through faith?" (Romans 3:31 KJV).

First, all who do not preach faith *do* make void the law, either directly and grossly, by limitations and comments that eat out all the spirit of the text; or indirectly, by not pointing out the only means whereby it is possible to perform it.

Secondly, we establish the law both by showing its full extent and spiritual meaning and by calling everyone to that living way, whereby the righteousness of the law may be fulfilled in them.

While these believers trust in the blood of Christ alone, they use all the ordinances He has appointed, do all the good works which "He had before prepared that they should walk therein." And they enjoy and manifest all holy and heavenly tempers, even the same mind that was in Christ Jesus.

Faith vs. Pride

Grace. . .not of yourselves.
EPHESIANS 2:8 NASB

Does preaching this faith lead men and women into pride?

Accidentally, it may: Therefore, every believer ought to be earnestly cautioned by the words of the great apostle: "Because of unbelief they (the first branches) were broken off, and you stand by faith. Do not be haughty, but fear. For if God did not spare the natural branches, He may not spare you either. Therefore consider the goodness and severity of God: on those who fell, severity; but toward you, goodness, if you continue in His goodness. Otherwise you also will be cut off" (Romans 11:20–22 NKJV).

And while believers continue in that goodness, they will remember those words of St. Paul, foreseeing and answering this very objection (Romans 3:27 NKJV): "Where is boasting then? It is excluded. By what law? Of works? No, but by the law of faith." If a man or woman were justified by their works, they would have something of which to glory. But there is no glorying for the one who does not work but believes on Him who justifies the ungodly (Romans 4:5).

Everything is of God. The faith by which salvation is given as well as the salvation itself are both the free gift of God. There is nothing of which a man or a woman can boast.

An Undeserved Gift

Not by works, so that no one can boast.
EPHESIANS 2:9 NIV

We have nothing of which to glory. The apostle used words to this effect in the verses preceding the above text (Ephesians 2:4–8 NKJV): "God, who is rich in mercy. . .even when we were dead in trespasses, made us alive together with Christ (by grace you have been saved). . .that. . .He might show the exceeding riches of His grace in His kindness toward us in Christ Jesus. For by grace you have been saved through faith, and that not of yourselves. . ." Of yourselves comes neither your faith nor your salvation: "It is the gift of God"; the free, undeserved gift. The faith through which you are saved, as well as the salvation which He attaches to it, is of His own good pleasure, His mere favor. That you believe is one instance of His grace; that in believing you are saved is another. Not of works, lest anyone should boast. All our works, all our righteousness, which were before our believing, merited nothing of God but condemnation, so far removed were they from deserving faith. Therefore, whenever faith is given, it is not of works.

Neither is salvation of the works we do *when* we believe; for then it is *God* that works in us. Therefore, He gives a reward for what He Himself has worked; this only commends the riches of His mercy but still leaves us nothing of which to glory.

The Goodness of God

Shall we go on sinning so that grace may increase?
By no means!
ROMANS 6:1–2 NIV

It may be that some do not speak of the mercy of God saving or justifying us freely by faith because they believe it encourages people in sin. Indeed, it may and will. Many will continue to sin that grace may increase, but their blood is upon their own heads. The goodness of God ought to lead them to repentance, and so it will those who are sincere of heart.

When penitent seekers know there is yet forgiveness with God, they will cry aloud that He would blot out their sins also, through faith which is in Jesus. And if they earnestly cry and faint not, if they seek Him in all the means He has appointed, if they refuse to be comforted till He come, He will come, and will not tarry (Hebrews 10:37). And He can do much work in a short time.

The Acts of the Apostles records many examples of God's working this faith in men's and women's hearts, even like lightning falling from heaven. In the same hour that Paul and Silas began to preach, the jailer repented, believed, and was baptized. It was the same with the three thousand on the day of Pentecost who repented and believed at St. Peter's first preaching. And, blessed be God, there are now many living proofs that God is still "mighty to save."

The Righteousness of God

Whoever believes on Him will not be put to shame.

ROMANS 9:33 NKJV

Simple faith is too "hard" for many people. They make this objection: "If a person cannot be saved by all he or she can do, it will drive them to despair."

True, to despair of being saved by their own works, their own merits, or righteousness. And so it ought, for none can trust in the merits of Christ till he has utterly renounced his own.

The one who goes about to establish his own righteousness—his own method of acceptance with God—cannot receive the righteousness of God, which is the way of justification that He has fixed.

The design of the law was to bring men and women to believe in Christ for justification and salvation. The righteousness which is of faith cannot be given a person while he is trusting in that which is of the law: namely, his own works.

It is sometimes called *the righteousness of God*—the whole benefit of God through Christ for the salvation of a sinner—and it is called this because God planned and prepared, reveals and gives, approves and crowns it; and it is shown to us only by the gospel.

Rich in Mercy

*It does not. . .depend on man's desire or effort,
but on God's mercy.*
ROMANS 9:16 NIV

Salvation by faith is an uncomfortable doctrine to the self-righteous. The devil speaks like himself (without either truth or shame) when he declares its discomfort, for salvation by faith is the only comfortable doctrine, very full of comfort, to all self-destroyed, self-condemned sinners. Whoever believes on Him will not be ashamed: And the same Lord over all is rich unto all that call upon Him. Here is comfort, high as heaven, stronger than death!

What! Mercy for all? For Zaccheus, a public robber? For Mary Magdalene, a common harlot? Then one may say, "Then I, even I, may hope for mercy!" And so you may, afflicted one, whom no one has comforted! God will not cast out your prayer. Perhaps He may say the very next hour, "Be of good cheer, your sins are forgiven." So forgiven that they shall reign over you no more. Yes, and the Holy Spirit will bear witness with your spirit that you are a child of God.

O glad tidings of great joy, sent unto all people! To everyone who thirsts, come to the waters: And you who have no money, come, buy, and eat (see Isaiah 55:1). Though your sins be red like crimson, though more than the hairs of your head, return unto the Lord, and He will have mercy upon you; and to our God, for He will abundantly pardon.

First of All, and To All

*"Whoever believes in Him should not perish
but have eternal life."*
JOHN 3:15 NKJV

Salvation by faith must be preached as the first doctrine, and it must be preached to all. The Holy Spirit says, through St. Paul, "No other foundation can anyone lay than that which is laid, which is Jesus Christ" (1 Corinthians 3:11 NKJV).

"Whoever believes on Him shall be saved" is, and must be, the foundation to all else. That is, it must be preached *first,* and it must be preached to *all.* We must exclude no one. Not the poor: They have a peculiar right to have the gospel preached to them. Not the unlearned: God has revealed these things unto the unlearned and ignorant from the beginning. Not the young: "Suffer these" to come to Christ, "and forbid them not." Not sinners, least of all. He "came not to call the righteous, but sinners to repentance."

If we were to exclude any, it might be the rich, the intellectual, the reputable, moral people. It is true that, too often, these exclude themselves from hearing. Yet we must speak the words of our Lord and give them also a simple presentation of the Word of truth. For our commission is, "Go and preach the gospel to *every* creature." If anyone twists it, or any part of it, to his destruction, he must bear his own burden. But still, as the Lord lives, whatever He says to us, that will we speak.

The Righteousness of Faith

A man is justified by faith
apart from observing the law.
ROMANS 3:28 NIV

Never has maintaining this doctrine been more seasonable than at this day. Nothing but this can effectually prevent the increase of delusions among us. It is endless to attack, one by one, all the errors that assail us. But salvation by faith strikes at the root, and all errors fall at once where this truth is established. It was this doctrine, justly called the strong rock and foundation of the Christian religion, that first established Christianity on this continent. It is this alone that can save us now. Nothing but this can give a check to the immorality which has overspread the land as a flood. Can you empty the great ocean drop by drop? If so, then you may reform us by persuasion from individual vices. But let the righteousness which is of God by faith be brought in, and the waves shall be stayed. Nothing but this can stop the mouths of those who "glory in their shame" and openly deny the Lord that bought them.

Bring in the gospel. Begin with the righteousness of faith, with Christ, "the end of the law to everyone who believes." And those who till now appeared almost, if not altogether, Christians, stand confessed as sons of perdition—as far from life and salvation as the depth of hell is from the height of heaven. *God, be merciful unto them.*

Conquering and to Conquer

This is the victory that has overcome the world,
even our faith.
1 JOHN 5:4 NIV

Declaring salvation by faith to the world strikes at the very foundations of hell. For this reason, our adversary stirred up earth and hell to destroy those who first preached it. Likewise, knowing that faith alone could overturn the foundations of his kingdom, he called forth all his forces and employed all his arts of lies and slander, to frighten Martin Luther from reviving this truth.

Nor can we wonder at this. Luther himself observed, "How would it enrage a proud, armed, strong man to be stopped and set at naught by a little child coming against him with a stick in his hand!" And especially when he knew that little child would surely overthrow him and tread him underfoot. Even so, Lord Jesus! Your strength has always been "made perfect in weakness!"

Go forth then, O little child who believes in Him, and His "right hand shall teach you terrible things!" Though you are helpless and weak as a young infant, the strong man, Satan, will not be able to stand before you. You will prevail over him, and subdue him, and overthrow him, and trample him under your feet. March on, under the great captain of your salvation, conquering and to conquer, until all your enemies are destroyed, and "death is swallowed up in victory" (1 Corinthians 15:54 KJV). Thanks be to God!

The Kingdom of God; The Kingdom of Heaven

"Repent, for the kingdom of heaven is near."
MATTHEW 3:2; 4:17 NIV

The kingdom of heaven and the kingdom of God are two phrases for the same thing. They mean not merely a future happy state in heaven, but a state to be enjoyed on earth—the proper disposition for the glory of heaven rather than the possession of it. In this text, it properly signifies the gospel dispensation, in which subjects were to be gathered to God by His Son, and a society to be formed (the Church), which was to exist first on earth and afterwards with God in glory for those who "endure to the end."

The Jews understood it as a temporal kingdom, but Christ's and John the Baptist's demand of repentance, as previous to it, showed it was a spiritual kingdom. It is the peculiar business of Christ to establish the kingdom of heaven in the hearts of men and women. Yet, it is observable that He begins His preaching in the same words as John the Baptist: *"Repent!"* He thus shows that no wicked person could possibly be a subject of this kingdom, and that the repentance which John had taught still was, and ever will be, the necessary preparation for that present, inward kingdom of righteousness, peace and joy in the Holy Spirit.

Parable of the Sower

"A farmer went out to sow his seed."
MATTHEW 13:3 NIV

A parable signifies not only a comparison but, sometimes, a proverb. It is any kind of instructive speech in which spiritual things are explained and illustrated by natural. The story is the literal sense; the interpretation (explanation) is the spiritual. Resting in the literal sense is deadly. The spiritual sense gives life.

The manner of speaking in parables was extremely common in Middle Eastern countries. It drew and fixed the attention and caused the truths spoken to sink deeper into humble and serious hearers. Yet, by an awful mixture of justice and mercy, it hid them from the proud and careless.

How exquisitely proper is this parable an introduction to all the rest. In this one, our Lord answers an obvious and most important question: The same sower, Christ, and the same preachers sent by Him always sow the same seed—why does it not always have the same effect?

Our Lord points out the grand hindrances of our bearing fruit in the same order as they occur. The first danger is that "birds" will devour the seed. If it escapes this, there is another danger, namely, lest it be scorched and wither away. It is long after this that the thorns spring up and choke the good seed, so that few bring forth fruit to perfection.

Oh, Lord, may we be among those few.

Stony Places of the Heart

"They withered because they had no root."
MATTHEW 13:6 NIV

A preacher of the gospel casts the seed into the hearts of the hearers. The greatest philosophers cannot explain how the earth produces food from the seed sown. Neither can a preacher of the gospel explain how the soul of a person brings forth first weak graces, then stronger, then full holiness.

It is a curious kind of mechanism in whch the spring of motion is within itself. Yet observe the amazing exactness of the comparison. The earth brings forth no food nor does the soul bring forth holiness without both the care and toil of men and women and the gracious influence of heaven.

One hears the word *and considers it not.* This is the first and most general cause of unfruitfulness. *The wicked one comes,* either inwardly, filling the mind with thoughts of other things—or by those who talk of other subjects when people should be considering what they have heard.

The seed sown *on stony places sprang up* soon, received with joy, perhaps with ecstasy, struck with the beauty of truth and drawn by the grace of God.

Yet he had no root in himself—no deep work of grace, no change in the ground of the heart, no deep conviction. Good desires soon wither away, and *he is offended,* finding a thousand plausible pretences for leaving so narrow and rugged a way.

Lord God, may we have deep roots in good soil.

Thorns Spring Up

*"The worries of this life,
the deceitfulness of wealth and the desires
for other things come in and choke the word."*

MARK 4:19 NIV

A vast majority of those who hear the Word of God receive the seed of the gospel as by the highway side. Many of those who do not lose it by the birds—Satan or his agents—receive it as on stony places where it springs up with no deep root. Some who receive it in a better soil still permit the thorns to grow up and choke it. Yet, in all these cases, it is not the will of God that hinders, but the person's voluntary perverseness.

The seed that fell among thorns was choked out and became unfruitful. One who *received the seed among the thorns* heard the Word and considered it in spite of Satan and all his agents, *has root in himself,* is deeply convinced and in great measure inwardly changed. He does not draw back *when tribulation and persecution* arise. Yet, perhaps unperceived at first, *thorns spring up* with the good seed till they gradually destroy all its life and power, *and it becomes unfruitful.*

Cares are thorns to the poor; wealth, to the rich; desire of other things, to all. The desire of anything that does not lead to happiness in God tends to barrenness of soul. And, these *enter in* where they were not before, some perhaps never known till now. If you have received and retained the Word, see to it that no other desire enters in.

Lord, may we hold close the Word of the gospel.

Good Ground: Hearers and Doers of the Word

*"Which in an honest and good heart,
having heard the word, [they] keep it,
and bring forth fruit with patience."*
LUKE 8:15 KJV

Those who keep the good word have avoided *the deceitfulness of riches*. Deceitful indeed, for they smile and betray, put out the eyes, harden the heart, and steal away all the life of God in the soul, filling it with pride, anger, and love of the world. It makes men and women enemies to the whole cross of Christ; yet, all the while, riches are eagerly desired and vehemently pursued, even by those who believe there is a God.

One who receives seed *on the good ground* is one who *hears the word, considers it, and keeps it. . .with perseverance.* The ground is soft, not like that by the wayside; deep, not like the stony ground; and purged, not full of thorns.

In this parable Jesus told, the ground bore fruit, *some a hundredfold, some sixty, some thirty.* It was in various proportions, some abundantly more than others; but all were fruitful hearers of the word—because when they *heard the word, they considered it.* St. Paul wrote to Timothy, *Meditate on these things. . .that thy profiting may appear in all things.*

True meditation is faith, hope, love, and joy, melted down together by the fire of God's Holy Spirit and offered up to God in secret.

Lord, may we consider and be fruitful.

The Way to the Kingdom

"The kingdom of God is at hand;
repent and believe in the gospel."

MARK 1:15 NASB

These words naturally lead us to consider, first, the nature of true religion, here termed by our Lord "the kingdom of God," which, He said, "is at hand"; and secondly, the way to it, which He points out in the words, "Repent and believe in the gospel."

As to the nature of true religion, termed by our Lord "the kingdom of God," it is explained in the Epistle to the Romans by the apostle Paul: The kingdom of God is not food and drink, "but righteousness and peace and joy in the Holy Spirit" (Romans 14:17 NKJV).

Not only unconverted Jews but also great numbers of those who had received the faith of Christ were still zealous for the law (Acts 21:20), even the ceremonial law of Moses. Whatever they found written there, either concerning meat (food) and drink offerings, or the distinction between clean and unclean foods, they not only observed themselves but vehemently pressed upon those among the Gentiles who had turned to God. Some even taught that unless those were circumcised, and kept the whole law (the whole ritual law), " 'you cannot be saved' " (Acts 15:1, 24 NASB). In opposition to this, the apostle stated: *The kingdom is not food and drink.*

Not an Outward Religion

The kingdom of God is not a matter of eating and drinking.
ROMANS 14:17 NIV

In the above Scripture and others, the apostle Paul declares that true religion does not consist in food and drink: not in any ritual observances—no outward thing, nothing exterior to the heart. The whole substance of true religion lies in "righteousness, peace and joy in the Holy Spirit" (v. 17 NIV).

Not in any *outward thing* such as *forms or ceremonies,* even of the most excellent kind. Supposing these to be ever so decent and significant, ever so expressive of inward things; supposing them to be ever so helpful; even supposing them to be, as in the case of the Jews, appointed by God Himself. Yet true religion does not *principally* consist in these; and, *strictly speaking,* not at all. How much more must this hold true concerning such rites and forms as are only of human appointment!

The religion of Christ rises infinitely higher and lies immensely deeper than all these. These are good in their place, just so far as they are in fact subservient to true religion. And it is superstition to object against them while they are applied only as occasional helps to human weakness. But let no one carry them further. Let none dream that they have any intrinsic worth, or that religion cannot exist without them. This makes them an abomination to the Lord.

The religion of Christ is inward.

True Religion is Inward

*The kingdom of God is. . .
righteousness, peace and joy in the Holy Spirit.*

ROMANS 14:17 NIV

The nature of religion is so far from consisting in forms of worship or rites and ceremonies that it does not properly consist in any outward actions of any kind. It is true, a person cannot have true religion who is guilty of vicious, immoral actions, or who does to others what he would not they should do unto him if he were in the same circumstances. It is also true that one has no real religion who knows to do good and does it not.

Yet one may both abstain from outward evil and do good and still have no religion. Or two persons may do the same outward work, such as feeding the hungry, or clothing the naked. One of these may be truly religious and the other have no religion at all: For one may act from the love of God, and the other from the love of praise.

Although true religion naturally leads to every good word and work, the real nature of religion lies deeper still, in the hidden man of the heart. I say *of the heart,* for neither does religion consist in orthodoxy or right opinions. Although these are not properly outward things, they are not in the heart but in the *understanding.* One may have right opinions on every point, even zealously defend them, and still not have any more religion than a pagan. True religion is of the heart.

Peace, Joy, and Love

"Love the Lord your God. . .with all your soul."
MARK 12:30 NIV

Religion of the heart is more than having the right understanding of religious things. One may be orthodox in every point, holding only those opinions in harmony with Scripture, even defending them zealously on all sides; one may think justly concerning the incarnation of our Lord, concerning the ever-blessed Trinity, and every other doctrine contained in the oracles of God; one may assent to all three creeds—those called the Apostles', the Nicene, and the Athanasian. Yet, it is possible he or she may have no true religion at all, no more of that referred to by our Lord as the kingdom of God, than does a pagan, a Jew, or a Turk.

One may be almost as orthodox as the devil and all the while be as great a stranger to the religion of the heart as the devil is.

This alone is religion, truly so called: This alone is in the sight of God of great price. The apostle sums it up in three particulars: "righteousness, and peace, and joy in the Holy Spirit." And the first branch of Christian righteousness was summed up by our Lord: "Love the Lord your God with all your heart and with all your soul and with all your mind and with all your strength."

The Two Great Commandments

> *"You shall love."*
> MARK 12:30 NASB

Loving the Lord God with all your heart, mind, soul, and strength is the first great branch of Christian righteousness. You shall delight yourself in the Lord your God; seeking and finding all happiness in Him. You shall hear and fulfill His word, "My son, give me your heart." And having given Him your inmost soul to reign there without a rival, you may well cry out in the fulness of your heart, "I will love You, O my Lord, my strength. The Lord IS my strong rock; my Savior, my God, in whom I trust."

The second commandment, the second great branch of Christian righteousness, is closely and inseparably connected with the first: "Love your neighbor as yourself." *Love*—embrace with the most tender goodwill, the most earnest and cordial affection, the most inflamed desires of preventing or removing all evil and bringing every possible good. *Your neighbor*—not only your friends, kinfolk, or acquaintances; not only the virtuous ones who regard you, who extend or return your kindness, but every person, not excluding those you have never seen or know by name; not excluding those you know to be evil and unthankful, those who despitefully use you. Even those you shall love *as yourself* with the same invariable thirst after their happiness. Use the same unwearied care to screen them from whatever might grieve or hurt either their soul or body. This is love.

Love Is the Sum of True Religion

Love is the fulfillment of the law.
ROMANS 13:10 NIV

Now is not this love the fulfillment of the law—the sum of all inward and outward Christian righteousness? For it necessarily implies merciful affections and humbleness of mind ("love is not puffed up"), gentleness, meekness, long-suffering ("love is not provoked, but believes, hopes, endures all things"). And "love works no evil to his neighbor," either by word or deed. It cannot willingly hurt or grieve anyone but is full of mercy and good works.

But true religion, that is a heart right toward God and man, implies happiness as well as holiness. For it is also "peace and joy in the Holy Spirit." What peace? The peace of God, which only God can give, and the world cannot take away. It is a supernatural sensation, a divine taste, of "the powers of the world to come" such as a person in his natural, unconverted state does not know.

It is a peace that banishes all doubt and painful uncertainty because the Spirit of God bears witness with the spirit of a Christian that he or she is a child of God. It banishes tormenting fear: the fear of the wrath of God, the fear of hell, the fear of the devil, and in particular, the fear of death. The one who has the peace of God desires, as did the apostle Paul, if it be the will of God, "to depart and to be with Christ." The soul wants to be in the presence of the One it loves.

Peace Plus Joy Equals Happiness

Blessed is he whose transgressions are forgiven.

PSALM 32:1 NIV

Wherever the peace of God is fixed in the soul, there is also joy in the Holy Spirit, joy created in the heart by that Holy Spirit, the ever-blessed Spirit of God. He is the one who works in us that calm, humble rejoicing in God through Christ Jesus, by whom we have received the atonement, the reconciliation with God. And because of this reconciliation, the Holy Spirit enables us boldly to confirm the truth of the psalmist's declaration, "Happy is the one whose unrighteousness is forgiven, and whose sin is covered." The same Holy Spirit inspires the Christian soul with that even, solid joy arising from the testimony of the Spirit that one is a child of God. And that causes him or her to "rejoice with joy unspeakable, in hope of the glory of God." He has hope both of the glorious image of God, now in part and which shall be fully revealed in him; and of that crown of glory which fades not away, reserved in heaven for him.

This holiness and happiness, joined together, are sometimes styled in the sacred writings *the kingdom of God,* as in Mark 1:15, and sometimes the *kingdom of heaven.* It is termed *the kingdom of God* because it is the immediate fruit of God's reigning in the soul. It is called *the kingdom of heaven* because it is, in a degree, heaven opened in the soul right here on earth.

Heaven in Your Heart

He who has the Son has life.
1 JOHN 5:12 NIV

As soon as God takes unto Himself His mighty power and sets up His throne in a heart, it is instantly filled with righteousness and peace and joy in the Holy Ghost. This is, in a degree, heaven within the soul. Whoever experiences this can say assuredly before angels and men:

Everlasting life is won;
Glory is on earth begun.

This agrees with the constant meaning of Scripture, which bears record that God "has given us eternal life, and this life is in His Son. He who has the Son [reigning in his heart] has life," even life everlasting (1 John 5:11–12 NKJV). And life eternal is to "know You, the only true God, and Jesus Christ whom You have sent" (John 17:3 NKJV).

Those to whom this is given may confidently address God, though in the midst of a fiery furnace,

Where Thy presence is display'd is heaven.

And this kingdom of God, or of heaven, "is at hand," is near. As originally spoken, these words implied that "the time" was then fulfilled. God was "made manifest in the flesh," and He would set up His kingdom among men and reign in the hearts of His people. Wherever the gospel of Christ is preached, His kingdom is near, not far from everyone. You may this very hour enter in, if you will pay attention to His voice: *Repent and believe the gospel.*

The Way Is Simple

"Repent and believe in the gospel."
MARK 1:15 NASB

What is the way to the kingdom of heaven?

Repent and believe the gospel. To repent means, first of all, to know yourself. This is the *first* repentance, prior to faith—conviction or self-knowledge. Awake, then. *Know yourself to be a sinner,* and what manner of sinner you are. *Know* the corruption of your inmost nature by which you have gone very far from original righteousness—the corruption which is deep-seated hatred against God. It is not subject to the law of God, indeed, it cannot be.

Know, further, that you are corrupted in every power, every faculty of your soul; totally corrupted in every one of these, the whole foundation being out of line. Your understanding is darkened, and you cannot discern God or the things of God.

Know that the clouds of ignorance and error rest upon you and cover you with the shadow of death. Acknowledge that you know nothing yet as you ought to know—not God, not the world, not yourself.

Your will is totally perverse and distorted, averse to all good, prone to all evil. Your affections are alienated from God; your passions are either undue in degree or placed on undue objects. In your soul, from top to bottom, there is no soundness, only wounds and bruises and hateful disease.

Such is the self-knowledge, the dawn of repentance, the way to the kingdom of God.

What Kind of Fruit?

"A bad tree bears bad fruit."
MATTHEW 7:17 NIV

What manner of branches can one expect to grow from the evil root of inbred corruption of one's inmost nature? First, unbelief—asking "Who is the Lord that I should serve Him?" Then, independence—pretending to be like the Most High. Hence, pride in all its forms; teaching one to say, "I am rich and have need of nothing."

From this evil fountain flow vanity, thirst of praise, ambition, covetousness, the lust of the flesh, the lust of the eye, and the pride of life. From these arise anger, hatred, malice, revenge, envy, jealousy, evil surmisings, and all foolish and hurtful lusts which pierce the soul with many sorrows, and, if not prevented, drown the soul in everlasting damnation.

And what fruits can grow on such branches? Only those that are bitter and evil continually. From pride come contention and vain boasting. From lust of the flesh come gluttony or drunkenness, sensuality, fornication, uncleanness, and all manner of defiling the body which God designed for a temple of the Holy Spirit.

Time fails to tally all the idle words spoken which have provoked the Most High, all the works either themselves evil or at least not done to the glory of God. Actual sins are more than one can express. Who can number the sands of the sea, or the drops of rain, or one's iniquities?

God Is Just

The wages of sin is death.
ROMANS 6:23 NIV

The death here spoken of is not only temporal but eternal. The soul who sins shall die (Ezekiel 18:4). It shall die the second death. This is the sentence: to be punished with everlasting destruction, with never-ending death from the presence of the Lord (2 Thessalonians 1:9). The expression "in danger of hellfire" is far too weak; the meaning is rather "under the sentence of," doomed already, just dragging to execution. All are guilty of everlasting death as the just reward of their inward and outward wickedness. And it is justice that the sentence should now take place.

Do you see, do you feel this? Are you thoroughly convinced that you deserve God's wrath and everlasting damnation? Do you *know* that God would do you no wrong if He now commanded the earth to open and to swallow you up? And that He would be just if you were now to go down quick into the pit of hell, into the fire that shall never be quenched?

If God has given you to truly repent, you have a deep sense that these things are so, and that it is of His mere mercy that you are not consumed, swept away from the face of the earth and from His face forever.

This, too, is part of that true inward repentance which is the way to the kingdom of God.

We Need a Savior

"Salvation is found in no one else."
ACTS 4:12 NIV

What can one do to appease the wrath of God, to atone for all his or her sins, to escape the punishment so justly deserved? Alas, you can do nothing. Nothing you do will in any way make amends to God for even one evil work, word, or thought. If you could from now on do all things well and perform perfect, uninterrupted obedience, it would not atone for what is past. Not increasing your debt would not discharge it.

But suppose perfect obedience from this day forward could atone for the sins that are past; this would be of no profit, for you are not able to perform it in any point. Begin now to make the trial. Shake off that outward sin which constantly besets you. You cannot. How then will you change your entire life from all evil to all good? Indeed, it is impossible unless your heart first be changed.

And are you able to change your own heart from all sin to all holiness? No more than you are able to give life to a dead body and raise one who lies in the grave. You can do nothing in this matter; you are utterly without strength.

To be deeply sensible of this, how helpless you are—as well as how guilty and how sinful—is that repentance which is the forerunner of the kingdom of God. One step more, and you will enter in. You do *repent*. Now, *believe the gospel*.

We Have a Savior

Christ Jesus came into the world to save sinners.
1 TIMOTHY 1:15 NIV

The gospel is good tidings, good news for guilty, helpless sinners. In the largest sense of the word, it is the entire revelation made to men and women by Jesus Christ. Sometimes, it means the whole of what He did and suffered while He lived on earth.

The gospel is "Jesus Christ came into the world to save sinners." "God so loved the world, that He gave His only begotten Son, that we might not perish, but have everlasting life." "He was wounded for our transgressions, He was bruised for our iniquities; the chastisement for our peace was upon Him, and by His stripes we are healed."

Believe this, and the kingdom of God is yours. By faith, you attain the promise. He pardons and frees from guilt all that truly repent and genuinely believe His holy gospel. As soon as God speaks to your heart: "Be of good cheer; your sins are forgiven"; His kingdom comes. You have righteousness, peace, and joy in the Holy Spirit.

Only beware that you do not deceive your soul with regard to the nature of this faith. It is not a bare assent to the Bible or articles of any creed. It is a confidence in the pardoning mercy of God through Christ Jesus, who loved *you* and gave Himself for *you*, and a sure trust that *you* are now reconciled to God by the blood of the cross.

Christ Our Redeemer

In Him we have redemption through His blood.
EPHESIANS 1:7 NASB

Do you have a sure trust in the mercy of God through Christ Jesus, a confidence in a pardoning God? A divine evidence, a conviction that "God was in Christ reconciling the world to Himself, not imputing" your former trespasses? That "the Son of God has loved me, and given Himself for me"?

Are you convinced that "I, even I, am now reconciled to God by the blood of His cross"? Do you *thus* believe? Then the peace of God is in your heart, and sorrow and sighing flee away. You are no longer in doubt of the love of God. It is clear as the noonday sun. Your heart cries out about the loving-kindness of the Lord. You are no longer afraid of hell or death or him who once had the power of death—the devil—no, nor painfully afraid of God Himself. Only a tender concern not to offend Him.

When you *thus* believe, your soul magnifies the Lord, and your spirit rejoices in God your Savior. You rejoice that you have redemption through His blood, even the forgiveness of sins. You rejoice in the Spirit of adoption, the Holy Spirit, who cries within your heart, *Abba, Father!* You rejoice in a hope full of immortality and in reaching forward to the "mark for the prize of your high calling." You are reaching in earnest expectation of all the good things God has prepared for all those who love Him.

Enter the Kingdom

God has poured out his love into our hearts.
ROMANS 5:5 NIV

Do you now believe? Then the love of God is now poured out in your heart. You love Him, because He first loved us. And because you love God, you love your brother and sister, also. And having love, peace, and joy, you also have long-suffering, gentleness, fidelity, goodness, meekness, temperance, and all the other fruits of the same Spirit. In a word, you have whatever dispositions are holy, heavenly, or divine. And while you gaze with open face and heart at the glory of the Lord, which is His glorious love, and the glorious image in which you were created, you are changed inwardly into the same image from glory to glory by the Spirit of the Lord.

This repentance, this faith, this peace, joy, love; this change from glory to glory is what the wisdom of the world counts madness, utter foolish distraction. But regard that not; do not be moved from your steadfastness. You know in whom you have believed. Hold fast what you have already attained; hold fast, and follow on till you attain *all* the great and precious promises.

You who have not yet known Him, do not be terrified by those who speak evil of things they do not know. It is Christ who died and is now making intercession for you at the right hand of God. Cast yourself on the Lamb of God, with all your sins, and enter with joy into the kingdom of God.

Parable of the Prodigal Son

"A certain man had two sons."
LUKE 15:11 KJV

Our Lord in this parable shows first that the Jews had no cause to murmur at the reception of the Gentiles by God. He also shows that if the Pharisees were indeed as good as they fancied themselves to be, they still had no reason to murmur at the kind treatment of any sincere penitent.

We have in this parable a lively representation of the condition and behavior of sinners in their natural state. When enriched by the bounty of the great common Father, they ungratefully run from Him (vv. 12–13). Sensual pleasures are eagerly pursued, till all the grace of God is squandered away (v. 13). And while in this pursuit, not a serious thought of God can find a place in their minds. Even when afflictions come upon them (v. 14), still they will make hard shifts before they will let the grace of God, concurring with His providence, persuade them to think of a return (vv. 15–18).

When at last they see themselves naked, indigent, and undone, they recover the exercise of their reason (v. 17). They remember the blessings they have thrown away and attend to the misery they have incurred. Hereupon they resolve to return to their Father and put the resolution immediately into practice (vv. 18–20).

God Receives Sinners

*"This son of mine was dead
and is alive again."*

LUKE 15:24 NIV

Consider with wonder and pleasure the gracious reception returning sinners find from divine, injured goodness! When such a prodigal comes to his Father, He sees him afar off (v. 20). He pities, meets, embraces him. He even interrupts the acknowledgments with the token of His returning favor (v. 21). He arrays him with the robe of a Redeemer's righteousness—with inward and outward holiness—adorns him with all His sanctifying graces, and honors him with the tokens of adopting love (v. 22). And all this He does with unutterable delight because the one who was lost is now found (vv. 23–24).

The Father tells the older brother, *You are always with me, and all I have is yours.* This suggests a strong reason against murmuring at the indulgence shown to the greatest of sinners. The father's receiving the younger son did not cause him to disinherit the elder. Nor is God's receiving notorious sinners any loss to those who have always served Him, especially if they have made a greater progress in inward as well as outward holiness.

The elder brother calls the returning prodigal "your son." The father mildly reproves him: "your brother" (v. 32). Amazing intimation that the best of us ought to account the worst sinners our brethren when they are inclined to return!

Joy in Heaven

"Joy shall be in heaven
over one sinner that repenteth."
LUKE 15:7 KJV

We learn from this parable how God—in direct contrast to the Pharisees and scribes—receives sinners. First, Jesus said, there is a solemn and festive joy in heaven even in our blessed Lord Himself. Joy is also among the angels and spirits of just men and women. Not frivolous gaiety, but a solid, serious, heartfelt joy.

The sum of the parable of the returning prodigal son is this: A father particularly rejoices when an extravagant child, supposed to be utterly lost, comes to a thorough sense of his duty. The joy is greater than in the case of another one equally valuable but not in such danger. The angels in heaven likewise particularly rejoice in the conversion of the most abandoned sinners. God Himself so readily forgives and receives them that He may be represented as having part in the joy.

So let no elder brother—the one comparatively just and outwardly blameless—murmur at this indulgence, but rather welcome the prodigal back into the family.

And let those who have been thus received wander no more. Let them strive to equal the strictest devotion and constancy of those like the elder brother—those who have served the heavenly Father and not transgressed His commandments.

The Means of Grace

*"You have gone away from My ordinances
and have not kept them."*

MALACHI 3:7 NKJV

By "means of grace," I mean outward signs, words, or actions, ordained of God and appointed to be the ordinary channels whereby He might convey to people either preventing (drawing, convicting), or justifying, or sanctifying grace. I use this expression, "means of grace," because I know of none better; and because it has generally been used in the Christian church for many ages, directing us to bless God both for the means of grace and hope of glory; and teaching us that a sacrament is "an outward sign of inward grace, and a means whereby we receive the same."

In the above text from the Old Testament, God is speaking to His people. But are there any ordinances *now,* since life and immortality have been brought to light by the gospel? Are there, under the Christian dispensation, any *means ordained of God* as the usual channels of His grace?

This question could never have been proposed in the apostolic church except by an open heathen, for the constant practice of the whole body of Christians was that so long as all who believed were together, and had all things common, they continued steadfastly in the teachings of the apostles, and in breaking of bread, and in prayers (see Acts 2:42, 44).

Growing or Doing?

Grow in the grace and knowledge
of our Lord and Savior Jesus Christ.
2 PETER 3:18 NIV

The chief of the means of grace are prayer (whether in secret or in the great congregation); searching the Scriptures (which implies reading, hearing, and meditating thereon); and receiving the Lord's Supper (eating bread and drinking wine in remembrance of Him). These we believe to be ordained of God as the ordinary channels of conveying His grace to the souls of men and women.

So it was in the early church. But in process of time, the love of many grew cold. Some began to mistake the *means* for the *end*, and to place religion in *doing* those outward works rather than in a heart renewed after the image of God. Now, the whole value of the *means* depends on their actually serving the *end* of religion. Consequently, all these means—when separate from the end—are less than nothing and vanity. If they do not actually lead to the knowledge and love of God, they are not acceptable in His sight. They are rather an abomination before Him, a stink in His nostrils. He is weary of them. And if they are used to try to *fulfill* the religion they should only serve, they turn God's arms against Himself and keep Christianity out of the heart instead of being the *means* by which it is brought in.

Forgetting the "End"; Abusing the Means

> " 'These people honor me with their lips,
> but their hearts are far from me.' "
> MARK 7:6 NIV; SEE ALSO ISAIAH 29:13 NIV

As more and more time intervened from the days of the early apostles, people began to forget that the end of every commandment is love out of a pure heart, with unfeigned faith—loving the Lord God with all their heart and their neighbor as themselves, and being purified from pride, anger, and evil desire, by a faith of the operation of God. Others seemed to imagine, though religion did not mainly consist in these outward means, that there was something in them with which God was well pleased—something that would make them acceptable in His sight, even though they were not exact in the weightier matters of justice, mercy, and the love of God.

With such abuse, the ordinances did not lead to the end for which they had been ordained. The things which should have been for spiritual health were to them an occasion of falling. They were so far from receiving any blessing from them that they drew down only a curse upon their heads. So far were they from growing more heavenly in heart and life that they became more the children of hell than before. Seeing these results, others drew the erroneous conclusion that these *means* were *not* the means of conveying the grace of God. But the fault lay in the *abuse*, not in the *use*, of the means.

God Is the Giver

Every good and perfect gift is. . .
from the Father.
JAMES 1:17 NIV

It is true that outward religion is worth nothing without the religion of the heart. "God is a Spirit: and they that worship him must worship him in spirit and in truth" (John 4:24 KJV). Therefore, external worship is lost labor without a heart devoted to God. The outward ordinances of God profit much when they advance inward holiness. But when they do not advance it, they are unprofitable and void. And when they are used in the place of inward religion, they are an utter abomination to the Lord.

All outward means whatever, if separate from the Spirit of God, cannot profit at all, cannot lead in any degree either to the knowledge or the love of God. Without controversy, the help that is done upon earth, He doeth it Himself. It is He alone who, by His own almighty power, works in us what is pleasing in His sight. All outward things, unless He works in them and by them, are mere weak and beggarly elements. We know there is no inherent power in the words spoken in prayer, in the letter or the sound of the Scripture read, or in the bread and wine received in the Lord's Supper. It is God alone who is the giver of every good gift, the author of all grace. The whole power is of Him, whereby, through any of these, there is any blessing conveyed to our souls.

Christ Is All

Christ is all, and in all.
COLOSSIANS 3:11 NASB

We know that God is able to give His grace though there were no means on the face of the earth. In this sense, we may affirm that, with regard to God, there is no such thing as means, seeing He is equally able to work whatever pleases Him, by any means, or by none at all.

We know, further, that the use of *all means* whatever will never atone for one sin. It is the blood of Christ alone whereby any sinner can be reconciled to God. There is no other propitiation for our sins, no other fountain for sin and uncleanness.

Every believer in Christ is deeply convinced that there is no merit except in Him. There is no merit in any of their own works: not in uttering the prayer, or searching the Scripture, or hearing the Word of God, or eating that bread and drinking that cup of the Lord's Supper. If those who say, "Christ is the only means of grace," mean that He is the only meritorious cause of grace, it cannot be disputed by any who know the grace of God. For "Christ," as the apostle said, "is all, and in all."

The Merit of Christ Alone

Jesus has become the guarantee.
HEBREWS 7:22 NIV

It is a melancholy truth that a large proportion of those called Christians do to this (very) day abuse the means of grace to the destruction of their souls. This is doubtless the case with all those who rest content in the form of godliness without the power. Either they fondly presume they are Christians already because they do thus and thus (although Christ was never yet revealed nor the love of God poured out in their hearts). Or else they suppose they will infallibly become Christians just because they use these means. They idly dream (though perhaps hardly conscious of it) that there is some kind of power in these means by which sooner or later (they know not when) they shall certainly be made holy. Or that there is a sort of merit in using these means, which will surely move God to give them holiness or else to accept them without it.

So little do they understand that great foundation of the whole Christian building: *by grace we are saved*. Saved from our sins, from the guilt and the power of them, restored to the favor and image of God. Not for any works, merits, or worth of our own, but by the free grace, the mere mercy of God, through the merits of His well-beloved Son. We are thus saved, not by any power, wisdom, or strength in us or in any other, but only through the grace or power of the Holy Spirit, who works all in all.

How Are We to Wait?

Seek the LORD while he may be found;
call on him while he is near.

ISAIAH 55:6 NIV

Suppose one knows this salvation to be the gift and the work of God, and suppose further that he or she is convinced also that they do not have this gift, how might they attain to it?

If you say, "Believe, and you will be saved!" they answer, "True, but how shall I believe?" You reply, "Wait upon God."

"Well, but how am I to wait? Using the means of grace, or not? Am I to wait for the grace of God which brings salvation by using the means of grace or by laying them aside?"

It cannot be conceived that the Word of God should give no direction in so important a point; or that the Son of God, who came down from heaven for us and for our salvation, should have left us without direction with regard to a question in which our salvation is so nearly concerned. And, in fact, He has *not* left us undirected; He has shown us the way in which we should go. We have only to consult the Word of God. Inquire what is written there. If we simply abide by that, no possible doubt can remain.

According to Holy Scripture, all who desire the grace of God are to wait for it in the means which He has ordained—*in using, not in laying aside*, prayer; hearing, reading, and meditating on the Scriptures; and partaking of the Lord's Supper.

Ask, Seek, Knock

"Ask, and it will be given to you."
LUKE 11:9 NASB

All who desire the grace of God are to wait for it, first, in the way of prayer. This is the express direction of our Lord Himself. In His Sermon on the Mount, after explaining at length wherein religion consists and describing the main branches of it, He adds, "Ask, and it will be given to you; seek, and you will find; knock, and it will be opened to you. For everyone who asks receives, and he who seeks finds, and to him who knocks it will be opened" (Matthew 7:7–8 and Luke 11 NASB). In the plainest manner, we are here directed to ask in order to receive, or as a means of receiving; to seek, in order to find the grace of God, the pearl of great price; and to knock, to continue asking and seeking, if we would enter into His kingdom.

That no doubt might remain, our Lord gives a peculiar parable of a father who desires to give good gifts to his children, concluding with these words, " 'How much more will your heavenly Father give the Holy Spirit to those who ask Him?' " (Luke 11:13 NASB).

Jesus gives a direction to pray, with a positive promise that by this means we shall obtain our request: "Go into your room, and. . .pray to your Father who is in the secret place; and. . . [He]. . .will reward you openly" (Matthew 6:6 NKJV).

Pray and Persevere

"Lord, teach us to pray."
LUKE 11:1 NIV

Immediately after our Lord answered this (above) request of His disciples, He showed them the absolute necessity of using prayer if we would receive any gift from God.

He told the story of a man who begged his friend at midnight to get up and lend him three loaves of bread. Though the friend would not rise and give him because he was his friend, yet because of his troublesome persistence, his friend will rise and give him. Jesus said, "And I say unto you, Ask, and it shall be given you."

How could our blessed Lord more plainly declare the means—persistently asking—by which we may receive of God what otherwise we should not receive at all?

"He spoke also another parable, to this end, that men ought always to pray, and not lose heart"—to persevere until they receive of God whatever petition they have asked of Him: *There was in a city a judge. . .[and] there was a widow in that city; and she came unto him, saying, Avenge me of mine adversary. And he would not for a while: but afterward he said within himself, Though I fear not God, nor regard man; yet because this widow troubleth me, I will avenge her* (Luke 18:1–5 KJV).

Our Lord Himself made the application (v. 8) for those who cry day and night to Him: "I tell you that he will avenge them speedily" (KJV).

Ask in Faith

Ask in faith without any doubting.
JAMES 1:6 NASB

Regarding the use of prayer as a means of grace, the direction which God has given us by the apostle James is most clear. With regard to prayer of every kind, public or private, and the blessing attached to it, he says: "If any of you lacks wisdom, let him ask of God, who gives to all liberally and without reproach" (if they ask; otherwise "you do not have because you do not ask," James 1:5; 4:2 NKJV). If they ask, God does not reproach them but says "it will be given to [them]" (James 1:5 NKJV).

Because the apostle adds, "Let him ask in faith," some may object that this is not a direction to unbelievers (to seekers), to those who do not know the pardoning grace of God. I answer: The meaning of the word *faith in this place* is fixed by the apostle himself, as if it were on purpose to halt this objection. The words immediately following are, "nothing wavering," *without doubting.* Not doubting but that God hears his prayer and will fulfill the desire of his heart; will grant him the grace, the wisdom for which he asks.

We must conclude, therefore, that Scripture shows that all who desire the grace of God are to wait for it in the way of prayer.

Search the Scriptures

The holy Scriptures. . .
are able to make you wise for salvation
through faith in Christ Jesus.

2 TIMOTHY 3:15 NIV

All who desire the grace of God are to wait for it also by searching the Scriptures. Our Lord's direction with regard to the use of this means is plain and clear. "Search the Scriptures," He said to the unbelieving Jews, for they "testify of Me" (John 5:39 NKJV). And for this very end He directed them to search the Scriptures that they might believe in Him.

The objection that "this is not a command, but only an assertion that they did search the Scriptures," is shamelessly false. A command cannot be more clearly expressed; it is as peremptory as words can make it.

And what a blessing from God attends the use of this means appears from what is recorded concerning the Bereans. After hearing St. Paul, they "searched the Scriptures daily to find out whether these things were so. Therefore many of them believed." They found the grace of God in the way which He had ordained (see Acts 17:11–12 NKJV).

It is indeed probable that in some of those who had received the Word with all readiness of mind, faith came, as the same apostle speaks, "by hearing," and was only confirmed by reading the Scriptures. For under the general term *searching* are contained *hearing and reading and meditating.*

Scripture, a Gift from God

All Scripture is given. . .of God.
2 TIMOTHY 3:16 NKJV

Hearing, reading, and meditating on the Scriptures is a means whereby God not only gives, but also confirms and increases, true wisdom. St. Paul wrote to Timothy: "From childhood you have known the Holy Scriptures, which are able to make you wise for salvation through faith which is in Christ Jesus" (2 Timothy 3:15 NKJV). The same truth (namely that this is the great means God has ordained for conveying His manifold grace to man) is delivered in the fullest manner in the words that immediately follow: "All Scripture is given by inspiration of God." Consequently, all Scripture is infallibly true "and is profitable for doctrine, for reproof, for correction, for instruction in righteousness" to the end "that the man of God may be complete, thoroughly equipped for every good work" (vv. 16–17 NKJV).

This is spoken primarily and directly of the Old Testament Scriptures which Timothy had known from a child; the New Testament was not yet written. So St. Paul was very far from making light of the Old Testament! Of these, St. Peter wrote also, "you do well to heed as a light that shines in a dark place, until the day dawns and the morning star rises in your hearts" (2 Peter 1:19 NKJV).

Let all, then, who desire that day to dawn upon their hearts wait for it in searching the Scriptures.

In Remembrance of Me

Eat this bread and drink this cup.
1 CORINTHIANS 11:26 NIV

All who desire an increase of the grace of God are to wait for it, thirdly, in partaking of the Lord's Supper, for this also is a direction the Lord Himself gave. "The same night in which He was betrayed (He) took bread; and. . .broke it and said, 'Take, eat; this is My body' [that is, the sacred sign of My body]. . .'do this in remembrance of Me.' . . .He also took the cup. . .saying, 'This cup is the new covenant in My blood. This do. . .in remembrance of Me.' For as often as you eat this bread and drink this cup, you proclaim the Lord's death till He comes" again (1 Corinthians 11:23–26 NKJV). By these visible signs, we openly exhibit before God, angels, and our fellow creatures our solemn remembrance of His death till He returns in the clouds of heaven.

The direction for His remembrance first given by our Lord is expressly repeated by the apostle (v. 28). "Let him eat, let him drink"—both in the form of command. These words do not imply a bare permission only, but a clear, explicit command. It is a command to all those who already are filled with peace and joy in believing. It is likewise for those who can truly say, "The remembrance of our sins is grievous unto us, the burden of them is intolerable." All these persons may find a sweet means of grace in eating and drinking at the table of our Lord.

Mysteries of Faith

"Do this in remembrance of me."
LUKE 22:19 NIV

Partaking of the Lord's Supper is an ordinary, stated means of receiving the grace of God. This is evident from the words of the apostle: "The cup of blessing which we bless, is it not the communion," or communication, "of the blood of Christ? The bread which we break, is it not the communion of the body of Christ?" (1 Corinthians 10:16 NKJV). Is not the eating of this bread and the drinking of this cup, an outward, visible means whereby God conveys spiritual grace into our souls? Conveys all that righteousness, and peace, and joy in the Holy Spirit which were purchased by the body of Christ once broken, and the blood of Christ once shed for us? Therefore, let all who truly desire the grace of God, eat of that bread, and drink of that cup of the Lord's Supper.

Only let those first examine themselves, whether they understand the nature and design of this holy institution, and whether they really desire to be made conformable to the death of Christ. Then, nothing doubting, let them eat and drink.

God has plainly pointed out His way. Yet men and women, wise in their own eyes, have from time to time raised innumerable objections to it. It might be needful to consider a few of these, not because they have weight in themselves, but because they have so often been used to trouble and subvert those who did run well till Satan appeared as an angel of light.

Submit to Obey

Fear God and keep his commandments,
for this is the whole duty of man.

ECCLESIASTES 12:13 NIV

The first and chief objection to using the means of grace is, "You cannot use them without trusting in them." I pray, where is this written? I expect you should show me plain Scripture for your assertion. Otherwise I dare not receive it, because I am not convinced you are wiser than God. If it really had been as you claim, it is certain Christ must have known it. And if He had known it, He would surely have warned us. Because He has not—because there is nothing of this in the whole revelation of Jesus Christ—I am as fully assured your statement is false as that this revelation is of God.

You say, "Leave them off for a short time, to see whether you trusted in them or no." So I am to *disobey* God, in order to know whether I trust in *obeying* Him! And do you openly declare this advice? Do you deliberately teach folks to "do evil, that good may come?" O tremble at the sentence of God! The "condemnation is just."

You say, "If you are troubled when you leave them off, it is plain you trusted in them." By no means. If I am troubled when I willfully disobey God, it is plain His Spirit is still striving with me; but if I am not troubled at willful sin, it is plain I am given up to a reprobate mind.

Embrace the Promise

He who promised is faithful.

HEBREWS 10:23 NASB

But what is meant by *trusting in the means?* Looking for the blessing of God therein? Believing, that if I wait in this way, I shall attain what otherwise I should not? So I do. By the grace of God, I will *thus* trust in them, till the day of my death. That is, I will believe that whatever God has promised, He is faithful to perform. And seeing He has promised to bless me in this way, I *trust* it shall be according to His word.

It has been also objected, "This is seeking salvation by works." Do you know the meaning of the expression you use? What *is* seeking salvation by works? In the writings of St. Paul, it means either seeking to be saved by observing the ritual works of the Mosaic law, or expecting salvation for the sake of our own works, by the worthiness of our own righteousness. But how is either of these meanings implied in waiting in the way God has ordained, and expecting that He will meet me there because He has promised to do so?

I do expect that He will fulfill His word: He will meet and bless me in this way. Yet not for the merit of my righteousness, but through the merits, sufferings, and love of His Son, in whom He is always well pleased.

I Will Keep Your Law

*You have purified yourselves
by obeying the truth.*

1 PETER 1:22 NIV

It has been vehemently objected that Christ is the only means of grace. I answer, This is mere playing upon words. Explain your term, and the objection vanishes away. When we say, "Prayer is a means of grace," we understand a channel through which the grace of God is conveyed. When you say, "Christ is the means of grace," you mean the sole price and purchaser of it, that "no man comes unto the Father, but through Him." And who denies it?

But does not the Scripture (it has been objected, also) direct us to *wait* for salvation? Does not David say, "My soul waits for God; from Him comes my salvation?" Does not Isaiah teach us the same, saying, "O Lord, we have waited for You"?

All this cannot be denied. We are undoubtedly to *wait* on Him. But how shall we wait? Can you find a better way of waiting for Him than the way He Himself has appointed? Consider the very words of the prophet Isaiah. The whole sentence runs thus: "In the way of Your judgments [or ordinances], O LORD, we have waited for You" (Isaiah 26:8 NKJV). In the very same way did David wait: "Teach me, O LORD, the way of Your statutes, and I shall keep it to the end" (Psalm 119:33 NKJV).

Trust and Obey

The Lord is my strength and song,
and He has become my salvation.
EXODUS 15:2 NASB

"Yes," say some, "but God has appointed another way: 'Stand still and see the salvation of God.'" Let us examine the Scriptures to which you refer.

The first of them, with the context, runs thus:

> *And when Pharaoh drew near, the children of Israel*
> *lifted their eyes, and. . .they were very afraid, and. . .*
> *they said to Moses, "Because there were no graves in*
> *Egypt, have you taken us away to die in the wilder-*
> *ness?". . . And Moses said to the people, "Do not be*
> *afraid. Stand still, and see the salvation of the*
> *LORD.". . . And the LORD said to Moses. . ."Tell the*
> *children of Israel to go forward. But lift up your rod,*
> *and stretch out your hand over the sea and divide it.*
> *And the children of Israel shall go on dry ground*
> *through the midst of the sea."*
>
> EXODUS 14:10–16 NKJV

This was the salvation of God, which they stood still to see,
by marching forward with all their might!

So let us believe God and follow His commands, waiting on Him in His way, using the means of grace He has appointed.

Obedience Is Better

To obey is better than sacrifice.
1 SAMUEL 15:22 NIV

Another passage in which the expression "Stand still" occurs reads thus: "Then some came and told Jehoshaphat, saying, 'A great multitude is coming against you from beyond the sea.'. . . And Jehoshaphat feared, and set himself to seek the LORD, and proclaimed a fast throughout all Judah. So Judah gathered together to ask help from the LORD; and from all the cities of Judah they came to seek the LORD. Then Jehoshaphat stood in the assembly. . .in the house of the LORD. . . . Then the Spirit of the LORD came upon Jahaziel. . .and he said, 'Listen. . .Thus says the LORD to you:

> *Do not be afraid nor dismayed because of this great*
> *multitude. . . . Tomorrow go down against them. . . .*
> *You will not need to fight in this battle. Position your-*
> *selves, stand still and see the salvation of the LORD'. . . .*
> *So they rose early in the morning and went out. . . .*
> *Now when they began to sing and to praise, the LORD*
> *set ambushes against the people of Ammon, Moab, and*
> *Mount Seir. . .[and] they helped to destroy one another."*
>
> 2 CHRONICLES 20:2–23 NKJV

Such was the salvation that the children of Judah saw. They obeyed. *They sang and praised the Lord.* But how does all this prove that we ought *not* to wait for the grace of God in the means which He has ordained?

Wait in Faith and Obedience

"If anyone loves me, he will obey my teaching."
JOHN 14:23 NIV

I shall mention one more objection, which, in fact, does not properly belong to this subject. Nevertheless, because it has been so frequently urged, I may not wholly pass it by.

The objection is that St. Paul said, "If you died with Christ from the basic principles of the world, why. . .do you subject yourselves to regulations?" (Colossians 2:20 NKJV). Therefore, it is said, a Christian, one that is dead with Christ, need not use the ordinances, the means of grace, any more.

So one says, "If I am a Christian, I am not subject to the ordinances of Christ!" By the very absurdity of this, surely you see at first glance, that the regulations referred to cannot be the ordinances of Christ. They are the Jewish ordinances—to which it is certain a Christian is no longer subject.

This undeniably appears from the words immediately following, " 'Do not touch, do not taste, do not handle' " (v. 21 NKJV). These all evidently refer to the ancient ordinances of the Jewish law, so that this objection is the weakest of all.

So, in spite of all objections, that great truth must stand unshaken: All who desire the grace of God are to wait for it in the means which He Himself has ordained.

God's Way Is Perfect

*The precepts of the Lord are right,
giving joy to the heart.*

PSALM 19:8 NIV

There is a kind of order wherein God Himself is generally pleased to use these means in bringing a sinner to salvation. One goes senselessly on in his own way. God comes upon him unaware—by an awakening sermon or conversation, an awful providence, or a stroke of His convincing Spirit without any outward means. Having now a desire to flee from the wrath of God, he purposely goes to hear how it may be done. If he finds a preacher who speaks to the heart, he is amazed and begins searching the Scriptures.

The more he *hears* and *reads,* the more convinced he is; the more he meditates day and night. By these means, the arrows of conviction sink deeper into his soul. He begins to *talk* of the things of God and to *pray* to Him, scarce knowing what to say. Perhaps it is only in "groans which cannot be uttered," perhaps doubting whether the high and lofty God will regard such a sinner as he. So he goes to pray with those who know God, in the congregation. He observes others partaking of the Lord's Supper. He thinks, "Christ has said, 'Do this!' How is it that I do not? I am too great a sinner; I am not worthy."

He struggles awhile, finally breaking through; and so he continues in God's way: *in hearing, reading, meditating, praying, and partaking of the Lord's Supper;* till, in the manner that pleases Him, God speaks, "Your faith has saved you. Go in peace."

The Means of Grace and the Means to Grace

Teach me your way, O LORD;
lead me in a straight path.
PSALM 27:11 NIV

By observing the order in which God leads a sinner, we may learn what means to recommend to any particular soul. If any thing will reach a careless sinner, it is probably hearing, or conversation, if he ever has any thought about salvation. To one who begins to feel the weight of his sins, not only hearing the Word of God, but reading it, too, and perhaps other serious books, might be a means of deeper conviction. He is well advised also to meditate on what he reads that it may have its full force upon his heart. And to speak freely, particularly among those who walk in the same path. When trouble and heaviness take hold upon him, he should then be earnestly exhorted to pour out his soul before God, always to pray and not lose heart. And when he feels the worthlessness of his own prayers, remind him of going up into the house of the Lord, to pray with all who fear Him. But if he does this, the word of his Lord will soon be brought to his remembrance to eat and drink the Lord's Supper.

We should second the motions of the blessed Spirit, for one is thus led, step by step, through all the means God has ordained—not according to our own will, but just as the providence and the Spirit of God go before and open the way.

The Variety of the Spirit

In the night I remember your name, O LORD,
and I will keep your law.

PSALM 119:55 NIV

It has been already observed that there is an order in which God is generally pleased to use these means as He brings sinners to Himself. Yet we find no command in Holy Scripture for any particular order to be observed. Neither do the providence and the Spirit of God adhere to any without variation. The means in which different people are led, and in which they find the blessing of God, are varied, transposed, and combined together a thousand different ways.

Yet still our wisdom is to follow the leadings of His providence and His Spirit, more especially as to the means wherein we ourselves seek the grace of God. For He guides us partly by His outward providence, giving us the opportunity of using sometimes one means, sometimes another; and partly by our experience, whereby His free Spirit is pleased most to work in our hearts.

And in the meantime, the sure and general rule for all who groan for the salvation of God is this: Whenever opportunity serves, use all the means which God has ordained, for who knows in which of them God will meet you with the grace that brings salvation?

God Is the Doer

"He is the LORD;
let him do what is good in his eyes."
1 SAMUEL 3:18 NIV

It wholly depends on our manner of using the means of grace whether they shall convey any grace at all to us. It is necessary for us always to retain a lively sense that God is above all means. Beware of limiting the Almighty. He does whatever and whenever it pleases Him. He can convey His grace either in or out of any of the means which He has appointed. Who has known the mind of the Lord? or who has been His counselor?

Look, then, every moment for His appearing! Perhaps at the hour you are employed in His ordinances—or before or after; or when you are hindered from them. He is never hindered. He is always ready, always able, always willing to save.

Before you use any means, let it be deeply impressed on your soul: There is no *power* in this. It is, in itself, a poor, dead, empty thing. Separate from God it is a dry leaf, a shadow.

Neither is there any *merit* in my using this or that means; nothing intrinsically pleasing to God; nothing whereby I deserve any favor at His hands, not even a drop of water to cool my tongue. But because God bids, therefore I do. Because He directs me to wait in this way, therefore here I wait for His free mercy, whereof comes my salvation.

All Is of God

The blood of Christ, who through the eternal Spirit
offered Himself without blemish to God,
[shall] cleanse your conscience from dead works
to serve the living God.

HEBREWS 9:14 NASB

Settle this in your heart, that the mere work done profits nothing. There is no power to save but in the Spirit of God, no merit but in the blood of Christ. Consequently, even what God ordains conveys no grace to the soul if you do not trust in Him alone. On the other hand, he that does truly trust in Him cannot fall short of the grace of God, even though he were cut off from every outward ordinance, or shut up in the center of the earth.

In using all means, seek God alone. In and through every outward thing, look only to the *power* of His Spirit, and the *merits* of His Son. Beware you do not get stuck in the *work* itself; if you do, it is all lost labor. Nothing short of God can satisfy your soul. Therefore, fix on Him in all, through all, and above all. For all the power, and all the merit is of Him alone.

Remember also to use all means as *means*—as ordained, not for their own sake, but for the renewal of your soul in righteousness and true holiness. If, therefore, they actually tend to this, that is well; but if not, they are dung and dross.

Sing of His Love

Declares the Lord,
I will put my laws in their minds
and write them on their hearts. . . .
and will remember their sins no more.
HEBREWS 8:10, 12 NIV

After you have used any of these means of grace, take care how you value yourself on them; how you congratulate yourself as having done some great thing. This is turning all into poison. The cause of our redemption is not our own works or righteousness, but the kindness and love of God our Savior. . . according to His mercy. . .that we might become heirs of eternal life (see Titus 3:4–7).

Meantime, think, "If God was not there, what does using this means avail? Have I not been adding sin to sin? O Lord, save, or I perish! O lay not this sin to my charge!"

If God *was* there, if His love flowed into your heart, you have already forgotten the outward work. You see, you know, you feel, God is all in all. Be abased. Sink down before Him. Give Him all the praise. Let God in all things be glorified through Christ Jesus. Cry from the depth of your heart, "My song shall be always of the lovingkindness of the LORD, with my mouth I will ever be telling of Your truth from one generation to another!" (See Psalms 89:1 and 100:5.)

Repentance

"Produce fruit in keeping with repentance."
MATTHEW 3:8 NIV

Repentance is of two sorts. One, which is spoken of here, is termed *legal,* and it is a thorough conviction of sin. The other sort is termed *evangelical.* It is a change of heart and, consequently, of life, marked by a change from sin to holiness.

Jesus gives us an example of both sorts of repentance in the parable of the returning prodigal. He was first convicted of his condition, followed by an inward and outward change. There is joy in heaven, Jesus said, over one such sinner who repents and is thoroughly changed in heart and life (see Luke 15:7). *Legal repentance* is scarcely sufficient. There must be an entire change in the nature of the heart.

The believers in Judea asked Peter to account for his preaching to the Gentiles at the house of Cornelius. When he had concluded, they all said, " 'Then God has also granted to the Gentiles repentance to life' " (Acts 11:18 NKJV). Being fully satisfied, they glorified God that He had wrought this for the Gentiles—a change from spiritual death to spiritual life, leading to life everlasting.

The apostle Paul testified both to Jews and Gentiles *"repentance toward God* and faith toward our Lord Jesus Christ" (Acts 20:21 NKJV). The very first motion of the soul toward God is a kind of repentance. This must itself go before faith, which in turn produces the change from sin to holiness of heart and life.

Enter by the Narrow Gate

"Enter through the narrow gate."
MATTHEW 7:13 NIV

Jesus described, in what is commonly called the Sermon on the Mount (Matthew 5–7), true holiness and happiness, that is, the nature of true inward religion. And He pronounced as happy those who follow after that way.

After warning His hearers of some hindrances to holiness (7:1–12), He begins, in the above text, urging them to practice the way He had described.

At the same time, He gives a caution against hindrances of another kind: *ill example and ill advice.* By one or the other, many, perhaps thousands, who once went well in the way of God had drawn back into a state of damnation. And many of these were not novices in religion; they had made some progress in righteousness.

Our Lord presses His caution against ill example and ill advice with all possible earnestness. He repeats it again and again, in variety of expressions, lest we should let the point slip away.

To effectively guard against ill example, He said, *"Enter by the narrow gate;* for wide is the gate and broad is the way that leads to destruction, *and there are many who go in by it.* Because narrow is the gate and difficult is the way which leads to life, and there are few who find it." What a powerful force is *the many.* Oh, run from their evil example!

Flee the Wide Gate

"Wide is the gate and broad is the road
that leads to destruction,
and many enter through it."
MATTHEW 7:13 NIV

In these words we may observe the inseparable properties of the way to hell: The gate is wide; the road is broad; and many enter through it.

Wide indeed is the gate and broad the way that leads to destruction. For sin is the gate of hell and wickedness is the road to destruction. And how very wide is the gate of sin; how very broad is the way of wickedness.

The commandment of God is exceeding broad (see Psalm 119:96), extending to all our actions, to every word that goes out of our lips, every thought that rises in our hearts.

Sin is equally broad with the commandment, since any breach of the commandment is sin. Yes, it is a thousand times broader. There is only one way of keeping the commandment, but there are a thousand ways of breaking every commandment. So that this gate is wide indeed.

Consider how wide the parent-sins are: the carnal mind which is against God, pride of heart, self-will, and love of the world. Do they not diffuse themselves through all our thoughts and mingle with all our tempers? Do they not permeate the mass of our affections as yeast leavens a dough?

How kind is our Lord to warn us against these hindrances to progressing in His way!

Avoid the Broad Road

"Broad is the road that leads to destruction."
MATTHEW 7:13 NIV

Just as the gate of sin is very wide, so the way of wickedness is very broad. It is not something which the imagination might paint, but that which may be a matter of daily melancholy experience. Nor do you need to go around the earth to find them.

Survey any kingdom, any single country, city, or town. How plenteous is the harvest of wickedness. And it need not be a place that is still overspread with pagan darkness. Look at this one, a country that professes to see the light of the glorious gospel. This has been called a Christian land. But alas! who will carry the reformation of opinions into our hearts and lives? How innumerable are our sins! Do not the grossest abominations of every kind abound among us from day to day? Do not sins of every sort cover the land as the waters cover the sea? Who can count them? Rather go and count the drops of rain or the sands on the seashore. So wide is the gate and so broad the way that leads to destruction! And so many who enter through it!

And how well are we warned to avoid these. For we may otherwise be swept along by the force of so numerous examples conspiring with our own hearts to carry us away. But by the grace of God, we accomplish the difficult and move against the press to enter the narrow way.

Many Walk the Broad Road

> *"Wide is the gate. . .*
> *that leads to destruction, and many enter through it."*
> MATTHEW 7:13 NIV

There are many who walk in that way—almost as many as go in at the gate of death. It cannot be denied (we acknowledge it with shame and sorrow of heart) that even in this, which has been called a Christian country, the general part of every age and gender, of every profession and employment, of high and low, of rich and poor, is walking in the way of destruction. The far greater part of the inhabitants of every city lives in sin. Some are in habitual, gross, visible ungodliness or unrighteousness—some open violation of their duty either to God or to their fellow humans. No one denies: These are all in the way that leads to destruction.

Add those who have a fair name but are not alive to God. They appear outwardly alive but are inwardly full of uncleanness—full of pride or vanity, of anger or revenge, of ambition or covetousness. They love themselves and the world's pleasures more than they love God. They may be highly esteemed of men and women, but they are an abomination to the Lord.

Add all those who have something of the form of godliness but nothing of its power. They have not submitted to the righteousness which is of God by faith.

Take all these together and you see that, indeed, "Many go in at the wide gate." *Reader, where are you?*

The Broad Road Leads to Death

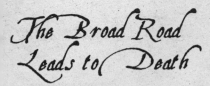

Flee the evil desires.
2 TIMOTHY 2:22 NIV

How terribly true is our Lord's assertion, "Wide is the gate and broad is the way that leads to destruction, and there are many who go in by it" (Matthew 7:13 NKJV).

Now this does not concern only the vulgar herd—the base, common part of humanity. Men and women of eminence in the world—those who have much possessions—are not excused from this description. On the contrary, their desire is toward the broad way. Many wise ones, according to the human methods of judging, many mighty in power of one kind or another, of courage, of riches, many noble ones are called into the broad way. Called by the forces of the world, by the base desires of their flesh, and by the devil. And they obey that calling.

Indeed, in general, the higher they are raised in fortune and power, the deeper they sink into wickedness. The more blessings they receive from God, the more sins they commit. They do not use their honor or riches, their learning or wisdom, as means of working out their salvation. They use what should be a blessing as means of excelling in vice. And so they ensure their own destruction.

The very reason why so many of these go on securely in the broad way is because it *is* broad. They do not consider that this very broadness is the inseparable quality of the way to destruction.

The Narrow Way

Pursue righteousness.
2 TIMOTHY 2:22 NASB

So many people enter the way to destruction because small is the gate and narrow the way that leads to life. Indeed, the narrowness is an inseparable quality of the way to heaven.

So narrow is the way that leads to life everlasting, so small the gate, that nothing unclean, nothing unholy, can enter. No sinner can pass through that gate until he or she is saved from their sins. Not only from outward sins, from evil lifestyles copied from their parents. It will not suffice that they have ceased doing evil and learned to do well. They must not only be saved from all sinful actions, from evil and useless conversation. They must be inwardly changed, thoroughly changed in the spirit of their mind. Otherwise, they cannot pass through the gate of life; they cannot enter into glory.

For narrow is the way that leads to life—the way of universal holiness. Narrow indeed is the way of poverty of spirit; the way of holy mourning; the way of meekness; the way of hungering and thirsting after righteousness. Narrow is the way of mercifulness; of love unfeigned; the way of purity of heart; of doing good to all; and of gladly suffering evil for righteousness' sake.

A narrow way indeed, but such is the inseparable quality of the way to heaven.

God Rejoices in the Few

"Narrow the road that leads to life,
and only a few find it."
MATTHEW 7:14 NIV

Alas! how few find even the way of primitive, heathen honesty! How few are there that do nothing to another which they would not want another to do to them! How few who are clear before God from acts of injustice or unkindness! How few who do not offend with their tongue, speaking nothing unkind or untrue! What a small proportion of men and women are innocent even of outward transgressions! And how much smaller a proportion have their hearts right before God, clean and holy in His sight!

Where are they whom His all-searching eye discerns to be truly humble, abhorring themselves in the presence of God their Savior? Where are the deeply serious, who sense their needs, as sojourners on this earth, meek and gentle? Where are the ones who are not overcome by evil but who overcome evil with good? Where are those thoroughly athirst for God, continually yearning for a renewal in His likeness?

How thinly scattered over the earth are they whose souls are enlarged in love for all mankind, who love God with all their strength. They have given Him their hearts and desire nothing else in earth or heaven! How few are they who spend their strength doing good to everyone, ready to suffer all things, even death itself, to save one soul from eternal death! *Are you one of these few?*

Hold Fast

"Lord, are only a few people going to be saved?"

LUKE 13:23 NIV

Few are found in the way of life. And while so many are in the way of destruction, there is great danger lest the torrent of ill example should bear us away with them. Even a single example, if it be always in our sight, is apt to make much impression upon us. Especially when it has nature on its side, when it falls in with our own inclinations! How great then must be the force of so numerous examples continually before our eyes, all conspiring with our own hearts to carry us down the stream of nature! How difficult must it be to stem the tide and to "keep ourselves unspotted in the world!"

What heightens the difficulty still more is that they are not the rude and senseless part of humanity (at least not these alone) who set us the ill example, who throng the downward way. The polite, the well-bred, the genteel, the wise, those who understand the world, those of knowledge, of deep and various learning, the rational, the eloquent are all, or nearly all, against us.

And how shall we stand against these? How can unlearned and ignorant men and women hold their own against those who are well versed in controversies and have learned all the arts of persuasion? We can hold on in the way of the kingdom only when we desire nothing more than God and resolutely cherish the desires we have from Him.

Worldly Wisdom

*A natural man does not accept
the things of the Spirit of God,
for they are foolishness to him.*
1 CORINTHIANS 2:14 NASB

The men and women of learning are so well versed in controversies and reasoning that it is a small thing with them to prove that their way is right because it is broad. They will show you that one who follows a multitude cannot do evil—only the one who will not follow them; that your way must be wrong because it is narrow and because so few people find it. They will further demonstrate that evil is good and good is evil—that the way of holiness is the way of destruction, and the way of the world is the only way to heaven.

Yet we must contend not only with these *wise ones* in the broad way. There are also many important, noble, and powerful men and women in the way that leads to destruction. These do not apply to your understanding but to your *fears*. This method seldom fails even where argument profits nothing. For everyone has the capacity to *fear* whether they can reason or not.

So that everyone who has not a firm trust in God, a sure reliance both on His power and love, does naturally fear to give offense to those who have the power of the world in their hands. It is no wonder, then, if the example of these powerful people is a law to all who do not know God.

Against All Odds

> "How hard it is for the rich to
> enter the kingdom of God!"
>
> LUKE 18:24 NIV

Many rich are likewise in the broad way. And these apply to the *hopes* of men and women, and to all their foolish desires, as strongly and as effectively as the mighty and noble do to their fears. So that you can hardly hold on in the way of the kingdom unless you are dead—crucified to the world and the world crucified to you. Unless you desire nothing but God.

How dark, uncomfortable, and forbidding is the prospect on the opposite side—a small gate, a narrow way, and few finding the gate or walking in the way. And these are not wise, not ones of learning or eloquence. Many of them are not able to reason either strongly or clearly. They do not know how to prove what they profess to believe, or to explain even what they say they experience. You think such advocates as these do not recommend the cause they have espoused, but rather discredit it.

Neither are they noble, honorable people. If they were, you would put up with them. But they are poor people, with no power or authority in the world. Therefore, there is nothing to be *feared;* there is nothing at all to *hope* from them. So that all your natural desires (except those you have received immediately from God) continually incline you to return to the broad way. Yet our Lord says, "Enter by the *narrow* gate."

While It's Still "Today"

> "Strive to enter through the narrow door."
> LUKE 13:24 NASB

In the Sermon on the Mount, our Lord earnestly exhorts, "Enter by the narrow gate." In the [above] passage from Luke, He uses a different expression: "Strive to enter in." In the original, the word means to strive as in agony. "For," He says, "many will seek to enter and will not be able." He said the master of the house calls them "evildoers."

They were commanded to depart because they had been doers of evil; because they had walked in the broad way. In other words, *they had not agonized to enter in at the narrow gate.* Probably they did *seek,* before the door was shut; but that did not suffice. And they did *strive,* after the door was shut, but then it was too late.

Therefore, *strive now,* today, to enter in at the small gate, the narrow way. And to do this, settle in your heart, and let it be uppermost in your thoughts, that if you are in a broad way, you are in the road that leads to destruction. If many go with you, as sure as God is true, both they and you are going to hell! If you are walking as the generality of men and women walk, you are all walking to the bottomless pit! Are many wise, many rich, many mighty or noble traveling in the same way? By this token, without going any farther, you know it does not lead to life.

Oh, leave the broad way and choose the narrow one. It leads to life everlasting.

True Wisdom

> *I press on toward the goal for the prize.*
> PHILIPPIANS 3:14 NASB

Here is a short, a plain, an infallible rule, before you enter into particulars. In whatever profession you are engaged, you must be singular—out of the ordinary—or be damned! The way to hell has nothing singular in it. The way to heaven is singularity all over. If you move but one step towards God, you are no longer as others. But do not regard this. It is far better to stand alone than to fall into the pit of hell.

Run, then, with patience the race that is before you, though your companions in it are but few. This will not always be so. After a while, you will come to an innumerable company of angels, to the general assembly and church of the firstborn, and to the spirits of just men made perfect (see Hebrews 12:22–23).

For now, *strive* to enter in by the narrow gate. Be penetrated with the deepest sense of the inexpressible danger your soul is in so long as you are in a broad way. Are you void of poverty of spirit and all that inward religion which the many, the rich, the wise, account madness?

Strive to enter in. Be pierced with sorrow and shame for having so long run on with the unthinking crowd. Have you been neglecting, perhaps despising, the "holiness without which no one can see the Lord"? Turn, and *strive;* be singular. Enter the narrow gate that leads to life.

Have a Holy Urgency

*See to it that you do not refuse him
who speaks [from heaven].*
HEBREWS 12:25 NIV

Strive to enter by the narrow door.

Strive, as in an agony of holy fear. A promise has been made of your entering into His rest (see Hebrews 4:9–11). *Strive,* lest you should come short of it.

Strive, in all the fervor of desire, with groans that words cannot express.

Strive by prayer without ceasing. At all times, in all places, lift up your heart to God. Give Him no rest till you, like the psalmist, "awake with God's likeness" and are satisfied with it.

To conclude: *Strive* to enter in at the narrow gate. *Strive,* not only by this agony of soul, of conviction, of sorrow, of shame, of desire, of fear, of unceasing prayer. *Strive,* likewise, by putting in order all your conversation, your whole life, by walking with all your strength in all the ways of God—the way of innocence, of piety, and of mercy. Shun all the appearance of evil. Do all possible good to all people. Deny your own will in all things, and take up your cross daily.

Be ready to cut off everything that would hinder, and to cast it from you. Be ready and willing to suffer the loss of possessions, of friends, of health—of all things on earth—so you may enter into the kingdom of heaven.

Take Up Your Cross

"If anyone wishes to come after Me,
he must deny himself, and take up his cross."

MATTHEW 16:24 NASB

If any will follow Christ, their very first step is to deny themselves—in place of their own will to substitute the will of God as their one overriding principle of action.

Note that Jesus said, *If anyone wishes, or desires.* No one is forced, but *if* any will be a Christian, it must be on these terms: *Let him deny himself, and take up his cross.* This rule can never be too much observed: Let each one in all things deny his or her own will, however pleasing, and do the will of God, however painful.

Should we not consider all crosses, all things painful to our human nature, as what they really are: as opportunities of embracing God's will at the expense of our own? Consequently, as so many steps by which we may advance toward perfection?

We will make swift progress in the spiritual life if we are faithful in this practice. Crosses are so frequent that whoever takes advantage of them will soon be a great gainer.

Great crosses are occasions of great improvement. And the little ones which come daily, even hourly, make up in number what they lack in weight. We may, in these daily and hourly crosses, make effectual sacrifice of our will to God. These, so frequently repeated, will soon mount to a great sum.

Even Little Crosses Have Significance

*"If anyone wishes to come after Me,
he must deny himself. . .and follow Me."*
MATTHEW 16:24 NASB

Let us remember that God is the author of all events. No circumstance is so small or inconsiderable as to escape His notice and direction. Every event, therefore, declares to us the will of God; to which thus declared, we should heartily submit. We should renounce our own will to embrace His; we should approve and choose what His choice warrants as best for us.

In this we should exercise ourselves continually; this should be our practice all the day long. We should in humility accept the little crosses that are dispensed to us as those that best suit our weakness.

Let us bear these little things, at least for God's sake, and prefer His will to our own in matters of so small importance. His goodness will accept these small sacrifices, for He does not despise small things.

Whoever desires to save his life at the expense of his conscience—that is, whoever in the highest instance of life itself will not renounce himself—will be lost eternally. But can anyone hope he should be able to renounce himself in this case if he cannot do so in the smallest instances? *And whoever loses his life shall find it:* What he loses on earth he will find in heaven.

How We Enter the Kingdom

> *"Not everyone who says to me,
> 'Lord, Lord,' will enter the kingdom of heaven."*
> MATTHEW 7:21 NIV

In the Sermon on the Mount, our Divine Teacher declared the whole counsel of God regarding the way of salvation. He also observed the chief hindrances to holiness for those who desire to walk in it. In the above verse, he sets His seal to His prophecy and impresses His authority on it that it might stand firm to all generations.

That no one may ever conceive there is any other way, our Lord said, *Not everyone. . .shall enter. . .only the one who does the will of My Father who is in heaven. Many will say to Me in that day, "Lord, Lord, have we not prophesied in Your name, cast out demons in Your name, and done many wonders in Your name?". . . Depart from Me, you that work iniquity. . . . Now everyone who hears these sayings of Mine, and does not do them, will be like a foolish man who built his house on the sand.*

This foolish one is the one of whom our Lord said, "Not everyone who says to Me, 'Lord, Lord' shall enter. . . ." And this is a decree which cannot pass away; it stands forever.

We must thoroughly understand the force of these words, of the expression, "That says to Me, 'Lord, Lord.' " It undoubtedly means *anyone who thinks of going to heaven by any other way than the one just [previously] described by our Lord.*

Not by Verbal Religion

"Not everyone . . .
will enter the kingdom of heaven."
MATTHEW 7:21 NIV

Our Lord's expression in this text implies (to begin at the lowest point) all good words, all verbal religion. It includes whatever creeds we may recite, whatever professions of faith we make, whatever numbers of prayers we may repeat, whatever thanksgivings we read or say to God.

We may speak well of His name and declare His lovingkindness to all. We may be talking of all His mighty acts, and telling of His salvation from day to day.

By comparing spiritual things with spiritual, we may show the meaning of the Word of God. We may explain the mysteries of the kingdom which have been hid from the beginning of the world.

We may speak with the tongue of angels rather than men concerning the deep things of God. We may proclaim to sinners, "Behold the Lamb of God, who takes away the sin of the world!"

Yes, and we may do this with such a measure of the power of God and such demonstration of His Spirit, as to save many souls from death and hide a multitude of sins. Yet it is very possible, all this may be no more than saying, "Lord, Lord." I may have thus successfully preached to others, snatching many souls from hell, yet still drop into it when I am done. *May God have mercy on us all.*

Not by Good Works

*"Not everyone who says. . .
'Lord, Lord,' will enter."*
MATTHEW 7:21 NIV

The above expression may also imply the doing no harm to anyone. We may abstain from every presumptuous sin, from every kind of outward wickedness. We may refrain from all those ways of acting or speaking which are forbidden in Holy Scripture. We may have a conscience free from any external offense towards God and people. We may be clear of all ungodliness and unrighteousness. But we are not hereby justified. If we go no further than this, we shall never enter the kingdom of heaven.

Saying, "Lord, Lord," may imply, likewise, many of what are called *good works*. One may hear abundance of excellent sermons, attend the Lord's Supper and omit no opportunity of using all the other means of grace. I may do good to my neighbor, give my bread to the hungry, and cover the naked with a garment. I may be so zealous that I may give all my goods to feed the poor. Yes, and I may do all this with a desire to please God, even a real belief that by these I *do* please Him (which is the case with those of whom our Lord speaks). And still I may have no part in the glory that shall be revealed. For how far short is all this of that righteousness and true holiness Christ has previously described. How widely different from the inward kingdom of heaven which is opened in the believing soul!

Building on the Sand

"Many will say to Me on that day,
'Lord, Lord, did we not prophesy in Your name?' "
MATTHEW 7:22 NASB

Our Lord frequently declared that none who have not the kingdom of God within them shall enter into the kingdom of heaven.

Yet He well knew that many would not receive that saying. So He confirms it yet again: "Many [not one; not a few only; it is not a *rare* thing] will say to Me in that day," not only have we said many prayers; we have spoken Your praise; we have done no evil; but what is much more: "we have prophesied in Your name." We have declared Your will to men and women, we have showed sinners the way to peace and glory. And we have done this "in Your name," according to the truth of Your gospel. In or by Your name, by the power of Your Word and of Your Spirit "have we cast out devils. And in Your name [by Your power, not ours] have we done many miracles."

But Jesus said, "And then I will declare to them, I never knew you"; I never knew you as My own, for your heart was not right toward God. You were not meek and lowly; you were not lovers of God and all mankind. You were not renewed in the image of God; you were not holy as I am holy. "Depart from Me, you" who, in spite of all this, are "workers of law-lessness"—transgressors of My law, My law of holy and perfect love. You have built upon the sand.

Hearing Requires Action

*"Everyone who hears these words of Mine
and does not act on them,
will be like a foolish man
who built his house upon the sand."*
MATTHEW 7:26 NASB

Our Lord declared clearly that there is no way to get around the narrow gate and the difficult way of entering the kingdom of heaven. "Many [said He] will say, Look what we have done in Your name, but I will say to them, Depart from Me; I never knew you."

To put this statement beyond all possibility of contradiction, He confirms it by this suitable comparison: *Everyone who hears these sayings of Mine, and does not do them, will be like a foolish man who built his house on the sand. And the rain descended, the floods came, and the winds blew and beat on that house*—as they surely do, sooner or later, upon every soul alive—floods of outward affliction or inward temptation; the storms of pride, anger, fear, or desire—*and it fell. And great was its fall,* so that it perished forever.

Such must be the portion of all who rest in anything short of that religion which has been described. And their fall will be the greater because they "heard those sayings" and yet they "did them not."

How different a case is it with those who, when they hear the words of Christ, *do* them, and in so doing, build their house upon the Rock, the living Rock of Ages.

Building upon the Rock

*"Everyone who hears these words of mine
and puts them into practice is like a wise man
who built his house on the rock."*
MATTHEW 7:24 NIV

Examine the wisdom of those who do the sayings of our Lord, those who build upon a rock. They are indeed wise, who do "the will of My Father who is in heaven." They are truly wise whose righteousness exceeds the righteousness of the scribes and Pharisees. They are poor in spirit, knowing themselves as also they are known. They see and feel all their sin and guilt until it is washed away by the atoning blood of Christ. They are conscious of their lost condition, of the wrath of God abiding on them, and of their utter inability to help themselves till they are filled with peace and joy in the Holy Spirit. Then they are meek and gentle, patient toward all, never returning evil for evil but rather a blessing, and thus overcome evil with good.

Their souls are athirst for nothing on earth, but only for the living God. These have love for all, even ready to lay down their lives for their enemies. They love the Lord their God with all their heart, mind, soul, and strength. Those alone shall enter into the kingdom of heaven who, in this spirit, do good to all, and who for that cause are hated, reproached, and persecuted, yet still rejoice and are exceeding glad. These know in whom they have believed and are assured that these light, momentary afflictions will work out for them "an eternal weight of glory."

Wise Builders

The fear of the LORD is the beginning of wisdom.
PSALM 111:10 NASB

How truly wise is the one who knows him or herself. They know they are everlasting spirits which came from God, sent into a house of clay, not to do their own will but the will of the One who sent them. They know the world. They are to pass a few days or years, not as inhabitants but as strangers and sojourners in the way to the everlasting habitations. Accordingly, they use the world as not abusing it and as knowing that the fashion of it passes away.

They know God as Father and as friend, the parent of all good; the center of the spirits of all flesh; the sole happiness of all intelligent beings. They see, clearer than the noonday sun, that this is the end, the purpose, of all human beings, to glorify the One who made us for Himself, and to love and enjoy Him forever.

And, with equal clearness, they see the means to that end, to the enjoyment of God in glory—to know, even now, to love, to imitate God, and to believe in Jesus Christ whom He has sent.

These are wise, even in God's account. For they are building their house upon a rock—upon the Rock of Ages, the everlasting Rock, the Lord Jesus Christ—and living a life of holiness and happiness, praising God and doing all things to His glory.

The Sure Foundation

Jesus Christ is the same
yesterday and today and forever.
HEBREWS 13:8 NASB

The Lord Jesus Christ is fitly called the everlasting Rock of Ages for He changes not. To Him, both the men of God of old and the apostle citing His words bear witness: " 'You, LORD, in the beginning laid the foundation of the earth, and the heavens are the work of Your hands. They will perish, but You remain; and they will all grow old like a garment; like a cloak You will fold them up, and they will be changed. But You are the same, and Your years will not fail' " (Hebrews 1:10–12 NKJV).

Wise, therefore, is the one who builds on Him; who lays Him as the only foundation; who builds only upon His blood and righteousness, upon what He has done and suffered for us. On this cornerstone, the wise one fixes his or her faith, and rests the whole weight of the soul upon it.

These are taught of God to say, "Lord, I have sinned! I deserve the nethermost hell, but I am justified freely by Your grace through the redemption that is in Jesus Christ. And the life that I now live, I live by faith in Him who loved me and gave Himself for me. The life I now live is a divine, heavenly life, a life that is hid with Christ in God."

I now live, even in the flesh, a life of love, of pure love both to God and to my fellows. And, thanks be to God, doing all to His glory.

The House on the Rock Stands Firm

*"And the rain. . .the floods. . .the winds. . .
slammed against that house; and yet it did not fall,
for it had been founded on the rock."*

MATTHEW 7:25 NASB

Let not even the one who builds on the everlasting Rock of Ages think that there will be no more warfare. He or she is not out of the reach of temptation. It still remains for God to prove the grace He has given. Even the wise ones will be tried as gold in the fire, tempted not less than those who do not know God—perhaps abundantly more. For Satan will not fail to try to the uttermost those he is not able to destroy.

The rain *will* furiously descend—only at such times and in such manner as seems good, not to the prince of the power of the air but to Him whose kingdom rules over all. The floods, the torrents, will come; they will lift up their waves and rage horribly. But the Lord sits above the waterfloods. He remains King forever, and He will say to them also, "Just to here shall you come and no farther. Here shall your proud waves be stayed." The winds will blow and beat upon that house as though they would tear it from the foundation. But they cannot prevail; it does not fall for it is founded upon a rock.

The wise ones build on Christ by faith and love; therefore, they shall not be cast down. Though the waters rage and swell, and the mountains shake at the tempest, still they are safe under the shadow of the Almighty.

What Is Your Foundation?

Examine yourselves to see
whether you are in the faith;
test yourselves.
2 CORINTHIANS 13:5 NIV

It closely concerns every one of us to apply personally and practically our Lord's teachings about building upon a sure foundation. We each need to diligently examine what foundation we have built upon, whether on a rock or on the sand.

How deeply are *you* concerned to ask, "What is the foundation of *my* hope?" On what do you build your expectation of entering into the kingdom of heaven? Is it built on your orthodoxy, your right opinions, which you have sadly misnamed *faith?* Is this not madness? Surely this is building on the sand, or rather, on the froth of the sea.

Or again, are you building your hope on what is equally unable to support it—perhaps, on belonging to an excellent church, one reformed after the true Scripture model, blessed with a pure doctrine, an apostolic form of government?

These are truly reasons for praising God, as they are certainly helps to holiness, but they are not themselves holiness. And if they are separate from it, they will profit nothing. Indeed, they will leave us all the more without excuse and exposed to the greater damnation.

So this foundation, likewise, is like building upon the sand. We cannot, we dare not, rest here.

Not by Harmlessness

Without faith it is impossible to please Him.
HEBREWS 11:6 NASB

If I. . .do not have love, it profits me nothing.
1 CORINTHIANS 13:3 NASB

Some men and women build their hope of salvation upon their innocence. Are you one of these? Do you build upon your doing no harm—not wronging or hurting anyone? You are just in all your dealings. You are downright honest, paying everyone what is due. You neither cheat nor extort; you act fairly with all. And you have a conscience toward God; you do not live in any known sin.

That is all well so far, but still it is not salvation. You may go thus far and yet never come to heaven. When all this harmlessness flows from a right principle, it is *the least part* of the religion of Christ. But if it does not flow from a right principle, it is *no part at all* of religion. So that in grounding your hope of salvation on this alone, you are still building upon the sand.

Do you go further yet? Do you add to your doing no harm? Observe all the means of grace? At all opportunities, observe the Lord's Supper, use public and private prayer, fast as often as you can, hear and search the Scriptures and meditate on them?

True, these things ought to be done. Yet these also are nothing if they are without faith, mercy, and the love of God; holiness of heart; heaven opened in the soul. If you have not these, you have still built upon the sand.

We Build by Faith

It is with your heart that you believe and are justified.
ROMANS 10:10 NIV

Friend, come up higher! Do not be content with good works: feeding the hungry, clothing the naked, visiting the fatherless and widowed in their affliction, or the sick and those in prison, and the stranger. Do you preach the truth of Jesus in the name of Christ? Do the influence of the Holy Spirit and the power of God enable you to bring sinners from darkness to light, from the power of Satan to God?

Then go and learn what you have taught: By grace you are saved through faith. . .not by our works of righteousness. . . but of His own mercy He saves us (see Ephesians 2:8, Titus 3:5).

Learn to hang naked upon the cross of Christ, counting all you have done just so much dross and dung. Apply to Him just in the spirit of the dying thief and the harlot with her seven devils! *Lord, save or I perish!* Else you are still on the sand; and after saving others, you will lose your own soul.

If you do now believe, pray, *Lord, increase my faith.* Or, if you have not faith, pray, *Give me this faith, though it be as a grain of mustard seed.* For only saving faith, the faith that builds upon a rock, stands firm when the floods rise and the winds blow. And this true saving faith will indeed be manifested in good works of righteousness.

Hearing and Doing by Faith

What does it profit. . .
if someone says he has faith
but does not have works?
JAMES 2:14 NKJV

Can such a faith of which the apostle speaks [above] save? O no! A faith which does not have works following, which does not produce both inward and outward holiness, is not a true Christian faith. The faith of the gospel, the faith that leads to glory, stamps the whole image of God on our hearts, purifying us as He is pure. Above all other snares of the devil, beware of resting on unholy, unsaving faith! If you build on this, you are lost forever: You are still building your house upon the sand. When the rain descends, and the floods come, the house will surely fall, and great will be the fall of it.

Now, therefore, build upon a rock. By the grace of God, know yourself. Know and feel that you were shaped in wickedness, conceived in iniquity, and that you have been heaping sin upon sin ever since you could discern good from evil. Own yourself guilty of eternal death, and renounce all hope of ever being able to save yourself. Be it all your hope to be washed in His blood and purified by His Spirit. For He bore all your sins when He died upon the cross. And if you do know that He has taken away your sins, so much the more abase yourself before Him in a continual sense of your dependence on Him for every good thought, word, and work, and of your utter inability to do any good unless He waters you with His grace every moment.

Wise for Eternity

Create in me a clean heart, O God.
PSALM 51:10 NASB

Do you know yourself a sinner? Weep for your sins, and mourn after God, till He turns your heaviness into joy. And even then, weep with those who weep, and for those who weep not for themselves. Mourn for the sins and miseries of all humanity. See the immense ocean of eternity without a bottom or a shore. It has swallowed up millions upon millions of people and is ready to devour those who yet remain.

Here is the house of God, eternal in the heavens. And there is hell and destruction, without a covering! And from this, learn the importance of every moment which just appears and then is gone forever.

To your seriousness, add meekness of wisdom. Hold an even scale to all your passions, but particularly anger, sorrow, and fear. Calmly acquiesce in whatever is the will of God. Learn to be content in whatever condition you are in. Be mild to the good; be gentle to all, but especially to the evil and the unthankful. Avoid outward expressions of anger, especially in speech. Beware also every inward emotion contrary to love, even though it goes no farther than your heart. Be angry at sin, as an affront to the Majesty of heaven, but still love the sinner, as did our Lord, who looked on the Pharisees with anger, "grieved for the hardness of their hearts"—grieved at the sinners; angry at sin. Be thus "angry and sin not."

An Everlasting Kingdom

And now abide faith, hope, love. . .
but the greatest of these is love.

1 CORINTHIANS 13:13 NKJV

Do you hunger and thirst for that which endures unto everlasting life? Then trample underfoot the world and the things of the world—all these riches, honors, pleasures. What is the world to you? Follow after the image of God. Beware of quenching that blessed thirst, if God has already excited it in your soul. Do not quench it by what is commonly called religion—a poor, dull farce of form, of outside show—which leaves the heart still clinging to the dust, as earthly and sensual as ever. Let nothing satisfy you but the power of godliness, a religion that is spirit and life, dwelling in God and God in you. Contend for being an inhabitant of eternity, entering in by the blood of sprinkling "within the veil," and "sitting in heavenly places with Christ Jesus!"

And seeing you can do all things through Christ strengthening you, be merciful as your Father in heaven is merciful. Love your neighbor—friends and enemies—as your own soul. Let your love be long-suffering and patient towards all. Let it be kind, soft and benign, inspiring you with amiable sweetness, fervent and tender goodwill. Rejoice in the truth that is after godliness. Cover all things in love; believe all good of your neighbor; hope all things in his favor. Endure all things, triumphing over all opposition; for true love never fails, in time or in eternity.

Entering the Kingdom

"Yet it did not fall,
for it had been founded upon the rock."
MATTHEW 7:25 NASB

Let your religion be the religion of the heart. Let it lie deep in your inmost soul. Through the power of His grace, be purified from every unholy affection: from pride, by deep poverty of spirit; from anger, every unkind or turbulent passion, by meekness and mercifulness; from every desire but to please and enjoy God, by a hunger and thirst after righteousness. Love the Lord your God with all your heart and with all your strength.

Be little and low (beyond what words can express) in your own eyes, amazed and humbled to the dust by the love of God which is in Christ Jesus.

Be serious. Let the whole stream of your thoughts, words, and actions flow from the deepest conviction that you, indeed everyone, stand on the edge of the great gulf, just ready to drop either into everlasting glory or everlasting burnings.

Let your soul be filled with mildness, gentleness, patience, long-suffering towards all. At the same time, let all that is in you be athirst for the living God, longing to awake after His likeness. Be a lover of God and of all men and women; in this spirit do and endure all things.

Thus show your faith by your works; thus do the will of your Father who is in heaven. So shall you reign with Him in glory as you now walk with Him on earth.

Flesh vs. Spirit

To be spiritually minded is life and peace.
ROMANS 8:6 NKJV

To be carnally minded—the words just prior to the above text—is to mind the things of the flesh, to have a mind focused on and controlled by the sinful nature. Those who are after (or according to) the flesh are those who remain under the guidance of corrupt nature, and they mind the things of the flesh.

That is, they have their thoughts and affections fixed on those things which gratify the corrupt nature with which they were born. Namely, on visible and temporal things—on things of the earth, on pleasure (of sense and imagination), praise, or riches. This, says the writer, *is death*— spiritual death now and the way to death everlasting.

But they who are after the Spirit—who are under His holy guidance—*mind the things of the Spirit.* They think of, relish, and love invisible, eternal things. These are the things which the Spirit has revealed and which He works in the heart of the Christian. He moves us toward these eternal things which He has promised to give us.

To be spiritually minded—to have a mind set on and controlled by the Holy Spirit of God—*is life,* a sure mark of *spiritual* life and the way to everlasting life. And it is attended with *peace,* the peace *of* God—the foretaste of life everlasting—and peace *with* God, opposite to the enmity of the mind controlled by corrupt nature (see v. 7).

Natural vs. Spiritual

The natural man does not receive
the things of the Spirit of God. . . .
But he who is spiritual judges all things.
1 CORINTHIANS 2:14–15 NKJV

The natural man or woman is one—everyone—who has not the Spirit of God. Such have no other way of obtaining knowledge than by natural senses and understanding. Such do not receive, do not understand or conceive, the things pertaining to God's nature or His kingdom that are revealed by His Spirit.

Verse fourteen reads, *they are foolishness to him.* He is so far from understanding that he utterly despises them. *Neither can he know them.* As he has not the will, so neither has he the power; *because they are spiritually discerned.* They can be discerned only by the aid of the Spirit and by those spiritual senses which a natural man does not have.

But the spiritual man or woman, one who has the Spirit of God, *discerns all things,* all the things of God of which the apostle has been writing. *For the Spirit searches. . . the deep things of God* (v. 10) and He reveals the hidden, mysterious depths, both of His nature and kingdom, to the spiritual one.

The natural man or woman does not understand the spiritual person nor understand what he or she says of the truths of God which He has revealed either in His Word or to His children's hearts. Yet the apostle Paul says that spiritual ones *have the mind of Christ* concerning the whole plan of gospel salvation.

Not Yet a Christian

"You almost persuade me to become a Christian."
ACTS 26:28 NKJV

Ever since the rise of Christianity, many in every age and nation have stood with King Agrippa in his words to the apostle Paul: Almost persuaded to be a Christian.

However, since it avails nothing with God to go only thus far, it is important to consider what it means being *almost,* and also being *altogether, a Christian.*

Implied in being *almost a Christian* is, first, primitive honesty. Not the honesty merely recommended in the writings of the uncivilized, godless philosophers but the sort which common pagans expected one of another, and many of them actually practiced. They were taught not to be *unjust.* Not to oppress the poor, nor to use extortion, nor cheat the poor or the rich, nor to defraud, and, if it were possible, to owe no one anything.

They commonly allowed that some regard be paid to *truth* as well as to justice. They held in abomination anyone who would call God to witness to a lie, or one who falsely accused another. Indeed, willful liars were counted disgraceful pests of society.

Again, there was a sort of *love and assistance* they expected from one another. This included not just the little deeds of humanity, but feeding the hungry, clothing the naked, and, in general, giving to the needy whatever they themselves had and did not need. Yet all this is merely *primitive honesty,* not Christianity.

An "Outside" Christian

Having a form of godliness.
2 TIMOTHY 3:5 NIV

One who is almost a Christian has the form of godliness, even the godliness prescribed in the gospel. He or she has the outside of a real Christian, doing nothing the gospel forbids: does not take the name of God in vain, nor treat the day of the Lord irreverently. They avoid actual adultery, fornication, and uncleanness as well as every word or look which might directly or indirectly lead or tend to it. They shun evil-speaking, cursing, talebearing, all foolish jesting (which is considered a virtue by some), or any conversation not good for building up themselves and others, or which might grieve the Holy Spirit of God.

They do not willingly wrong, hurt, or grieve anyone but in all things act and speak by that plain rule, "Whatever you would not one should do to you, do not do to another."

In doing good, they do not limit themselves to meaningless offers of goodwill but labor for the profit of many that they may help at least some. They endeavor to do good to the souls as well as the bodies of men and women, not merely feeding the hungry if they have food to spare, but labor, as they have opportunity, to bring them to the gospel of Christ. Yet this is having only the *outside form of a Christian*.

Still just an "Outside" Christian

Having a form of godliness.
2 TIMOTHY 3:5 NIV

One who has the outside form of a Christian abstains from "wine, wherein is excess" (Ephesians 5:18 KJV) and from reveling and gluttony. He or she avoids, as much as possible, all strife and contention, continually endeavoring to live peaceably with all. If they are treated wrongly, they do not avenge themselves, nor return evil for evil. They do not revile others, nor are they brawlers or scoffers at the faults or infirmities of their neighbors.

And in doing good, they do not confine themselves to cheap and easy instances of kindness, but they work, even suffer, for the benefit of as many as possible. In spite of toil or pain, whatever their hands find to do, they do with all their strength. It may be for friend or enemy, for an evil person or a good one. They are not slothful in this, but as they have opportunity, they do good to all, both in soul and body.

They reprove the wicked, instruct the ignorant, confirm the wavering, quicken the good, and comfort the afflicted. They labor to awaken those asleep in sin; to lead those already awakened to wash in the "fountain opened for sin and uncleanness"; and to stir up those who are saved through faith to adorn the gospel of Christ in all things. And all this from a mere *form of godliness.*

A Form of Godliness

Having a form of godliness but denying its power.
2 TIMOTHY 3:5 NIV

One who has the form of godliness does not merely abstain from all outward evil, doing all possible good. He or she also uses the means of grace at all opportunities, especially by attending the house of God as frequently as possible. Nor do they come in looking gaudy and acting impertinent, gazing about with careless indifference. They do not sleep or recline in sleeping posture; nor do they act as though God is asleep, talking with one another or merely seeming to use a prayer to God for His blessing.

No; they behave with seriousness and attention in every part of the solemn service, especially during the Lord's Supper. Theirs is not a careless behavior; but a deportment which says only "God be merciful to me a sinner."

If they are heads of families, they practice family prayer, and they set aside times also for private addresses to God.

Those who have the form of godliness, being *almost Christians,* have also a real, inward principle of religion, a *sincerity,* from which these outward actions flow. Indeed, without sincerity, one does not have even primitive honesty, for even pagans made a difference between those who avoided sin from fear of punishment and those who did so from a love of virtue. Without the inward principle of sincerity, one is not even *almost a Christian.* He is, rather, only a hypocrite altogether!

The Almost Christian

Holding to a form of godliness.
2 TIMOTHY 3:5 NASB

The almost Christian shuns all evil, does all possible good, observes the means of grace, and possesses sincerity of heart—a real design to serve God, a hearty desire to do His will—a sincere view of pleasing God in conversation, in all that is done or left undone. For the almost Christian, this design runs through all the tenor of his life. Sincerity is the moving principle in doing good, abstaining from evil, and using the ordinances of God, the means of grace.

Right here, it will probably be inquired, "Is it possible that anyone living should go so far as this and yet be *only almost a Christian?* What more can be implied in being a *Christian altogether?*"

I answer, first, it is possible to go thus far and yet be only *almost a Christian.* I learn this not only from the Word of God, but also from the sure testimony of experience. I did go thus far for many years, using all diligence to shun all evil and to have a conscience void of offense; redeeming the time; using every opportunity of doing good to all; constantly and carefully using all the public and private means of grace; striving after a steady seriousness of behavior. God is my record, I did this in all sincerity, with a real desire to please Him who had called me to lay hold of eternal life. Yet, my conscience bears me witness in the Holy Spirit, all that time I was but *almost a Christian.*

Altogether a Christian: The Love of God

" 'Love the Lord your God with all your heart.' "
MATTHEW 22:37 NASB

We come, second, to what is implied in being altogether a Christian.

First, the love of God. So says His Word: " 'You shall love the LORD your God with all your heart, with all your soul, with all your mind, and with all your strength' " (Mark 12:30 NKJV). Such a love as this occupies the whole heart, takes up all the affections, fills the entire capacity of the soul, and employs the utmost extent of all its faculties.

One who thus loves is continually rejoicing in God. His delight is in the Lord, his Lord and his all, to whom he gives thanks in all things. All his desire is toward God and to the remembrance of His name. His heart is always crying out, "Whom have I in heaven but Thee? and there is none on earth that I desire beside Thee."

Indeed, what can he desire but God? Not the world or the things of the world, for he is crucified to the world and the world is crucified to him. He is crucified to the desire of the flesh, the desire of the eye, and the pride of life. He is dead to pride of every kind: For "love is not puffed up." One who is dwelling in love, dwells in God, and God in him; and he is less than nothing in his own eyes. For the love of God is a mark of _the altogether Christian._

The Love of Our Neighbor

> " 'You shall love your neighbor as yourself.' "
> MATTHEW 22:39 NASB

The second thing implied in our being altogether a Christian is the love of our neighbor. Our Lord said, "You shall love your neighbor as yourself." If any ask, "Who is my neighbor?" we reply, "Everyone in the world; every child of His who is the Father of the spirits of all flesh" (see Hebrews 12:9).

Nor may we exclude our enemies, or the enemies of God and of their own souls. Every Christian loves these also as himself, even as Christ loved us.

If you would more fully understand what manner of love this is, consider St. Paul's description of it (see 1 Corinthians 13:4–8). It is long-suffering and kind. It does not envy; it is not rash or hasty. It is "not puffed up"—not arrogant—but makes the one who loves the servant of all. Love does not behave indecently but gives all men and women their due. Love does not seek its own advantage, only the good of others that they may be saved. Love is not provoked to sharpness or unkindness to anyone. It thinks no evil. Love does not rejoice in iniquity, but rejoices in the truth. It covers all evil which it knows of anyone. It believes all good things of others and puts the most favorable construction on everything. Love hopes whatever is for the best of anyone and endures whatever the injustice, malice and cruelty of others can inflict.

Faith, the Ground of All

And without faith it is impossible to please Him.
HEBREWS 11:6 NASB

We may separately consider faith as being implied in what it means to be altogether a Christian. Yet faith cannot actually be separated from the love of God and of our neighbor. It is, rather, the ground of both. Very excellent things are spoken of faith in the Word of God. Everyone who "believes. . .is born of God" (1 John 5:1 NASB); "as many as received Him, to them He gave the right to become children of God, even to those who believe in His name" (John 1:12 NASB); and "This is the victory that has overcome the world—our faith" (1 John 5:4 NASB). Our Lord Himself declared that one who believes in the Son has everlasting life and shall not come into judgment, but has passed from death into life (see John 5:24).

But let none deceive his or her own soul. The faith which does not result in repentance, love, and all good works is not that true, living faith but a dead and devilish one. Even the devils believe the Old and New Testaments. They believe that Christ was born of a virgin, that He worked miracles and declared Himself very God. They believe that He suffered death to redeem us from everlasting death, that He rose again, is at the Father's right hand, and will judge the living and the dead at the end of the world. Yet they are devils still, and remain in their damnable estate, lacking the true Christian faith. We must have a *living faith*.

Right and True Christian Faith

For in Christ Jesus. . .faith working through love.
GALATIANS 5:6 NASB

The right and true Christian faith is not only to believe that the Holy Scriptures and the creeds which express our beliefs are true. It is to have a sure trust and confidence to be saved from everlasting damnation by Christ. It is a sure trust and confidence which a person has in God that, by the merits of Christ, one's sins are forgiven, and he is now reconciled to the favor of God. From this comes a loving heart to obey His commandments.

This faith purifies the heart by the power of God who now dwells within. The heart is cleansed from pride, anger, wrong desire—from all unrighteousness, from "all filthiness of the flesh and spirit" (see 2 Corinthians 7:1 NKJV). And the heart is filled with a love stronger than death, both to God and to everyone. This love does the works of God, rejoicing to spend and be spent for all. This love endures with joy, not only reproach for the name of Christ, the being mocked, despised, and hated by men and women, but whatever the wisdom of God permits the malice of people or devils to inflict.

Whoever has *this* faith, thus working by or through love, is not only almost, but *altogether, a Christian.*

Our Hearts Tell Us

Thou God seest me.
GENESIS 16:13 KJV

Who are the living witnesses of this faith and this love? I implore you, as you are in the presence of the One who sees the hearts of men and women without a covering, that you ask your own heart: Am I of that number?

Do you even practice justice, mercy, and truth as far as an honest pagan? Do you have the *outside* of a Christian, the *form* of godliness? Do you abstain from evil—from whatever is forbidden in the Word of God? Do you do whatever good you can with all your might? Do you seriously attend the house of God and take part in the means He has given as channels of receiving His grace? And is all this done with a sincere design and desire to please God?

Can you frankly say you have even come up to the standard of pagan honesty, without which you are not even *almost a Christian?* Are you still without even the *form* of Christian godliness? Has God seen in you a real design of pleasing Him in all things? Have you intended to devote all your words and works, your business, your studies, your diversions, to His glory? Did you design or desire that whatever you did should be done "in the name of the Lord Jesus"? That it should be a spiritual sacrifice, acceptable to God through Christ?

But even good designs and good desires do not make a Christian unless they are brought to good effect. "Hell is paved," says one, "with good intentions." There remains a final question.

Being Altogether a Christian

*The love of God has been poured out within our hearts
through the Holy Spirit who was given to us.*

ROMANS 5:5 NASB

It is not enough to shun evil and do good at all opportunities, nor to seriously use all the means of grace with a sincere design and desire to please God.

The great question remains for each of us: Is the love of God poured out in my heart? Does my heart cry that He is my all? Am I happy in God? Is He my delight? And is it written in my heart that those who love God love their neighbor also?

Go further: Do I believe that Christ loved me and gave Himself for me? Do I have faith in His blood? Do I believe that the Lamb of God has taken away my sins and cast them as a stone into the depth of the sea, giving me redemption through His blood, even the remission of my sins? Does His Spirit testify with my spirit that I am a child of God?

Let no one persuade you to rest short of this prize of your high calling. Cry day and night unto Him who, "while we were without strength, died for the ungodly"; until you know Him in whom you have believed and know that you are indeed *altogether a Christian.*

Then, being justified freely by His grace by the redemption that is in Jesus, you will experience that blessed peace with God through Jesus Christ and know the love of God poured into your heart by the Holy Spirit given unto you!

As a Little Child

*"Unless you are converted and become as little children,
you will by no means enter the kingdom of heaven."*
MATTHEW 18:3 NKJV

The first step towards entering into the kingdom of grace is to become as little children—lowly in heart, knowing yourselves utterly ignorant and helpless, and hanging wholly on your Father in heaven for a supply of all your wants. It is further true that unless you are turned from darkness to light, from the power of Satan to God, except you are entirely, inwardly changed, renewed in the image of God, you cannot enter into the kingdom of glory. Thus must everyone be converted in this life, or he can never enter into life eternal.

All who are in this sense little children are unspeakably dear to our Lord. Therefore, help them all you can, as if it were Christ Himself in person. And see that you do not offend them, Jesus said (v. 6), or turn them out of the right way; neither hinder them in it.

Let us be careful, then, to receive and not to offend the very weakest believer in Christ. For as inconsiderable as some of these may appear to us, the very angels of God have a peculiar charge over them (v. 10). Indeed, these angels are of the highest order, who continually behold the face of the Father, continually appear at the throne of the Most High. And these "little children" are the very ones Christ came to save.

The New Birth

> " 'You must be born again.' "
>
> JOHN 3:7 NASB

If any doctrines of Christianity may be termed "fundamental," they are doubtless those of justification and the new birth. The former relates to that great work which God does for us, in forgiving our sins. The latter relates to the great work that God does in us, in renewing our fallen nature.

In order of *time,* neither of these is before the other. In the moment we are justified by the grace of God through the redemption that is in Jesus, we are also "born of the Spirit." But in order of *thinking,* as it is termed, justification precedes the new birth. We first conceive His wrath to be turned away, and then His Spirit to work in our hearts.

Of how great importance it is for everyone to thoroughly understand these fundamental doctrines. A full, clear account of them will enable us to give a satisfactory answer to three questions. First, Why must we be born again? (the foundation of this doctrine); secondly, How must we be born again? (the nature of the new birth); and thirdly, For what purpose must we be born again? (to what end is it necessary?)

Made in the Image of God

God created man in His own image.
GENESIS 1:27 NASB

Why must we be born again? The answer lies in the scriptural account of the creation. We read that the three-one God said, " 'Let Us make man in Our image, according to Our likeness. . . .' So God created man in His own image" (Genesis 1:26–27 NKJV).

This image was, first, *a natural image,* a picture of His own immortality, a spiritual being, with understanding, freedom of will, and various affections. It was, likewise, *a political image,* the governor of this lower world, having dominion over the fish of the sea and over all the earth. But it was chiefly God's *moral image* in which man was created, which, according to the apostle, is "righteousness and true holiness" (Ephesians 4:24 KJV). In this righteous and holy *moral image* of God, man was made.

"God is love" (1 John 4:8, 16 KJV). Accordingly, man, at his creation, was full of love; it was the sole principle of his tempers, thoughts, words, and actions. God is full of justice, mercy, and truth; so was man as he came from the hand of his Creator. God is spotless purity; and so was man, in the beginning, pure from every sinful blot. Otherwise, God could not have pronounced him "very good" (Genesis 1:31 KJV). There is no medium: An intelligent creature not loving God, not righteous and not holy, is not good at all, much less to be pronounced by God "very good."

So our state at creation was *very good.*

Rebellion in Paradise

*"From the tree of the knowledge of
good and evil you shall not eat."*

GENESIS 2:17 NASB

Man was made in the image of God, yet he was not made immutable, unchangeable. This would have been inconsistent with that state of trial in which God was pleased to place him. He was therefore created able to stand, yet liable to fall.

God Himself informed Adam of this and gave him a solemn warning about it. Nevertheless, he did not abide in honor; he fell from his high estate. He ate of the tree which God had commanded him, "You shall not eat thereof."

By this willful act of disobedience, this flat rebellion against his sovereign, Adam openly declared that he would no longer have God rule over him. He would be governed by his own will and not the will of the One who had created him. He would not seek his happiness in God but in the world.

Now, God had told him before, "In the day you eat of that fruit, you shall surely die." And the word of the Lord cannot be broken. Accordingly, in that day, he *did* die; he died to God—the most dreadful of all deaths. He lost the life of God, separated from the One in union with whom spiritual life consists. The body dies when it is separated from the soul; the soul, when it is separated from God. Adam sustained this separation in the very hour he disobeyed.

Losing the Life of God

*The man and his wife hid themselves from
the presence of the LORD God.*
GENESIS 3:8 NASB

When Adam disobeyed God and ate of the forbidden fruit (v. 6), he gave immediate proof of his separation from God. He showed by his behavior that the love of God was extinguished in his soul, which was now "alienated from the life of God" (Ephesians 4:18 NKJV). He was now under the power of servile fear, so that he fled from the presence of the Lord. So little did he retain even of the knowledge of Him who fills heaven and earth that he tried to hide himself among the trees of the garden. He had lost both the knowledge and the love of God, without which the image of God could not subsist. He was, therefore, deprived of this image at the same time and became unholy as well as unhappy. Instead of having the image of God, he had sunk into pride and self-will, the very image of the devil, and into sensual appetites and desires, the image of the beasts.

Some may argue that the threatening "in that day. . . you shall die" refers to the death of the body only. But to affirm this is flatly to make God a liar. For it is evident Adam did not die *in this sense* "in that day"; he lived another nine hundred (and more) years. Unless we impeach the veracity of God, this death *must* be understood of *spiritual death,* the loss of the life and image of God.

Why We Must Be Born Again

> *"You should not be surprised at my saying,*
> *'You must be born again.'"*
>
> JOHN 3:7 NIV

In Adam, all died (see Romans 5:5–21), all humankind, even those yet unborn. The natural consequence of this is that everyone descended from him comes into the world spiritually dead, dead to God, wholly dead in sin—entirely void of the life and image of God and of the righteousness and holiness in which Adam was created. Everyone born now bears the image of the devil in pride and self-will and the image of the beast in sensual appetites and desires.

The foundation for, the need of, the new birth is this entire corruption of our nature. Having been born in sin, we must be "born again." *Everyone born* must be *born again.*

But *how* must one be born again? What is the nature of the new birth? This is the second question of the highest importance. We ought to examine it with all possible care. We need to ponder it in our hearts until we fully understand this point and clearly see how we are to be born again.

Not that we are to expect any philosophical account of the manner how it is done. Our Lord guards us against any such expectation in His next words. He reminds Nicodemus of an indisputable fact of nature even the wisest ones are not able to fully explain. The precise manner of how the wind begins and ends, rises and falls, no one can tell.

Not a New Doctrine

"So is everyone who is born of the Spirit."
JOHN 3:8 NASB

"The wind blows where it wishes," Jesus told Nicodemus. "You hear the sound of it [you are assured that it does blow] but cannot tell where it comes from and where it goes." Even the wisest ones under the sun are not able to fully explain it.

So is everyone who is born of the Spirit. You may be as absolutely assured of the fact as of the blowing of the wind. But the precise manner how it is done, how the Holy Spirit works this in the soul, neither you nor the wisest ones are able to explain. Yet without descending into curious, critical inquiries, we can give a plain scriptural account of the nature of the new birth.

The expression *being born again* was not *first* used by our Lord in His conversation with Nicodemus. It was well known before that time and was in common use among the Jews when our Savior appeared among them.

When an adult heathen was convinced that the Jewish religion was of God and desired to join it, it was the custom to baptize him first before he was admitted to circumcision. When he was baptized, he was said to be *born again.* By this, they meant that one who was before a child of the devil was now adopted into the family of God and accounted one of His children. Our Lord used this same expression, but in a stronger sense than Nicodemus was accustomed to.

How Can These Things Be?

"How can a man be born when he is old?
He cannot enter a second time into
his mother's womb and be born, can he?"
JOHN 3:4 NASB

These things cannot be, literally, but they may, spiritually. One may be born from above, born of God, born of the Spirit, in a manner bearing a very near analogy to the natural birth.

Before a child is born he has eyes, but does not see; he has ears, but does not hear. He has an imperfect use of all other senses. He has no knowledge or natural understanding of any of the things of the world. As soon as he is born, he begins to see the light and the objects around him. His ears are opened, and he hears the sounds which strike upon them. At the same time, all other organs of sense begin to be exercised upon their proper objects. He now breathes and lives in a manner totally different from before.

How exactly does the parallel hold in all these instances! While one is in a mere "natural" state, before he is born of God, he has—in a spiritual sense—eyes and sees not. A thick, impenetrable veil lies upon them. He has ears, but hears not. He is deaf to that which is of the most concern to hear. His other spiritual senses are all locked up. Hence he has no knowledge of God or the things of God, either of spiritual or eternal things. Although he is a living man, he is a dead Christian. But all this changes as soon as he is born again of the Spirit.

A Total Change in the Senses

*"That which is born of the flesh is flesh,
and that which is born of the Spirit is spirit."*
JOHN 3:6 NASB

As soon as a person is born of God, there is a total change in all his spiritual senses. The eyes of his understanding are opened (see Ephesians 1:18). God, who of old time commanded light to shine out of darkness, now shines on his heart, and he sees the light of the glory of God in the face of Jesus Christ. His ears are opened, and he hears the inward voice of God saying, "Be of good cheer; your sins are forgiven." This is the meaning of what God speaks to his heart, though perhaps not in these very words. He is now ready to hear whatever God is pleased from time to time to reveal to him.

He feels in his heart the mighty working of the Spirit of God—not in a gross, carnal sense as those in the world willfully misunderstand the expression. We mean neither more nor less than this: One feels, is inwardly sensible of, the graces which the Spirit of God works in his heart. He feels, he is conscious of, a peace which passes all understanding. He often feels a joy in God that is "unspeakable and full of glory." He feels the love of God poured into his heart by the Holy Spirit which is given unto him. His spiritual senses are now exercised to discern spiritual good and evil. By their use, he daily increases in the knowledge of God, of Jesus Christ, and of the things pertaining to His inward kingdom.

The Nature of the New Birth

Created in Christ Jesus.
EPHESIANS 2:10 NASB

Having been born again from above, one may now be properly said to live. God has quickened him by His Spirit, and he is alive to God through Jesus Christ. He lives a life which the world knows not—a life which is "hid with Christ in God." God is continually breathing upon the soul, as by a kind of spiritual respiration, and the soul is breathing unto God. Grace is descending into the heart, and prayer and praise are ascending to heaven. By this communion between God and himself, this fellowship with the Father and the Son, the life of God in the soul is sustained. The child of God grows up, till he comes to the full measure of the stature of Christ (see Ephesians 4:13).

We see that the nature of the new birth is *that great change which God works in the soul when He brings it to life, raising it from the death of sin to the life of righteousness.* It is the change wrought in the whole soul by the almighty Spirit of God when the soul is created anew in Christ Jesus, renewed after the image of God in righteousness and true holiness (see Ephesians 4:24). The love of the world is changed into the love of God; pride into humility; passion into meekness; hatred, envy, malice into a sincere, tender love for all. In a word, it is the change whereby the earthly, sensual, devilish mind is turned into the mind that was in Christ Jesus. This is the nature of the new birth: *"So is everyone who is born of the Spirit."*

The Necessity of the New Birth

Put on the new self,
created to be like God
in true righteousness and holiness.
EPHESIANS 4:24 NIV

For what purpose is the new birth necessary? First, in order to holiness. For gospel holiness is not a bare external religion, with a round of outward duties. No: Gospel holiness is no less than the image of God stamped upon the heart. It is no other than the whole mind that was in Christ Jesus. It consists of all heavenly affections and tempers mingled together in one. It implies such a continual, thankful love to Him who gave us His only Son that makes it natural to us to love everyone, and fills us with mercy, kindness, gentleness, and long-suffering. This love of God teaches us to be blameless in our conversation and enables us to present our souls and bodies—words, thoughts, and actions—a continual sacrifice to God, acceptable through Christ Jesus.

Now, this holiness can have no existence till we are renewed in the image of our mind. It cannot commence in the soul till that change is wrought; till by the power of the Highest overshadowing us we are brought from darkness to light, from the power of Satan to God—that is, till we are born again. Therefore, the new birth is absolutely necessary in order to holiness. And, "without holiness no one shall see the Lord," shall see the face of God in glory. Of consequence, *the new birth is absolutely necessary in order to eternal salvation.*

The New Birth: The Entrance to Heaven

> *"Unless one is born of water and the Spirit he cannot enter into the kingdom of God."*
>
> JOHN 3:5 NASB

Men and women may indeed flatter themselves (so desperately wicked and so deceitful is the human heart) that they may live in their sins till they come to their last gasp and yet afterwards live with God.

Thousands do really believe they have found a broad way that does not lead to destruction. "What danger," say they, "can a woman be in who is so *harmless and virtuous?* What fear is there that so *honest* a man, one of so *strict morality,* should miss heaven? Especially, if over and above all this, these constantly attend church and observe the sacraments?"

One of these will ask with all assurance, "What! shall not I do as well as my neighbors?" Yes, as well as your unholy neighbors; as well as your neighbors who die in their sins! For you will all drop into the pit together, into the nethermost hell! You will all lie together in the lake of fire, "the lake of fire burning with brimstone." Then, at length, you will see (but God grant you may see it before that) the necessity of holiness in order to glory. And, consequently, of the new birth, since none can be holy unless they are born again.

The Key to Happiness

Believing,
you rejoice with joy inexpressible and full of glory.
1 PETER 1:8 NKJV

Unless one is born again he cannot be happy even in this world. For it is not possible, in the nature of things, that one can be happy who is not holy. Even the poor, ungodly poet could tell us, "No wicked man is happy."

The reason is plain: All unholy tempers are uneasy tempers. Not only malice, hatred, envy, jealousy, and revenge create a hell in the heart. Even the softer passions, if not kept within due bounds, give a thousand times more pain than pleasure. Hope, when deferred (and how often this is the case) "makes the heart sick." Every desire which is not according to the will of God is liable to pierce us through with many sorrows. And all those general sources of sin—pride, self-will, and idolatry—are, in the same proportion as they prevail, general sources of misery.

Therefore, as long as these reign in any soul, happiness has no place there. But they must, and do, reign till the bent of our nature is changed, that is, till we are *born again.*

Consequently, the new birth is absolutely necessary in order to find happiness in this world as well as in the world to come.

New Birth:
Not the Same as Baptism

". . .born of water and the Spirit."
JOHN 3:5 NASB

An obvious conclusion from the above Scripture is that baptism and the new birth are not one and the same thing. Yet many seem to imagine that they are just the same; at least they speak as if they thought so.

Baptism is considered a sacrament in nearly every Christian denomination, a sacrament being an outward and visible sign of an inward and spiritual grace. But the parts of a sacrament are two: one, the outward and sensible sign; the other, an inward and spiritual grace. Baptism is a sacrament wherein Christ has ordained the washing with water—the person being baptized in the name of the Father, the Son, and the Holy Spirit—as a sign and seal of regeneration by His Spirit—a death unto sin and a new birth unto righteousness.

So, baptism, the outward sign, is distinct from regeneration, which is the inner grace being signified. What could be more plain? The one is an external, the other an internal, work. The one is a visible, the other an invisible, thing and, therefore, wholly different from each other. The one is an act of man, purifying the body; the other a change wrought by God in the soul. So that the former is just as distinguishable from the latter as the soul is from the body, or as water is from the Holy Spirit.

Whose Servant Are You?

. . .buried. . .by baptism into death: that. . .
we also should walk in newness of life.
ROMANS 6:4 KJV

Just as the new birth and baptism are not the same, they do not always accompany each other. One may possibly be "born of water" and yet not be "born of the Spirit." There may sometimes be the outward sign where there is no inward grace. (I do not now speak with regard to infants. While we cannot comprehend how this work can be wrought in infants, neither can we comprehend how it is wrought in an adult.) Whatever the case is with infants, it is sure that all of mature years who are baptized are not at the same time born again. "The tree is known by its fruits," and it is too plain to be denied, that many of those who were children of the devil before they were baptized continue the same afterward. "For the works of their father they do." They continue servants of sin with no pretense to either inward or outward holiness.

But neither is the new birth the same with sanctification. This is a *part* of sanctification, but not the whole. It is the gate, the entrance into it. When we are born again, our inward and outward holiness begins. Then we gradually "grow up in Him who is our Head"; just as a child is born in a short space of time and afterward gradually grows up. The same relation which there is between our natural birth and our growth also exists between our new birth and our sanctification.

In the Name of Charity?

Love does no wrong to a neighbor.
ROMANS 13:10 NASB

What must one say who loves the souls of men and women? We see them treating the Lord's Day irreverently, living in drunkenness or other willful sin, and we are grieved. What can one say, other than "You must be born again"? "No," says another. "That cannot be. How can you speak so uncharitably to people? Have they not been already baptized? They cannot be born again now."

Can they not? Do you really affirm this? Then they cannot be saved. Though one be as old as Nicodemus was, yet unless he is born again, he cannot see the kingdom of God. Therefore in saying, "They cannot be born again," you, in effect, deliver them over to damnation. Where is the uncharitableness now? On my side or yours? I say they may be born again. You say, "They cannot be." If so, they must inevitably perish! So you block up their way to salvation and send them to hell, out of mere charity?!

Perhaps it is the sinner himself, to whom in real charity we say, "You must be born again," who responds, "I defy your new doctrine. I need not be born again. I was born again when I was baptized. Would you have me deny my baptism?"

I answer, you have already denied it by every willful sin you have done. Baptized or unbaptized, "you must be born again," or you cannot be inwardly holy. And without holiness, no one will see the Lord in glory.

Did You Renounce the Devil?

Resist the devil and he will flee from you.
JAMES 4:7 NASB

Consider the case of the one who affirms he was born again in baptism yet remains an open sinner. I say to that one, if you have been baptized, do not admit it. For how highly it aggravates your guilt, and how it will increase your damnation!

You were devoted to God in your baptism and yet all along have been devoting yourself to the devil? You were consecrated to God the Father, the Son, and the Holy Spirit and ever since have been flying in the face of God in giving yourself to Satan? You have done all this even though you were once solemnly given up to God?

O be ashamed! Blush! Hide yourself in the earth! Never again boast of what ought to fill you with confusion, to make you ashamed before God and all mankind.

You have denied your baptism in the most effectual manner a thousand times, and day by day. For in baptism, you renounced the devil and all his works. Whenever you give place to him again by doing any of the works of the devil, you then deny your baptism.

But whether you are baptized or unbaptized, you must be born again. Otherwise, it is not possible you should be inwardly holy. And without inward as well as outward holiness, you cannot be happy even in this world, much less in the world to come.

Born from Above

> Born again, not of corruptible seed but incorruptible,
> through the word of God which lives and abides forever.
>
> 1 PETER 1:23 NKJV

It does not matter if you have done no harm and do not live in any willful sin. You must go further yet, or you cannot be saved. Even if you also do all the good you can and have improved *all opportunities* of doing good, yet this does not alter the case. Still, you must be born again.

Without this, nothing will do any good to your poor, sinful, polluted soul. You may faithfully go to church and observe the sacraments, say ever so many prayers in private; hear ever so many good sermons; read ever so many good books. Still, "you must be born again." None of these things—nor anything else under heaven—will stand in the place of the new birth to keep you from hell; you must be born again.

If you have not already experienced this inward work of God, let this be your continual prayer: "Lord, add this to all your blessings—let me be born again. Deny me not this: Let me be 'born from above.' Take away whatever seems good to You—reputation, fortune, friends, health—only give me this, to be born of the Spirit, to be received among the children of God. Let me be born of the incorruptible seed by the word of God. And then let me daily 'grow in grace and in the knowledge of our Lord and Savior Jesus Christ!'"

The Spirit Witnesses

*The Spirit Himself bears witness with our spirit
that we are children of God.*
ROMANS 8:16 NKJV

Many vain men and women have twisted this Scripture to their spiritual detriment. Many have mistaken the voice of their imagination for this witness of the Spirit of God. Then they idly presumed they were children of God while they were doing the works of the devil.

Many reasonable men and women have seen the dreadful effects of this delusion. But in laboring to keep at the utmost distance from it, they have leaned to the opposite extreme and questioned whether the testimony spoken of here is the privilege of *ordinary* Christians. They have rather supposed it to be an *extraordinary* gift that belonged only to the apostolic age.

But we need not run to either one or the other extreme. We may steer a middle course, keeping a sufficient distance from the spirit of error and enthusiasm without denying the gift of God and giving up the great privilege of His children.

The experience of all real Christians shows what many other texts of Scripture also reveal. There is, in every believer, both the testimony of God's Spirit, and the testimony of his own spirit, that he or she is a child of God. The testimony of our own spirit is a rational one, but the witness of God's Spirit is a *divine* testimony, an intimate conviction manifested to our hearts.

The Testimony of Our Own Spirit

[He] bears witness with our spirit.

ROMANS 8:16 NKJV

What is the witness or testimony of our own spirit? The foundation for this is found in the numerous texts of Scripture which plainly describe the marks of the children of God. And by the reason or understanding which God has given, everyone may apply those scriptural marks to himself and know whether he or she is a child of God.

First, "as many as are led by the Spirit of God" into all holy tempers and actions, "these are sons—[children]—of God" (Romans 8:14 NKJV). Secondly, I am thus "led by the Spirit of God." So I easily conclude, "Therefore, I am a child of God." Then, "by this we know that we know Him, if we keep His commandments" (1 John 2:3 NKJV, and many other such marks in the third and fourth chapters). It is highly probable there never were any children of God from the beginning until now who were further advanced in the grace of God and the knowledge of our Lord Jesus Christ than the apostle John and the fathers in Christ to whom he wrote those lines. Those Christians were far from despising these marks of being the children of God and applied them to their own souls for the confirmation of their faith.

Yet this is all only rational evidence to our reason. Those who have these marks are children of God. We have these marks; therefore, we are children of God.

This is the testimony of our own spirit.

Ask Your Conscience

In your thinking be mature.
1 CORINTHIANS 14:20 NASB

How does it appear that we have the marks of the children of God? That we do love God and our neighbor? And that we keep His commandments? That is, how does it appear to ourselves, not to others?

How does it appear that you are now in ease, and not in pain? By the same consciousness, you will know if your soul is alive to God; if you are saved from the spirit of proud wrath and have an even, quiet spirit. By the same means you will perceive if you love, rejoice, and delight in God. By the same, you must be directly assured if you love your neighbor as yourself; if you are kindly affectioned to all humankind, and full of gentleness and long-suffering.

And with regard to the outward mark of the children of God—the keeping His commandments—you know within yourself, if, by the grace of God, it belongs to you. Your conscience informs you from day to day if you have the name of God on your lips only in devotion and reverence; if you remember the Lord's Day and keep it holy; if you honor your father and mother; if you do to all as you would they should do to you; if you keep your body pure and set aside as the temple of the Lord; and if, whether you eat or drink, you are temperate and do all things to the glory of God. This, likewise, is the testimony of your own conscience.

Two Testimonies

[He] bears witness with our spirit.
ROMANS 8:16 NKJV

By an immediate consciousness of the inner workings of our own heart, we have the testimony of our own spirit that God has given us to be holy of heart and holy in our outward life. It is a consciousness of having received, in and by the Spirit of adoption, the heavenly tempers written in the Word of God as belonging to His adopted children: a loving heart toward God and toward all mankind; a childlike confidence toward God our Father, desiring nothing but Him and casting all our care upon Him; embracing every human with earnest, tender affection; and a consciousness that we are inwardly conformed by the Spirit of God to the image of His Son. And that we walk before Him in justice, mercy, and truth, doing the things that are pleasing in His sight.

But what is the testimony of *God's Spirit,* which is added to and joined with this? How does He "bear witness with our spirit" that we are His children? There are no words in human language to adequately express what the children of God experience. But perhaps one might say the testimony of the Spirit is an *inward impression on the soul,* whereby the Spirit of God directly witnesses to my spirit that I am a child of God; that Jesus Christ has loved me and given Himself for me; that all my sins are blotted out, and I, even I, am reconciled to God.

He First Loved Us

We love Him because He first loved us.
1 JOHN 4:19 NKJV

The testimony of the Spirit of God that we are His children must, in the nature of things, be before the testimony of our own spirit. We cannot be conscious that we are holy of heart and holy in life before we actually are. We must be inwardly and outwardly holy before we can have the testimony of our spirit that we are such.

But we must love God before we can be holy at all, for this love is the root of holiness, and we cannot love God till we know He loves us. *We love Him because He first loved us.* And we cannot *know* His pardoning love till His Spirit witnesses it to our spirit. Since this testimony of His Spirit must precede our love of God and all holiness, consequently *it must precede our inward consciousness of them,* or the testimony of our own spirit concerning them.

Then, and not until the Spirit of God has testified of His pardoning love, do we love Him who has first loved us and, for His sake, we love our "brother," also. His Spirit assures us that God has loved us and given His Son to be the propitiation, the satisfaction, for our sins and has washed us from our sins in His blood. And of this we are conscious to ourselves. We know that we love God and keep His commandments, and as long as we continue thus, this testimony continues joined with the testimony of God's Spirit that we are His children.

That We May Know

*We have received. . .
the spirit which is of God;
that we might know the things that
are freely given to us of God.*
1 CORINTHIANS 2:12 KJV

The operation of the Spirit of God is present even in the testimony of our own spirit that we are His children. He works in us everything that is good and shines upon His own work, clearly showing what He has done. St. Paul wrote the above words to show one great purpose for our receiving God's Spirit: that He may strengthen the testimony of our own conscience. He also gives us to see in a fuller and stronger light that we now do that which pleases Him.

One may still inquire *how does* the Spirit of God bear witness with our spirit that we are His children, excluding all doubt of our sonship? First, the soul intimately and evidently perceives when it loves, delights, and rejoices in God as when it loves and delights in anything on earth. The proper scriptural reasoning is: One who loves God, delights and rejoices in Him with a humble joy, holy delight, and obedient love, is a child of God. One says, "I thus love, delight, and rejoice in God. Therefore, I am a child of God."

The *manner* how the *divine* testimony is manifested to the heart I cannot explain. The *fact* we know: The Spirit of God does give a believer such a clear testimony of his adoption that he can no more doubt it than he doubts the blaze of the noonday sun.

Avoiding Presumption

These things I have written. . .
that you may know that you have eternal life.
1 JOHN 5:13 NASB

How is the joint testimony of God's Spirit with our spirit distinguished from the presumption of the natural mind and the delusion of the devil?

First, as to avoiding presumption. One who has never been convinced of sin is always ready to flatter himself, especially in spiritual things. Yet the Holy Scriptures abound with distinctive marks: describing the circumstances which go before, which accompany, and which follow the true, genuine testimony of the Spirit of God with the spirit of a believer. From these, one may surely know the difference between the real and the pretended witness of the Spirit.

For instance, the Scripture describes *repentance,* or conviction of sin, as constantly going before the witness of pardon, both in the Gospels and in the Book of Acts. " 'Repent and believe in the gospel' " (Mark 1:15 NASB). " 'Repent. . .and be converted. . .' " (Acts 3:19 NKJV). A stranger to this repentance has never known a broken and contrite heart. The remembrance of his sins was never grievous to him, nor the burden of them intolerable. One may repeat words without meaning them, and from a lack of true conviction of sin be grasping a mere shadow. He or she does not know the privilege of the children of God. Repentance precedes pardon and the witness of it.

From Darkness to Light

The darkness is past, and the true light now shineth.
1 JOHN 2:8 KJV

Being born of God must precede His witness that we are His children. The Scriptures describe this new birth as a vast and mighty change. A change from darkness to light as well as "from the power of Satan to God" (Acts 26:18 NKJV); a passing " 'from death unto life' " (1 John 3:14 KJV); a resurrection from the dead.

"You He made alive, who were dead in trespasses and sins" (Ephesians 2:1 NKJV). "When we were dead in trespasses, [He] made us alive together with Christ. . .and raised us up together, and made us sit together in the heavenly places in Christ Jesus" (vv. 5–6 NKJV).

But the one who presumes he or she has the witness of being a child of God does not know, has not experienced, any such change as this. He is altogether unacquainted with this whole matter.

This is a language he does not understand. He tells you he always was a Christian. He knows no time when he had need of such a change. By this also, if he would give himself permission to think, he might know that he is not born of the Spirit, that he has never known God. He has mistaken the voice of his natural mind for the voice of God.

And what are the marks of one's present deportment in comparison with Scripture? Do they agree with the scriptural description of a child of God?

The Present Marks of a Christian

You greatly rejoice with joy inexpressible and full of glory.
1 PETER 1:8 NASB

Whatever one has or has not experienced in time past, there are certain present marks by which we may distinguish a child of God from a presumptuous self-deceiver. The Scriptures describe that joy in the Lord which accompanies the witness of the Spirit as a lowly, humble joy, one that causes a pardoned sinner to exclaim, "Now that I see You, O God, I abhor myself! What am I but a vile worm of the dust!" With this lowliness is meekness, patience, gentleness, long-suffering. There is a soft, yielding spirit, a mildness, sweetness, and tenderness of soul that words cannot express.

The fruits which accompany the *supposed* testimony of the Spirit *in a presumptuous person* are just the reverse. The more confident one is of the favor of God, the more he is lifted up; the more haughty and assuming is the whole behavior. The stronger witness he imagines himself to have, the more overbearing he is to all around him. He is the more incapable of receiving reproof; the more impatient of contradiction. Instead of being more meek, gentle, and teachable, he is more unready to learn of anyone, more fiery and vehement in his temper, with a fierce impulsiveness in his speaking, in his whole deportment—as if he would take matters out of God's hands and would himself devour his adversaries.

Love Rejoices to Obey

*"By this all men will know
that you are My disciples,
if you have love."*
JOHN 13:35 NASB

The Scriptures teach, "This is the love of God [the sure mark of this], that we keep His commandments" (1 John 5:3 NASB). Our Lord Himself said, " 'He who has my commandments and keeps them, it is he who loves Me' " (John 14:21 NKJV).

Love rejoices to obey, to do in every point whatever is acceptable to one's beloved. A true lover of God hastens to do His will on earth as it is done in heaven. But is this the character of the presumptuous pretender to the love of God? No; *his* love gives him liberty to disobey, to break not keep, the commandments of God. He looks on himself as "not under the law" and thinks he is no longer obliged to observe it. He is less zealous, less careful, less watchful, less earnest since he fancies himself to be *at liberty.* He no longer "exercises himself unto godliness," has ceased "wrestling with principalities and powers," has stopped enduring hardships and "agonizing to enter the narrow gate." He supposes he has found an easier way to heaven: a broad, smooth, flowery path in which he says to his soul, "Be at ease." It undeniably follows that he has not the true testimony of his own spirit. He cannot be conscious of having those marks which he does not have. Nor can the Spirit of God bear witness to a lie, that one is a child of God who is manifestly a child of the devil.

Awake, O Sleeper!

"Awake, sleeper. . .
and Christ will shine on you."
EPHESIANS 5:14 NASB

Discover yourself! If you are one of the poor self-deceivers, awake! Is your confidence a self-confidence that you have the witness in yourself that you are a child of God, and thus defy all your enemies?

Alas! You are weighed in the balance and found lacking. The word of the Lord has tried your soul and proved it to be reprobate silver. You are not lowly of heart, therefore you have not yet received the Spirit of Jesus. You are not gentle and meek, even tempered. Therefore, your joy is worth nothing; it is not joy in the Lord. You do not keep His commandments; therefore, you do not love Him, nor are you a partaker of the Holy Spirit. It is as certain and as evident as the Word of God can make it: His Spirit does not bear witness with your spirit that you are a child of God.

Cry unto Him that the scales may fall off your eyes, that you may know yourself as He knows you: a poor, undeserving, hell-bound sinner. Pray that you may receive the sentence of death within yourself, until you hear the voice that raises the dead, saying, "Be of good cheer. Your sins are forgiven. Go in peace; your faith has made you whole"; and His Spirit witnesses with your spirit that you are His child.

An Inherent, Essential Difference!

"And I. . .heard a voice saying. . .
'Arise and go on into Damascus.' "
ACTS 22:7, 10 NKJV

The genuine witness is distinguished from presumption as day from night or a glimmering candle from the light of the noonday sun. There is an inherent, obvious, essential difference between the one and the other. In like manner, there is an inherent, essential difference between spiritual light and spiritual darkness; between the light by which the Sun of Righteousness shines upon our heart and the glimmering light which is of our own kindling. The apostle Paul did not explain to King Agrippa by what criteria or manner he distinguished the voice on the Damascus road to be the voice of God. For how he knew this, who is able to explain? Perhaps neither man nor angel.

The God who gives this witness, "Your sins are forgiven," is willing that the soul should know His voice. Otherwise, He would speak in vain. Also, He is able to, and does, perform it so that the soul is absolutely assured, "This voice is the voice of God." Yet, one who has this witness is not able to explain it to one who has it not, because the things of the Spirit are spiritually discerned.

You may indeed be assured that your spiritual senses are rightly disposed, that you do not mistake the voice of the Spirit. Examine the testimony of your own spirit; see if your heart has the fruit of the Spirit ruling there: love, joy, and peace.

Be Your Own Fruit Inspector

The fruit of the Spirit is love, joy, peace, longsuffering, kindness, goodness, faithfulness, gentleness, self-control.
GALATIANS 5:22–23 NKJV

These are the immediate fruits of the Spirit ruling in the heart. The outward fruits are doing good to others; doing no evil to any; and walking in the light—a hearty, uniform obedience to all the commandments of God.

By the inner fruits you are able to distinguish the voice of God from any delusion of the devil. That proud spirit cannot be humble. Nor can he give you a soft heart that melts into mourning before God and then into the love of His child. It is not God's adversary who enables you to love your neighbor, or to put on meekness, gentleness, patience, temperance, and the whole armor of God. No, it is none other than the Son of God who comes "to destroy the works of the devil." As surely as holiness is of God and as sin is the work of the devil, so surely is the witness you have in yourself not of Satan but of God. You may well say, "Thanks be to God for His unspeakable gift! Thanks be to God who has sent forth the Spirit of His Son into my heart, crying *Abba, Father;* bearing witness with my spirit that I am His child!"

Now let your life show forth His praise. Cleanse yourself from all filthiness of the flesh and spirit, perfecting holiness in the fear of God. Then your thoughts, words, and works will be a spiritual sacrifice, holy, acceptable to God through Christ Jesus!

New Testament Grace

"Abundant grace was upon them all."
ACTS 4:33 NASB

In the New Testament, there are three distinct ways the word *grace* is used. First, it was the merciful dispensation of the gospel as opposed to the law. The law was a dispensation of terror and bondage, which only showed sin, without enabling one to conquer it. The dispensation of grace, on the other hand, brought complete victory over sin to everyone under the powerful influence of the Spirit of Christ.

In general, however, *grace* meant the glorious, free love of God without any desert on our part; the abundant overflowings of His free mercy and favor in and through His Son. It implied the favor of Christ Jesus by which alone we can come to the Father. When joined with *peace,* it also implied the favor of God with all temporal and eternal blessings, the free love of the Lord Jesus and all its fruits.

In the passage above quoted, it means a large measure of the inward power of the Holy Spirit, which *was upon them* directing all their thoughts, words, and actions. So that *grace* has mainly to do with the gift of God to us, entirely undeserved and unmerited.

But it is also used in another sense. St. Peter admonished the believers to *grow in grace.* And, in this sense, he means to grow in every Christian temper, becoming daily, in thought, word, and action, more and more like Him who is our Head.

Growing in Grace

Grow in grace.
2 PETER 3:18 KJV

There may be, for a time, grace without growth, as there may be natural life without growth. But such sickly life, of soul or body, will end in death and every day draw closer to it. Health is the means of both natural and spiritual growth. If the remaining evil of our fallen nature be not daily mortified, it will, like an evil humor in the body, destroy the whole person.

But "if you through the Spirit do mortify the deeds of the body" (only so far as we do this), "you shall live" the life of faith, holiness, and happiness. The *end and design* of grace being purchased and bestowed upon us is to destroy the image of the earthly and restore us to that of the heavenly. And so far as grace does this, it truly profits us and also makes way for more of the heavenly gift that we may at last be filled with all the fulness of God.

The strength and well-being of a Christian depend on what his soul feeds on, as the health of the body depends on whatever we make our daily food. If we feed on what is according to our nature, we grow. If not, we pine away and die. The soul is of the nature of God, and nothing but what is according to His holiness can agree with it. Sin of every kind starves the soul and makes it consume away. So let us feed our souls on His Word and on Him by faith, that we may daily grow in grace.

Heavenly Consolations

*Grow in the grace and knowledge of
our Lord and Savior Jesus Christ.*
2 PETER 3:18 NASB

In the New Testament, *grace* generally means the abundant love of God through the favor of our Lord Jesus Christ and a measure of the inward power of the Holy Spirit.

Let us not try to invert the order of God in His new creation: We shall only deceive ourselves. It is easy to forsake the will of God and follow our own; but this will bring leanness into the soul. It is easy to satisfy ourselves without being possessed of the holiness and happiness of the gospel by calling these "moods and feelings" and to oppose faith to one and Christ to the other.

But *these* "moods" are no other than heavenly tempers, "the mind that was in Christ." And such *feelings* are the divine consolations of the Holy Spirit poured into the heart of the one who truly believes. Wherever faith is, and wherever Christ is, there are these blessings. If they are not in us, it is a sure sign that, though the wilderness had become a pool, the pool has become a wilderness again.

To grow *in the knowledge of Christ* is to grow also in *faith*, which is the root of true gospel religion. This we are to do until the day of eternity: a day without night, without interruption, without end.

Be Strong

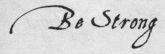

Be strong. . .in the power of His might.
EPHESIANS 6:10 NKJV

Be strong. Nothing less will suffice for fighting the good fight of faith (see 1 Timothy 6:12). To be weak and remain so is the way to perish. *In the power of His might* is a very uncommon expression. It plainly denotes what great assistance we need. As if His might would not do; it must be the *powerful exertion* of His might.

Put on the whole armor of God. The Greek word means a complete suit of armor. Believers are said to *put on* the girdle, breastplate, shoes, but *to take* the shield of faith and the sword of the Spirit. *The whole armor* (Ephesians 6:11 NKJV)—as if the *armor* would scarcely do; it must be the *whole* armor. This is repeated (v. 13) because of the strength and subtlety of our adversaries, and because of an "evil day" of extreme trial being at hand.

For our wrestling is not only, not chiefly, *against flesh and blood,* against weak men and women, or fleshly appetites, *but against principalities, against powers*—the mighty princes of all the infernal regions. Great is their power and that of the legions they command in the citadel of their kingdom of spiritual darkness. *Against the rulers of the world*—those other evil spirits who roam the provinces of the world given to them. *Against wicked spirits* who continually oppose faith, love, holiness, either by force or by fraud. Against all these we need nothing less than *the whole armor of God.*

Able to Stand

Put on the whole armor of God,
that you may be able to stand.
EPHESIANS 6:11 NKJV

Against wicked spirits who continually strive to infuse unbelief, pride, idolatry, malice, envy, anger, hatred *in heavenly places* which were once their dwelling place, and which they still aspire to as far as they are permitted. And so we need *the whole armor of God.*

In the evil day (v. 13). The war is perpetual, but the fight is one day less, another more, violent. *The evil day* is either at the approach of death, or in life. It may be longer or shorter, and admits of numberless varieties.

That you may still keep your armor on and still stand upon your guard, you must still watch and pray. Thus, you will be enabled to endure unto the end and *stand* with joy before the face of the Son of Man at "the last day."

So that you may be ready for every motion, have *your loins girt about with truth.* Not only with the truths of the gospel, but with "truth in the inward parts" (Psalm 51:6 NKJV). So our Lord is described (Isaiah 11:5). Without inward truth, all our knowledge of divine truth will prove but a poor "girdle" in *the evil day.* And as a girded man or woman is always ready to go forward, so this seems to indicate an obedient heart and a ready will, the inseparable companions of faith and love.

No Armor for Our Backs

And having done all, to stand. Stand therefore.
EPHESIANS 6:13–14 NKJV

Our Lord added "lights burning" (Luke 12:35 KJV) to "loins girded." By this, He showed that watching and ready obedience are paired with faith and love.

And having on the breastplate of righteousness—the righteousness of spotless purity. Our Lord is described with this *breastplate* (Isaiah 59:17). In this, Christ will present us faultless before God, through the merit of His own blood. The seat of conscience is in the breast, which is guarded by righteousness. No armor for the back is mentioned. We are always to face our enemies.

And your feet shod with the preparation of the gospel. Let the gospel always direct and confirm you in every step. This part of the armor, for the feet, is needful considering what a journey we have to go, what a race to run. Our feet must be so shod that our footsteps do not slip.

To order our lives and conversation rightly, we are *prepared* by the gospel blessing, the peace and love of God ruling in the heart (Colossians 3:14–15). Only by this can we tread the rough ways, surmount our difficulties, and hold out to the end.

St. Paul includes all these and a thousand more in saying, *Put on the Lord Jesus Christ* (Romans 13:14 NKJV), a strong and beautiful expression for the most intimate union with Him.

Faith over All

> *Above all, taking the shield of faith*
> *with which you will be able to*
> *quench all the fiery darts of the wicked one.*
>
> EPHESIANS 6:16 NKJV

As a sort of universal covering *above or over* every other part of the armor itself, continually exercise a strong and lively *faith.* This you may use as a *shield,* which will *quench all the fiery darts,* the furious temptations, and the violent and sudden injections *of the devil.*

And take for a helmet the hope *of salvation* (1 Thessalonians 5:8). The head is that part which needs to be defended most carefully. One stroke here may prove fatal. The armor for this is *the hope of salvation.* The lowest degree of this hope is a confidence that God will work the whole work of faith in us. The highest is a full assurance of future glory, added to the experiential knowledge of God's pardoning love. Armed with this *helmet,* the hope of the joy set before Him, Christ endured the cross and despised the shame (Hebrews 12:2).

And [take] the sword of the Spirit, which is the word of God. Satan cannot withstand this when it is edged and wielded by faith.

Till now, our armor has been only defensive. But we are to attack Satan as well as defend ourselves—the shield in one hand, the sword in the other. Whoever fights the powers of hell will need both. One who is covered in armor from head to foot and neglects the *sword* will be foiled after all.

The Crowning Weapon

Praying always with all prayer
and supplication in the Spirit,
being watchful. . .with all perseverance. . .
for all the saints.
EPHESIANS 6:18 NKJV

The description of the whole armor of God shows us how great a thing it is to be a Christian. The lack of any one thing makes us incomplete. Though one has his loins girded, has on the breastplate, his feet shod, the shield of faith, and sword of the Spirit, yet one more thing is needed: *praying always*. At all times and occasions, in the midst of all actions, inwardly *praying without ceasing. By the Spirit*—through the influence of the Holy Spirit. *With all prayer*—all sort of prayer: public, private, mental, vocal. Do not be diligent in one kind of prayer and negligent in others; if we desire our petitions answered, let us use all. Some use only mental prayer, thinking it is a way of worship superior to any other. But it requires far more grace to be enabled to pour out a fervent and continued prayer than to offer up mental aspirations.

Supplication—repeating and urging our prayer, as Christ did in the garden; *watching*—inwardly attending on God, to know His will, gain power to do it, and attain to the blessings we desire. *With all perseverance for all the saints*—persevering in this holy exercise that others may do all the will of God and be steadfast to the end. Perhaps we receive few answers to prayer because we do not intercede enough for others.

The Best Gifts, and the More Excellent

Earnestly desire the best gifts.
And yet. . .
1 CORINTHIANS 12:31 NKJV

In the verses preceding the above, St. Paul was speaking of the extraordinary gifts of the Holy Spirit, such as healing the sick; prophesying in the proper sense of foretelling things to come; speaking with strange tongues such as the speaker had never learned; and the miraculous interpretation of tongues. These gifts the apostle allows to be desirable. He exhorts the Corinthians, at least the teachers among them, to covet them earnestly in order to be even more useful to both Christians and the unconverted.

It does not appear that those extraordinary gifts of the Holy Spirit were common in the church much after Emperor Constantine declared himself a Christian. From a vain imagination of promoting the Christian cause, he heaped riches, power, and honor upon the Christians, especially the clergy. From that time, very few instances of these extraordinary gifts were found. Not because all the world had become Christian, but because the love of the Christians began to wane. The Christians had again become pagans and had only a dead form left.

Thus we need to examine the next words of St. Paul, "the more excellent way," which he described to the Corinthians, one far more desirable than all others together: the way of love, the love of God.

Covet These Also

The greater gifts. . .
a still more excellent way.
1 CORINTHIANS 12:31 NASB

I will not at present write of the extraordinary gifts of the Holy Spirit, but of the ordinary ones. These we also may *covet earnestly,* to be more useful in our generation. With this view, we may covet the gift of *convincing speech* to "sound" the unbelieving heart, and the gift of *persuasion,* to move the affections and enlighten the understanding. We may covet *knowledge,* both of the Word and the works of God, of providence and grace. We may desire a measure of that *faith* which goes far beyond the power of natural causes when it is for the glory of God and the happiness of men and women. We may desire a pleasing manner of speaking, or any other gift which would enable us to be useful wherever we are.

All these we may innocently desire. But there is a "more excellent way." The way of love—of loving all for God's sake, of humble, gentle, patient love—is what St. Paul so admirably describes in the chapter following the text. Without this love, he assures us, all eloquence, all knowledge, all faith, all works, and all sufferings are of no more value in the sight of God than sounding brass or rumbling cymbal. They are of no avail toward our eternal salvation. Without this love, all we know, believe, do, or suffer will profit us nothing in the great day of accounts.

A More Excellent Way

I show you a still more excellent way.
1 CORINTHIANS 12:31 NASB

There is another view of these words: a "more excellent way" in a different sense. An ancient writer has observed that, from the beginning, there have been two orders of Christians. The one lived an innocent life, conforming in all things not sinful to the customs and fashions of the world. They did many good works, abstained from gross evil and used the means of grace, the ordinances of God. In general, they endeavored to have a conscience void of offense in their behavior, not aiming at any particular strictness, being in most things like their neighbors.

The other Christians not only abstained from all appearance of evil, were steady in good works in every kind, and attended all the ordinances of God. But they likewise used all diligence to attain the whole mind that was in Christ and labored to walk, in every point, as their beloved Master.

To do this, they walked in a constant path of universal self-denial, trampling on every pleasure which they were not divinely conscious prepared them for taking pleasure in God. They took up their cross daily. They consistently strove to enter in at the narrow gate. They single-mindedly spared no pains to arrive at the summit of Christian holiness: "Leaving the first principles. . .to go on to perfection" and know all that love of God which passes knowledge, and to be "filled with all the fulness of God."

Choose a Higher Path

Forgetting what lies behind.
PHILIPPIANS 3:13 NASB

From long experience and observation, I am inclined to think that whoever finds redemption in the blood of Jesus has, at that time, the choice of walking in the higher or the lower path. I believe the Holy Spirit then sets before one the "more excellent way" and incites him or her to walk in it; to choose the narrowest path in the narrow way; to aspire after the heights and depths of holiness after the entire image of God. But if he or she does not accept this offer, they insensibly decline into the lower order of Christians. They still go on in what may be called a good way, serving God in a degree, and find mercy at the close of life, through the blood of the covenant.

I am far from quenching the smoking flax—from discouraging those that serve God in a low degree. But I wish them to not stop here. I encourage them to come up higher. Without thundering hell and damnation in their ears, without condemning the way they are in by telling them it is the way that leads to destruction, I will endeavor to point out to them what is, in every respect, a "more excellent way."

I do not affirm that all who do not walk in this way are in the high road to hell. But this much I must affirm: they will not have so high a place in heaven, will have fewer stars in their crown of glory than they would if they had chosen the better part.

Begin at the Beginning

Early will I seek You.
PSALM 63:1 NKJV

How do you begin your day? The generality of Christians, if they are not obliged to work for their living, rise at eight or nine in the morning after eight, nine, or more hours of sleep. I do not say (as I was apt to do fifty years ago) all who do this are in the way to hell. But neither can I say they are in the way to heaven, denying themselves and taking up their cross daily. From more than sixty years' observation, I can say that men in health require an average of six to seven hours of sleep and healthy women from seven to eight each twenty-four hours. This quantity of sleep is advantageous to body and soul, preferable to any medicine I have known, both for preventing and removing nervous disorders. In defiance of fashion and custom, it is, therefore, the most excellent way to take just so much sleep as experience proves our nature to require. It is indisputably most conducive both to bodily and spiritual health.

And why should you not? Because it is difficult? True; with men it is impossible. But all things are possible with God; and by His grace, all things will be possible to you. Only be instant in prayer and it will be not only possible, but easy. And, it is far easier to rise early always than only sometimes. Just begin at the right end: To rise early, you must sleep early. Then, the difficulty will cease. Its advantage will remain forever.

Wait on the Lord

My soul waits. . .for God only.
PSALM 62:1 NASB

The generality of Christians are accustomed to use some kind of *prayer*. Now, perhaps you are one who still uses the same form you used when you were a child. But surely, there is a "more excellent way" of ordering our private devotions. Consider both your inward and outward state and vary your prayers accordingly. Suppose you are healthy, at ease, and have kind relations, good neighbors, and agreeable friends. Then your outward state obviously calls for praise and thanksgiving to God.

On the other hand, if you are in adversity, in poverty or need, in distress or danger, or in pain or sickness, then you are called to pour out your soul before God in prayer suited to your circumstances.

In like manner, you may suit your devotions to your inward state, the present state of your mind. Are you in heaviness, either from a sense of sin or from manifold temptations? Let your prayer consist of the confessions, petitions, and supplications that agree with your distressed state of mind.

On the contrary, is your soul in peace? Are you rejoicing in God? Are His consolations large toward you? Then say with the psalmist, "You are my God and I will love You. . .I will praise You." Reading and meditating on a psalm of praise is the natural rising of a thankful heart. "A more excellent way" than any form.

The Business of Your Calling

"Do not work for the food which perishes."
JOHN 6:27 NASB

For what *purpose* do you undertake and follow your worldly business? "To provide things necessary for myself and my family." A good enough answer *as far as it goes,* but it does not go far enough for a Christian. We must go abundantly farther. Our purpose in all things is to please God. To do, not our own will, but the will of God on earth as the angels do in heaven. We work for that which endures to everlasting life.

Again, in what *manner* do you transact your worldly business? I trust with diligence, with all your might. And in justice: rendering to all their due in every circumstance. And in mercy: doing unto everyone as you would they should do to you. But Christians are called to go still farther: to add piety to justice; to intermix prayer—the prayer of the heart—with all the work of their hands. Without this, all the diligence and justice only show them to be honest persons. We must walk a "more excellent way" than honest pagans.

In what *spirit* do you go through your business? in the spirit of the world, or in the spirit of Christ? If you act in the spirit of Christ, you do everything in the spirit of sacrifice, giving up your will to the will of God. You continually aim, not at ease, or pleasure, or riches; not at anything other than the glory of God. This is the most excellent way of pursuing worldly business!

Taking Care of The Body

Whether, then, you eat or drink or whatever you do,
do all to the glory of God.
1 CORINTHIANS 10:31 NASB

These "houses of clay" which clothe our spirits require constant reparation, or they will sink into the earth even sooner than nature requires. Daily *food* is necessary to prevent this, to repair the decays of nature. It was common in the heathen world, when they were about to eat, to pour out a little drink to the honor of their god (although the heathen gods were but devils—see 1 Corinthians 10:19–21). There was once just such a common custom in this land. Would it not be a more excellent way if every head of family were to ask a blessing from God on what was about to be eaten and to return thanks to the giver of all blessings?

As to the *quantity* of food, good sorts of people do not usually eat to excess; at least not so as to make themselves sick with food or to intoxicate themselves with drink. As to the manner of eating, it is usually innocent, mixed with a little mirth, which is said to aid digestion. Provided they take only that measure of plain, wholesome food which most promotes health both of body and mind, there will be no cause of blame. Hunger is said to be a "good sauce" for the appetite; but a still better sauce is cheerful thankfulness, and the food so seasoned is the most agreeable kind. You may thus receive every morsel as God's pledge of life eternal.

A Refreshing "Side Dish"

Let your speech always be with grace.
COLOSSIANS 4:6 NASB

Our times of taking food are usually times of *conversation*. It is natural to refresh our minds while we refresh our bodies. One hopes the subjects of conversation would be harmless, modest, true, and kind, with no talebearing, backbiting, or evil-speaking. But it must also be good: good in itself and on a good subject. You must indeed speak of worldly things, otherwise you may as well go out of this world. But it should be only so far as is needful, then return to a better subject. Secondly, the conversation must be useful to build up either the speaker, the listeners, or both: Lift them up in faith, or love, or holiness. Thirdly, see that it gives not only entertainment, but in one way or another, ministers grace to the hearers. This is "a more excellent way" than mere harmlessness.

But we cannot always be intent upon business; both our minds and bodies require relaxation. Diversions are of various kinds, and which are "more excellent" for a Christian? A diversion may be indifferent in itself yet the surroundings be irreverent, base and vile, or with such a tendency. Even innocent pastimes may be superceded by those which are useful as well as innocent, such as visiting the sick, poor, the widows, and fatherless. Or by the reading of useful subjects and by prayer, the most useful of all pastimes, and indeed "a more excellent way."

A More Excellent Use of Money

"Do not lay up for yourselves treasures upon earth."
MATTHEW 6:19 NKJV

The generality of Christians set apart one-tenth or more of their income from whatever source for charitable uses. I praise God for all of you who act in such manner. May you never be weary of well-doing! May God restore what you give, sevenfold, into your own heart! But yet I show you "a more excellent way."

You may consider yourself one in whose hands the proprietor of heaven and earth, and all that is in them, has placed a part of His goods to be disposed of according to His direction. That is, consider yourself as one of a number of indigent persons to be provided for out of that portion of goods with which you are entrusted. This gives you two advantages: One, "it is more blessed to give than to receive" and the other, that you are to serve yourself first and others afterwards.

To be more particular: First, if you have no family, after you have provided for yourself, give away all that remains so that:

Each Christmas your accounts may clear
And wind your [ending] round the year.

Secondly, if you have a family, seriously consider before God how much each member requires to have what is needful for life and godliness. Thirdly, this being done, fix your purpose not to increase your substance. As it comes, daily or yearly or however often, let it go; do not "lay up treasures upon earth."

All My Goods, All My Heart

Do all to the glory of God.
1 CORINTHIANS 10:31 NASB

Laying up treasures on earth is as flatly forbidden by our Lord as murder or adultery. By doing so, you are laying up "wrath against the day of wrath and revelation of the righteous judgment of God."

But suppose it were not forbidden? Can you, on principle of reason, spend your money in a way which God may *possibly forgive,* instead of spending it in a manner which He will *certainly reward?* You will have no reward in heaven for what you *lay up;* you will for what you *lay out.* Every dollar you put into the earthly bank is sunk; it brings no interest above. But every dollar you give to the poor is put into the bank of heaven. And it will bring glorious interest, accumulating to all eternity.

Who then is the wise one, endued with knowledge, among you? Let that one resolve this day, this hour, this moment, the Lord assisting him, to choose in all particulars the "more excellent way." And let him or her steadily keep that resolve with regard to sleep, prayer, work, food, conversation, and diversions, but particularly with regard to the employment of that important talent, money. Let your heart answer to the call of God, "From this moment, God being my helper, I will lay up no more treasure upon earth. I will lay up treasure in heaven. I will give to God the things that are His: all my goods and all my heart."

Marks of the New Birth

"So is everyone who is born of the Spirit."
JOHN 3:8 NASB

It is of the deepest importance to know what is implied in the being a child of God, in having the Spirit of adoption. Since "except a man be born again [born of the Spirit] he cannot see the kingdom of God," I shall lay down the marks of the new birth just as they are in Scripture: faith, hope, and love.

The first, and the foundation of all the rest, is *faith*. St. Paul wrote, "You are all sons of God through faith in Christ Jesus" (Galatians 3:26 NASB); and St. John: "To them He gave the right to become children of God, even to those who believe in His name, who were born [when they believed], not of blood nor of the will of the flesh [by natural generation] nor of the will of man [by adoption—in whom no inward change is thereby wrought], but of God" (John 1:12–13 NASB). Again, "Whoever believes that Jesus is the Christ is born of God" (1 John 5:1 NASB).

But it is not a speculative faith which is spoken of by the apostles. Nor is it a bare assent to the proposition that Jesus is the Christ, nor to all those propositions in the creeds or in the Old and New Testaments. For even the devils believe that Jesus is the Christ and that Scripture is true as God is true. Yet, they are still "reserved in everlasting chains [of] darkness unto the judgment of the great day" (see Jude 6 KJV). For theirs is a dead faith. We must go beyond a mere assent to truth, to a living faith.

A Living Faith

But My righteous one shall live by faith.
HEBREWS 10:38 NASB

Whoever is born of God has a true, living, Christian faith. This living faith is not only assent, an act of the understanding, but a disposition which God has wrought in the heart. It is a sure trust and confidence in God that, through the merits of Christ, one's sins are forgiven, and he or she is reconciled to the favor of God.

This implies that one first renounce him or herself. In order to be "found in Christ," to be accepted through Him, one totally rejects all confidence in the flesh. He knows that "having nothing to pay"—no trust of any kind in his own works or righteousness—he comes to God as a lost, miserable, self-destroyed, self-condemned, undone, helpless sinner. His mouth is utterly stopped, being altogether guilty before God.

Such a sense of sin is commonly called despair by those who speak evil of things they do not know. But this sense of sin, together with a full conviction that our salvation comes only of Christ and an earnest longing for that salvation, all must precede a living faith. This *living* faith is a trust in Him who for us paid our ransom by His death and fulfilled the law in His life. So this faith whereby we are born of God is not only a belief in right and proper truths, but also one's true personal confidence of the mercy of God through our Lord Jesus Christ.

The Fruit of Living Faith

We. . .believe to the saving of the soul.
HEBREWS 10:39 NKJV

We find immediate and constant fruit of this true, living, Christian faith whereby we are born of God. These are power over sin (inward and outward) and peace. Whenever the blood of Christ is applied to a soul, it "purges the conscience from dead works." As St. Paul describes in the sixth chapter of his Epistle to the Romans, it purifies the heart from every unholy desire and temper. In his First Epistle, St. John strongly asserts this same invaluable privilege (see 1 John 3:1–9).

Being justified by this true, living faith, having all our sins blotted out, we also have peace: *peace with God through our Lord Jesus Christ* (see Romans 5:1 KJV). This is that peace of God which passes all human understanding. It is a serenity of soul that has not entered into the heart of the "natural" (unconverted) person to conceive. Nor is it possible for even the spiritual man or woman to describe it. It is a peace which all the powers of earth and hell are unable to take from the one who has this living faith.

Waves and storms beat upon it, but cannot shake it; it is founded upon a rock—the Rock of Ages. It keeps the hearts and minds of the children of God at all times, in all places. They have learned to be content in every condition of life. Their hearts stand fast, believing in the Lord and His goodness.

Power over Sin

Sin shall not be master over you.
ROMANS 6:14 NASB

When we have the true, living faith by which we are born of God from above, a fruit that cannot be separated from it is power over outward sin of every kind, over every evil word and action. Wherever the blood of Christ is by faith applied to a heart, it purges the conscience from dead works (see Hebrews 9:14). It gives power over inward sin also, for it purifies the heart from unholy affections and tempers. "How," said St. Paul, "shall we," who by faith "died to sin live any longer in it?" (Romans 6:2 NKJV). For "our old man is crucified with him, that the body of sin might be destroyed, that henceforth we should not serve sin" (v. 6 KJV). "For sin shall not have dominion over you. . . . Being then made free from sin, ye became the servants of righteousness" (vv. 14, 18 KJV).

St. John asserts the same privilege of power over outward sin: "Whoever has been born of God does not sin, for His seed remains in him; and he cannot sin, because he has been born of God" (1 John 3:9 NKJV). Some say, this means not to commit sin *habitually.* But that is not in the Book; and who are you to mend the Word of God? God plainly says, "He does not continue to sin" and one adds *habitually?* This comment swallows up the text, takes away the whole meaning and spirit of the passage, and leaves only a dead letter. By this human trickery the precious promise is utterly lost, and the Word of God is made of no effect.

Let No One Deceive You

You know that He appeared in order to take away sins;
and in Him there is no sin.
1 JOHN 3:5 NASB

Shall we let the apostle interpret his own words? Examine the whole tenor of his address. From the above verse, St. John draws this inference: "Whoever abides in Him does not sin. Whoever sins has neither seen Him nor known Him" (v. 6). To his enforcement of this important doctrine, he adds this highly necessary caution: "Little children, let no one deceive you [for many will endeavor to do so, to persuade you that you may be unrighteous, that you may commit sin, and yet be children of God]. He who practices righteousness is righteous, just as He is righteous. He who sins is of the devil, for the devil has sinned from the beginning" (v. 7–8). Then follows: "Whoever has been born of God does not sin, for His seed remains in him; and he cannot sin, because he has been born of God" (v. 9). "In this, adds the apostle, "the children of God and the children of the devil are manifest" (v. 10). By this plain mark (the committing or not committing sin), the children of God and the children of the devil are distinguished from each other. To the same effect are these words in his fifth chapter: "We know that whoever is born of God does not sin; but he who has been born of God keeps himself, and the wicked one does not touch him" (v. 18 NKJV).

Peace That Passes Understanding

The peace of God, which surpasses all understanding, will guard your hearts and minds through Christ Jesus.

PHILIPPIANS 4:7 NKJV

Another fruit of the true, living, Christian faith is peace. For "having been justified by faith," having all our sins blotted out, "we have peace with God through our Lord Jesus Christ" (Romans 5:1 NASB). This indeed our Lord Himself, the night before His death, solemnly conveyed to all His followers. "Peace," said He, "I leave with you [you who believe in God and believe also in Me], My peace I give to you; not as the world gives do I give to you. Let not your heart be troubled, neither let it be afraid" (John 14:27 NKJV). And again, " 'These things I have spoken to you, that in Me you may have peace' " (John 16:33 NKJV). This is that peace of God which passes all understanding: that serenity of soul which the unconverted man or woman cannot conceive. Nor can even the spiritual man or woman describe it.

All the powers of earth and hell cannot take away this peace. Trouble and adversity cannot shake it because it is founded upon a rock. It holds steadfast the hearts and minds of the children of God. Whether they are in ease or in pain, in sickness or health, in abundance or want, they are happy in God. In every state, they have learned to be content and to give thanks to God through Christ Jesus. They are well assured that "whatever is, is best," because it is the will of God concerning them. And their hearts stand fast in faith.

A Living Hope

This hope we have as an anchor of the soul,
a hope both sure and steadfast.
HEBREWS 6:19 NASB

A second scriptural mark of those who are born of God is *hope*. St. Peter wrote to all the children of God scattered about, "Blessed be the God and Father of our Lord Jesus Christ, which according to his abundant mercy hath begotten us again unto a lively hope" (1 Peter 1:3 KJV). He called this a lively or living hope, because there is a dead hope as well as a dead faith. A dead hope is from the enemy of God, as evidenced by its fruits. As it is the offspring of pride, it is the parent of every evil word and action. On the other hand, everyone who has the living hope within him is "holy as He (God) that calls him is holy." He can truly say to his brothers and sisters in Christ, "Beloved, now are we the children of God, and we shall see Him as He is." That one "purifies himself, even as God is pure."

This *living hope* implies the testimony of our own spirit, or conscience, that we walk in simplicity and godly sincerity (see 2 Corinthians 1:12). It also implies the testimony of the Spirit of God bearing "witness with [or to] our spirit, that we are the children of God: And if children, then heirs; heirs of God, and joint-heirs with Christ" (Romans 8:16–17 KJV). What a glorious privilege of the children of God that *the Spirit of God Himself* bears witness that we are His children and, being such, are His heirs, joint-heirs with Christ the Son. *This* is that *living* hope!

The Privilege of Assurance

*The Spirit Himself bears witness with our spirit
that we are children of God.*

ROMANS 8:16 NKJV; SEE ALSO GALATIANS 4:6.

It is well for us to observe what God Himself teaches touching this glorious privilege of His children. Who is it that is bearing witness? Not our spirit only, but the Spirit of *God Himself* who bears witness with our spirit. And what is it He is bearing witness of? That we are the children of God "and if children, then heirs. . .of God, and joint-heirs with Christ" (Romans 8:16–17 KJV)—if we suffer with Him, if we deny ourselves, take up our cross daily, cheerfully endure persecution or reproach for His sake, "that we may be also glorified together."

And in whom does the Spirit of God bear this witness? In all who are the children of God. By this very argument does the apostle Paul prove, in the preceding verses, that they are so: "As many as are led by the Spirit of God, these are sons [children] of God. For you did not receive the spirit of bondage again to fear, but. . .the Spirit of adoption by whom we cry out, 'Abba, Father!' "

It follows, "the Spirit Himself bears witness with our spirit that we are children of God" (vv. 14–16 NKJV). And thus is the Scripture fulfilled, "Blessed are they that mourn, for they shall be comforted." Their fear and sorrow at being under the wrath of God is changed into joy when the Comforter Himself comes with the witness that they are now His children.

Adopted!

You received the Spirit of adoption
by whom we cry out, "Abba, Father."
ROMANS 8:15 NKJV

Note the expressions in this verse. *You:* as many as are the children of God, have, by virtue of your adoption, received that selfsame Spirit whereby *we* cry, "Abba, Father"; *we* being the apostles, prophets, teachers. *We:* through whom *you* believed; *we:* the "ministers of Christ and stewards of the mysteries of God." As *we* and *you* have one Lord, so we have one Spirit. As we have one faith, so we have one hope also. *We* and *you* are sealed with one "Spirit of promise," the earnest or down payment of *your* and *our* inheritance—the same Spirit bearing witness with *your* and *our* spirit "that we are children of God."

And thus it is easy to understand the great comfort which comes with the assurance of such a great inward transaction. For sorrow, and to some degree fear, has accompanied us while we groaned under a sense of the wrath of God. Yet as soon as we sensed this witness of God within us, our sorrow was turned to inexpressible joy that we have this state of grace, of favor, or reconciliation with God.

Whatever our pain may have been before, as soon as that hour is come, we no longer remember the anguish. Instead, there is only joy that we have been born of God and are no longer aliens from the commonwealth of the Israel of God.

Joy Inexpressible!

Believing, you rejoice with joy inexpressible
and full of glory.

1 PETER 1:8 NKJV

St. Peter describes believers as those whom God has begotten again unto a living hope; then he describes their great joy, that the trial of their faith "might be found unto praise, and honour, and glory at the appearing of Jesus Christ: in whom, though now ye see him not. . .ye rejoice with joy unspeakable and full of glory." Inexpressible indeed! The tongues of men and women have no power to describe this joy in the Holy Spirit. It is the hidden manna, which no one knows except those who receive it (see Revelation 2:17).

This we do know: It not only remains, but overflows in the depth of affliction. His consolations with His children are large when earthly comforts fail. When sufferings most abound, the consolations of His Spirit do much more abound. So much so that the children of God, those who bear the inward witness, can laugh inwardly at destruction, at deprivation, pain, hell, and the grave. They know the One who has the keys of death and hell, the One who will cast these enemies into the bottomless pit. Through their living hope, they even now hear that great voice from heaven, " 'God will wipe away every tear from their eyes; there shall be no more death, nor sorrow, nor crying' " and. . ." 'no more pain' " (Revelation 21:4 NKJV).

Love in the Heart

*The love of God has been poured out in our hearts
by the Holy Spirit who was given to us.*
ROMANS 5:5 NKJV

A third scriptural mark of those who are born of God, and the greatest mark of all, is *love*. It is the love of God which is poured into our hearts by the Holy Spirit when we are born again of the Spirit of God. "Because you are sons," St. Paul wrote to the Galatians, "God has sent forth the Spirit of His Son into your hearts, crying out, 'Abba Father!' " (Galatians 4:6 NKJV). By this Spirit, continually looking up to God as their reconciled and loving Father, they cry to Him for their daily bread, for all things needful, whether for soul or body. They continually pour out their hearts before Him, knowing they have those petitions they ask of Him (see 1 John 5:14–15). Their delight is in Him; He is the joy of their hearts. The desire of their soul is toward Him; it is their great satisfaction to do His will.

They love God as their Savior. They love the Lord Jesus Christ in sincerity. They are so joined unto the Lord as to be one spirit. Their souls hang upon the Lord Jesus and count Him the chief among ten thousand. They know what it means of which the psalmist wrote: "You are fairer than the sons of men; Grace is poured upon Your lips; Therefore God has blessed You forever" (Psalm 45:2 NKJV).

Loving Our Neighbor

*Love is of God;
and everyone who loves is
born of God and knows God.*
1 JOHN 4:7 NKJV

When the love of God has been poured into the heart of the born again person, the necessary fruit of that love is the love of our neighbor. This means every soul whom God has made, including our enemies. We cannot exclude those who are now despitefully using and persecuting us, for the love of God is a love by which we love everyone as we love ourselves.

Our Lord has expressed it strongly, teaching us to love one another, even as He has loved us; and while we were yet sinners, He loved us and laid down His life for us. Accordingly, this commandment is written in the hearts of all those that love God, " 'As I have loved you, so you must love one another' " (John 13:34 NIV).

Now we see the love of God "in that He laid down His life for us," and so, says the apostle, "we ought to lay down our lives for the brethren." If we sense we are ready to do this, then we truly love our neighbor. "We know that we have passed from death to life, because we love our brothers" (see 1 John 3:14–16 NIV).

The apostle continues, "Everyone who loves is born of God and knows God. . . . By this we know that we abide in Him. . . because He has given us of His [loving] Spirit" (1 John 4:7, 13 NKJV). *We love thus, because we have been born of God.*

Obedience, a Fruit of Love

This is love for God: to obey his commands.
1 JOHN 5:3 NIV

This *obedience* is the love of our neighbor also in the same sense as it is the love of God. But keeping the outward commandments is not all that is implied in loving God with all your heart, all your mind, all your soul, all your strength, and in loving your neighbor as yourself. The love of God is not an *outward service* merely, nor even a course of *outward works*. It is an affection of the soul, a disposition of the heart.

The meaning of the text is this: The *sign* of the love of God, the *proof* of our keeping the first and greatest commandment is to keep all the rest of His commandments also! True love, if it be once poured into our hearts, will *constrain* us to keep them, for whoever loves God with all his heart cannot help but serve Him with all his strength.

So that, a second fruit of the love of God in the heart is universal *obedience* to the One we love, and conformity to His will. We yield obedience to all the commands of God, internal and external, obedience of the heart and of the life. In every temper and in all manner of conversation.

One of the most obvious results is the being "zealous of good works." There is a hungering and thirsting to do good in every possible way unto everyone. There is a rejoicing to expend one's energy to the utmost for their benefit, looking for recompense only in the world to come.

Faith, Hope, Love

" 'Be holy because I, the Lord your God, am holy.' "
LEVITICUS 19:2; SEE ALSO 1 PETER 1:16 NIV

In the Scriptures we find plainly laid out the marks of the new birth, for God Himself has answered the weighty question of what it means to be born of God. In the judgment of the Spirit of God, declared in His Word, to be a child of God means: (1) so to *believe* in God, through Christ, as "not to commit sin" and to enjoy at all times and places that "peace of God which passes all understanding"; (2) so to *hope* in God through the Son of His love as to have not only the "testimony of a good conscience" but also the Spirit of God "bearing witness with your spirits that you are the children of God," from which springs the rejoicing in "Him through whom you have received the atonement"; (3) so to *love* God who has thus loved you as you never did love any creature and by it being constrained to love others as you love yourself—with a love ever burning in your hearts and flaming out in all your actions and words, making your whole life one "labor of love."

So, there is one continued obedience to the commands of God: *Be merciful as God is merciful; Be holy as I am holy; Be perfect as your Father. . .in heaven is perfect.* These souls purify themselves as He is pure; because they are "sons," the Spirit of love and of glory rests upon them, cleansing them from all filthiness of flesh and spirit, and teaching them to perfect holiness in the fear of God!

What Are You Now?

Examine yourselves to see whether you are in the faith.
2 CORINTHIANS 13:5 NIV

You who are born of God according to the marks laid down in His Word well know that you are His children. Your hearts are assured before Him. Everyone who has observed these marks can sense and know of a truth at this very moment whether, in the sight of God, you are thus His child.

The question is not anything else: What are you *now?* Is the Spirit of adoption *now* in your heart? Make the appeal to your own heart: Are you *now* the temple of the Holy Spirit? Does He *now* dwell within you?

Perhaps you are resting in a transaction made at your baptism, but does the Spirit of Christ and of glory *now* rest upon you, or has the light that was within you become darkness again? To you also I say, "You must be born again." You have read what are the marks of the children of God. All who do not have these on their souls, whether baptized or unbaptized, must needs receive them or without doubt they will perish eternally.

Lord Jesus! May everyone who prepares his or her heart to seek Your face receive that Spirit of adoption and be enabled to cry out, "Abba, Father." Let them now have power so to believe in Your name as to become children of God and know and sense redemption through Your blood and the forgiveness of sins.

Always Rejoice; Pray; Give Thanks

Rejoice always;
pray without ceasing. . .
give thanks.
1 THESSALONIANS 5:16–18 NASB

Rejoice always in uninterrupted happiness in God. *Pray without ceasing,* which is the fruit of *always rejoicing* in the Lord. *In everything give thanks,* which is the fruit of both the former. *This* is Christian perfection. Further than this we cannot go, and we need not stop short of it.

Our Lord has purchased joy, as well as righteousness, for us. It is the very design of the gospel that, being saved from guilt, we should be happy in the love of Christ.

Prayer may be said to be the breath of our spiritual life. One who lives cannot possibly cease breathing. So much as we really enjoy of God's presence, so much prayer and praise do we offer up *without ceasing;* else our rejoicing is but delusion.

Thanksgiving is inseparable from true prayer; it is almost essentially connected with it. One who always prays is ever giving praise, whether in ease or pain, both for prosperity and for the greatest adversity. He blesses God for all things, looks on them as coming from Him, and receives them only for His sake—not choosing nor refusing, liking nor disliking, anything, but only as it is agreeable or disagreeable to His perfect will.

For this, that you should thus rejoice, pray, give thanks, *is the will of God,* always good, always pointing at our salvation!

The Whole of You

May the God of peace Himself sanctify you entirely.
1 THESSALONIANS 5:23 NASB

The God of peace sanctifies by the peace which He works in us, which is a great means of sanctification. The word used in the original signifies *wholly and perfectly*—every part and all that concerns us.

And may the whole of you, the apostle continues, *the spirit and the soul and the body, be preserved blameless.* He shows that he wished their spiritual state to be preserved entirely, as well as desiring the health of their natural state.

To explain this a little further: Only the soul and the body are the natural constituent parts of men and women. The *spirit* is not in the fundamental nature of humans but is the supernatural gift of God, *to be found in Christians only.*

To encourage the Thessalonian Christians, St. Paul added, *Faithful is He who calls you, who also will do it* (v. 24), if you do not quench the Spirit, for which purpose he had already written (v. 19). For wherever the Spirit is, it burns. It flames in holy love, in joy, prayer, thanksgiving.

Oh, quench it not, damp it not in yourself or others, either by neglecting to do good, or by doing evil! As a great means of preventing this, he wrote, *Rejoice evermore; pray without ceasing; in everything give thanks.* A blessed admonition, even in our day!

Mortify the Deeds of the Flesh

Mortify the deeds of the body [and] ye shall live.
ROMANS 8:13, *Explanatory Notes*

The deeds of the flesh are not only evil actions but evil desires, tempers, thoughts. If you *mortify*, kill, destroy these, you shall live the life of faith more abundantly here, and hereafter, the life of glory.

Bitterness, or *the gall or root of bitterness,* is the highest degree of wickedness and is misery to the soul. It is a root of envy, anger, and suspicion and is the height of settled anger, opposite to kindness. *Wrath* is lasting displeasure toward the ignorant, and those who are out of the way to the kingdom. It is opposite to tenderheartedness. *Anger* is the first rising of disgust at those who injure you, opposite to forgiving one another. *Evil-speaking,* be it in ever so mild and soft a tone or with many professions of kindness, is owing to a lack of love toward God and neighbor.

Mortify, St. Paul wrote to the Colossians, *your members which are upon the earth.* Put to death, slay with one continued stroke, your members, which together make up the body of sin. These are *upon the earth* where they find their nourishment. They include *uncleanness* in act, word, or thought. *Inordinate affection*—every passion which does not flow from and lead to the love of God. *Evil desire* and *covetousness* are properly and directly *idolatry,* giving the heart to a creature, not the Creator. *These,* said the apostle, *we put to death that we may live!*

Repentance and Faith in Believers

"Repent and believe in the gospel."
MARK 1:15 NASB

It is generally supposed that repentance and faith are only the gate of religion, that they are necessary only at the beginning of our Christian course when we are first setting out in the way to the kingdom.

It is doubtless true that there is a repentance and a faith which are necessary at the beginning: (1) A *repentance,* which is a conviction of our utter sinfulness, guiltiness, and helplessness, and which precedes our receiving that inner kingdom of God; and (2) a *faith,* by which we receive that kingdom of righteousness, peace, and joy in the Holy Spirit.

Yet taking the words in another sense, a sense not quite the same nor yet entirely different, there is also a repentance and a faith which are required *after* we have believed the gospel. Indeed, we need these *in every subsequent stage* of our Christian course or we cannot run the race. *This* repentance and *this* faith are as necessary to our continuance and growth in grace as the former repentance and faith were to our *entering* into the kingdom of God.

This repentance is a knowing ourselves as guilty, helpless sinners while we also know we are children of God. *This* faith answers to such repentance, believing the glad tidings of full salvation from a sinful heart, which God has prepared for all people.

Why Should Believers Repent?

> *"Remember, therefore,*
> *what you have received and heard;*
> *obey it, and repent."*
> REVELATION 3:3 NIV

In what sense are we to repent and believe after we are justified?

Repentance frequently means an inward change, a change of mind from sin to holiness. But after we are justified, we speak of it in a quite different sense, as a kind of self-knowledge—the knowing ourselves to be sinners before God, indeed, guilty, helpless sinners, even though we know we are children of God.

When we are first born again, and the love of God is poured out into our hearts, it is natural to suppose that we are no longer sinners—that all our sins are not only covered but destroyed. We feel no evil in our hearts, so we readily imagine none is there. Though we readily acknowledge that he who believes is born of God, and "he that is born of God does not *commit* sin," yet we cannot allow that he does not *feel* it within. Sin does not *reign,* but it does *remain;* and a conviction of the sin which remains in the heart of the believers is one great branch of the repentance we are now speaking of.

For it is seldom long before one who imagined all sin was gone feels there is still *pride* in his heart. And yet he knows he is in the favor of God. He cannot, and ought not to, cast away his confidence, for the Spirit still witnesses with his spirit that he is a child of God.

Contrary to the Love of God

"Those whom I love I rebuke. . . .
So be earnest, and repent."
REVELATION 3:19 NIV

Sooner or later after he is justified, the believer feels *self-will*, a will contrary to the will of God. Now a *will* is an essential part of the nature of every intelligent being, even of our blessed Lord Himself. But His human will was always subject to the will of His Father.

The case with even true believers in Christ is that they frequently find their will more or less exalting itself against the will of God. They fight against this self-will with all their might, and thus they continue in the faith.

But self-will, as well as pride, is a species of *idolatry*. Both are directly contrary to the love of God, as is *the love of the world*. It is true, when one first passes from death unto life, he desires nothing more but God. He can truly say, "There is none upon earth that I desire beside You!"

But it is not always so. If he does not continually watch and pray, he feels not only the love of the world but also *lust* reviving and the assaults of *inordinate affection*. He feels the strongest urges toward loving the creature more than the Creator—be it a child, a parent, a husband, a wife, or a well-beloved friend. To the extent he yields to the desire of earthly things or pleasures, he is prone to forget God. And for this, even the true believer in Christ needs to repent.

Where Do You Look for Praise?

*"How can you believe if
you accept praise from one another,
yet make no effort to obtain the praise that
comes from the only God?"*

JOHN 5:44 NIV

The need for repentance in the believer further extends to his sense or feelings of desire to gratify the imagination with something great, beautiful, or uncommon. In how many ways does this desire assault the soul? Perhaps with the poorest trifles, such as dress or furnishings—things never designed to satisfy the immortal spirit.

How hard it is, even for believers, to conquer just one branch of the desire of the eye, *curiosity,* to constantly trample it under their feet and desire nothing merely because it is new!

How hard is it even for the children of God wholly to conquer the *pride of life!* St. John seems to mean by this nearly the same with what the world terms *the sense of honor.* This is no other than a desire of, and a delight in, the honor that comes from men: a desire and love of praise. And always joined with this is a proportional *fear of dispraise.* Nearly allied to this is *evil shame,* the being ashamed of that in which we should glory. This is seldom divided from the *fear of man,* which brings a thousand snares upon the soul.

A thorough conviction of the remains of these evil tempers in the heart is the repentance belonging to true believers.

Contrary to the Love of Our Neighbor

See to it. . .
that no root of bitterness
springing up causes trouble.
HEBREWS 12:15 NASB

A believer in Christ often feels other tempers that are as contrary to the love of our neighbor as to the love of God. For example, *jealousies, evil surmisings,* often groundless or unreasonable *suspicions*. The one who is clear in these respects may cast the first stone at his neighbor.

Who does not sometimes feel other tempers or inward motions which are contrary to brotherly love? If nothing of *malice, hatred, or bitterness,* is there no touch of *envy,* particularly toward those who enjoy some real or supposed good which we desire but cannot attain?

Do we never find any degree of *resentment* when we are injured or affronted—especially by those whom we loved or had most labored to help or oblige? Does injustice or ingratitude never excite in us any desire of *revenge?* Any desire of returning evil for evil instead of overcoming evil with good?

Covetousness, of whatever degree, is as contrary to the love of our neighbor as it is to the love of God, being either *the love of money* or a desire of *having more*.

All these show how much is still in our hearts which is contrary to the love of our neighbor. We are, as yet, only in part "crucified to the world," for the evil root still remains in the heart, until our Lord speaks, "Be clean!"

Sin in the Heart

The carnal mind is. . .against God.
ROMANS 8:7 NKJV

There does still remain, even in those who are justified, a *mind* which is, in some measure, *carnal.* So the apostle Paul tells the believers at Corinth: "You are still carnal"—walking after the flesh (1 Corinthians 3:3 NKJV). They had a *heart bent to backsliding,* still ever ready to depart from the living God.

A reading of this Epistle shows they had a proneness to pride, self-will, anger, revenge, love of the world—in short, of all evil. If the restraint were taken off for a moment, the root of bitterness would instantly spring up. It was such a depth of corruption that we cannot possibly conceive without clear light from God.

Now, a conviction of all this sin *remaining in their hearts* is the repentance which belongs to those who are justified.

But we should also be convinced that, as sin remains in our hearts, so it *cleaves* to all our words and actions. Indeed it is to be feared that many of our words are more than *mixed* with sin; they are sinful altogether. Such undoubtedly is all *uncharitable conversation*—all which does not spring from brotherly love, all which does not agree with that golden rule: "What you would that others should do to you, even so do unto them."

Let Your Speech Be with Grace

The tongue also is a fire,
a world of evil among the parts of the body.
JAMES 3:6 NIV

How few are there, even among believers, who steadily observe the good old rule: "Of the dead and the absent [speak] nothing but good."

And suppose they do, do they likewise abstain from *unprofitable conversation?* Yet this also is unquestionably sinful and grieves the Holy Spirit of God. Indeed, "for every idle word men may speak, they will give account of it in the day of judgment" (Matthew 12:36 NKJV).

Now suppose they set a watch before their mouth and keep the door of their lips. When they endeavor to speak for God, are their words pure, free from unholy mixtures?

Do they find everything pure in their very *intention?* Do they speak merely to please God, and not partly to please themselves? When they are reproving sin, do they feel no anger or unkind temper toward the sinner?

When they are comforting the afflicted or any such, do they never perceive any inward self-commendation: *Now you have spoken well?*

In some or all of these respects, how much sin cleaves to the best *conversation* even of believers! The conviction of this is another branch of the repentance which belongs to those who are justified.

What Is Your Inward Temper?

"They should repent. . .
and prove their repentance by their deeds."
ACTS 26:20 NIV

If the conscience of a believer is thoroughly awake, how much sin does he or she find cleaving to *their actions* also? Indeed, are there not many, whom the world would not condemn, who cannot be commended nor even excused if we judge by the Word of God?

Many of their actions are not to the glory of God; frequently they did not even aim at His glory. Many are doing their own will as least as much as His and seeking to please themselves as much if not more than to please God.

While they are endeavoring to do good to their neighbor, do they not feel wrong tempers of various kinds? Hence, their good actions, their *works of mercy,* are polluted with a mixture of evil. Is it not the same case when they are offering up their prayers to God, public or private, or engaged in the most solemn service? Are not their hearts often wandering to the ends of the earth?

Again, how many *sins of omission* are they chargeable with! We know the words of the apostle James, "To him who knows to do good and does not do it. . .it is sin" (James 4:17 NKJV). And do they not find in themselves a lack of love and holy tempers, and other *inward defects* without number? So that they cry, with Job, "I abhor myself, and *repent in dust and ashes"* (Job 42:6 KJV).

Why We Need an Advocate

If anyone sins,
we have an Advocate with the Father, Jesus Christ.
1 JOHN 2:1 NASB

A conviction of their *guiltiness* is another branch of that repentance which belongs to the children of God. But this is cautiously to be understood, and in a peculiar sense. For it is certain, there is "no condemnation to those who are in Christ Jesus"—that believe in Him—and in the power of that faith "do not walk according to the flesh, but according to the Spirit" (Romans 8:1 NKJV).

Yet they can no more bear the *strict justice* of God now than before they believed. Such pronounces them to be still *worthy of death,* on all the preceding accounts. It would absolutely condemn them to death, were it not for *the atoning blood of Christ.* Thus, they are thoroughly convinced that they still *deserve* punishment, although by the merits of Christ's blood it is turned aside from them.

But here are extremes on both sides, and few people steer clear of them. Most people strike on one side or the other, either thinking themselves condemned when they are not, or else thinking they *deserve* to be acquitted. No; the truth lies between: They still *deserve,* strictly speaking, only the damnation of hell. But what they deserve does not come upon them because they "have an advocate with the Father." Christ's life, death, and intercession still interpose between them and condemnation.

No Strength of Our Own

> *"The flesh is weak."*
> MARK 14:38 NASB

A conviction of their *utter helplessness* is yet another branch of the repentance of believers. By this, I mean (1) that they are no more able now *of themselves* to think one good word or do one good work than before they were justified. They still have no strength *of their own* to do good or to resist evil, no ability to conquer or even withstand the world, the devil, or their evil nature. *They can, it is certain, do all these things;* but it is not by their own strength. *It is the mere gift of God.*

By this helplessness, I mean (2) an absolute *inability to deliver ourselves* from the guiltiness and desert of punishment of which we are still conscious; (3) *by all the grace we have,* the inability to remove the pride, self-will, love of the world, anger, and general proneness to depart from God—which we know from experience to *remain* in our hearts. Or the evil which, in spite of all our endeavors, clings to all our words and actions; (4) an utter inability in ourselves to wholly avoid uncharitable, unprofitable conversations, and to avoid sins of omission, or to supply our numberless inward defects, especially *the lack of love and other right tempers* to God and our fellow creatures.

In this sense, we are to repent after we are justified. We can go no further till we do, for till we are sensible of our disease, it admits of no cure.

Repent and Believe the Gospel

"All things are possible with God."
MARK 10:27 NIV

It is such general experience of the children of God wherever they live that, however they differ in other points, they generally agree in this: Although we may "by the Spirit, mortify the deeds of the body," and weaken our enemies day by day, yet *we* cannot drive them out. By all the grace given at justification *we* cannot extirpate them. Though we watch and pray ever so much, *we* cannot wholly cleanse either our hearts or our hands.

Most sure, we cannot, till it please our Lord to speak to our hearts again, to speak the second time, "Be clean!" Then only is the leprosy cleansed. Then only the evil root, the carnal mind, is destroyed, and inbred sin subsists no more.

When, in this sense, we have repented, then we are called to "believe the gospel." This also is to be understood in a peculiar sense, different from that wherein we believed in order to be justified. We are to believe the glad tidings of the great, the full, salvation which God has prepared. Believe that the One who is the brightness of His Father's glory, is "able to save to the uttermost all that come to God through Him." He is able to save you from all the sin that still remains in your heart and to supply whatever is lacking in you. This is impossible with man, but with God-Man, all things are possible.

Believe God's Promises

"I will save you from all your uncleanness."
EZEKIEL 36:29 NIV

Can our Lord truly save us from all the sin that still clings to our hearts, our words, our actions?

What can be too hard for the One who has all power in heaven and in earth?

But His bare power to accomplish is not a sufficient foundation for our faith that He *will* do it, unless He has promised it. And *this* He has done, over and over and in the strongest terms. He has given us exceeding great and precious promises in both the Old and the New Testaments.

So we read in the law (Deuteronomy 30:6 NKJV), "The LORD your God will circumcise your heart. . .to love [Him] with all your heart and with all your soul." He repeats the promise in the Psalms [Psalm 130:8] and in the Prophets [Ezekiel 36:25].

In the New Testament we read, " 'Blessed is the Lord God of Israel, for He has visited and redeemed His people. . . that we. . .might serve Him. . .in holiness and righteousness before Him all the days of our life" (Luke 1:68, 74–75 NKJV).

You have good reason to believe He is not only able but *willing* to do this—to cleanse you from all your filthiness of flesh and spirit—to save you from all your uncleanness. This is the thing you now long for, the *faith* you now particularly need: namely, "that the Great Physician, the lover of my soul, is willing to make me clean."

Today Is the Accepted Time

Now is the day of salvation.
2 CORINTHIANS 6:2 NIV

Is our Lord willing to make you clean tomorrow or today? Let Him answer for Himself: " 'Today, if you will hear [My] voice, do not harden your hearts' " (Hebrews 3:7–8 NKJV). If you put it off till tomorrow, you harden your heart; you refuse to hear His voice. Believe, therefore, that He is willing to save you from sin *today*. He is willing to save you *now*. "Behold, now is the accepted time" (2 Corinthians 6:2 KJV).

He *now* says, "Be thou clean!" Only believe, and you also will immediately find that "all things are possible to him that believeth."

Continue to believe in Him who loved you and gave Himself for you. He bore all your sins in His own body on the cross. And He saves you from all condemnation by His blood continually applied.

Thus it is that we continue in a justified state. And when we go "from faith to faith," when we have faith to be cleansed from indwelling sin—to be saved from all our uncleanness— we are likewise saved from all that *guilt*, that *desert of punishment*, which we felt before. So that then we may say, not only,

Every moment, Lord, I need
The merit of Thy death!

but likewise, in the full assurance of faith,

Every moment, Lord, I have
The merit of Thy death!

The Full Assurance of Faith

*Let us draw near with a true heart
in full assurance of faith.*
HEBREWS 10:22 NKJV

By that faith in His life, death, and intercession for us, renewed from moment to moment, we are every whit clean. There is not only now no condemnation for us, but no such desert of punishment as was before, the Lord cleansing both our hearts and our lives.

By the same faith, we feel the power of Christ every moment resting upon us, by which alone we are what we are. By this alone, we are enabled to continue in spiritual life. Without this, regardless of all our present holiness, we should be devils the next moment.

But as long as we retain our faith in Him, we draw water out of the wells of salvation. We lean on our beloved, even Christ in us the hope of glory, who dwells in our hearts by faith.

He likewise is interceding for us at the right hand of God; we receive help from Him to think, speak, and act what is acceptable in His sight.

Thus does He go before us in all our doings, so that all our designs, conversations, and actions are begun, continued, and ended in Him.

Thus also does He cleanse the thoughts of our hearts by the inspiration of His Holy Spirit, that we may perfectly love Him, and worthily magnify His holy name.

Faith Answers Repentance

This is the victory. . .even our faith.
1 JOHN 5:4 NIV

Repentance and faith, in the children of God, exactly answer each other. By repentance, we feel the sin remaining in our hearts and clinging to our words and actions. By faith, we receive the power of God in Christ, purifying our hearts and cleansing our hands.

By repentance, we are still sensible that we deserve punishment for all our tempers, words, and actions. By faith, we are conscious that our Advocate with the Father is continually pleading for us, and thereby continually turning aside all condemnation and punishment from us.

By repentance, we have an abiding conviction that there is no help in us. By faith, we receive not only mercy but grace to help in *every* time of need.

Repentance disclaims the very possibility of any other help. Faith accepts all the help we stand in need of, from the One who has all power in heaven and earth.

Repentance says, "Without Him I can do nothing." Faith says, "I can do all things through Christ strengthening me."

Through Him, I can not only overcome but expel all the enemies of my soul. Through Him, I can love the Lord my God with all my heart, mind, soul, and strength.

Yes, I can "walk in holiness and righteousness before Him all the days of my life."

A Desperate Necessity

Casting down. . .every high thing. . .
bringing every thought. . .to the obedience of Christ.
2 CORINTHIANS 10:5 NKJV

An accurate view of the nature of repentance and faith in believers is needful in order to avoid the mischief of the opinion that we have no need for further change. For, "they that are whole need not a physician." If we think we are quite made whole already, there is no room to seek further healing.

On the contrary, a deep conviction that we are not yet whole constrains us to groan for a full deliverance to Him that is mighty to save—to implore that He will

Break off the yoke of inbred sin and fully set my spirit free!
I cannot rest till pure within, till I am wholly lost in Thee.

An accurate view of *this* repentance and *this* faith, coupled with a deep conviction of our *demerit* and our *guilt,* is absolutely necessary in order to our seeing the true value of the atoning blood. We need such in order to sense that we need this as much after we are justified as we ever did before—to know that:

He ever lives above for us to intercede—
His all-atoning love, His precious blood, to plead.

Lastly, an accurate view of the repentance and faith of believers brings a deep conviction of our utter *helplessness* to retain anything we have received, by which we are brought to magnify *Him,* so that *every* temper, thought, word, and work is brought to the obedience of Christ.

The Blood of Christ

How much more shall the blood of Christ. . .
purge your conscience?
HEBREWS 9:14 KJV

The *blood of Christ* is used to signify the merit of all His suffering. The writer tells us He offered Himself to God *through the eternal Spirit*, the work of redemption being the work of the Trinity. Neither is the Second Person (Christ) alone concerned even in the amazing condescension needful to complete it. The Father delivers up the kingdom to the Son; the Holy Spirit becomes the gift of the Messiah, being sent according to His good pleasure.

He *offered Himself*, infinitely more precious than any created victim, and that *without spot to God*. This precious offering purges our inmost soul *from dead works*, from all the inward and outward works of the devil.

These dead works spring from spiritual death in the soul, and lead to death everlasting. We are purged *to serve the living God* in the life of faith, in perfect love and spotless holiness.

The Lord Jesus accomplished all this that we *might receive the eternal inheritance* promised to Abraham, not by means of legal sacrifices, but of Christ's meritorious death.

He never went into the Holy of Holies *made with hands* in the temple at Jerusalem, *but into heaven itself, to appear in the presence of God for us* as our glorious High Priest and powerful intercessor (v. 24).

Grace and Peace Be Multiplied

*His divine power has given to us
all things that pertain to life and godliness.*
2 PETER 1:3 NKJV; SEE ALSO VERSES 4 AND 5.

Grace and peace are multiplied to us through the divine, experiential *knowledge of God and of Christ,* because *His divine power has given us all things. Through* that divine *knowledge of* (Christ) *who has called us by* His own glorious power, to eternal *glory* as the end, by Christian *fortitude* as the means.

Through which glory and fortitude *He has given us exceeding great,* and inconceivably *precious promises*—the promises and the things promised, which follow in their due season, that, sustained and encouraged by the promises, we may obtain all that He has promised.

That, having escaped the manifold *corruption which is in the world* from evil *desire, you may become partakers of the divine nature*—being renewed in the image of God, and having communion with Him so as to dwell in God and God in you.

For this very reason, because God has given you so great blessings, *giving all diligence*—a very uncommon word which we render *giving.* It signifies *bringing in over and above:* implying that God works the work, yet not unless we are diligent. Our diligence is to follow the gift of God. And diligence is followed by an increase of all His gifts.

Add to Your Faith

Add to your faith virtue.
2 PETER 1:5 KJV

The apostle Peter writes, because you have received this faith, *give all diligence to add to it.* Add the latter while increasing in the former. The Greek word properly means *lead up* as in a dance, one of these after the other, in a beautiful order. *Your faith:* that "evidence of things not seen," "the knowledge of God and of Jesus our Lord" (v. 2); faith, the root of all Christian graces. *Courage* by which you may conquer all enemies and difficulties, and execute whatever faith dictates.

In this beautiful connection, each preceding grace leads to the following; each following one tempers and perfects the preceding. They are set down in the order of nature rather than the order of time. For though every grace bears a relation to every other, yet here they are so nicely arranged that those which have the closest dependence on each other are placed together.

And to your courage, knowledge—wisdom, teaching how to execute courage on all occasions. *And to your knowledge, temperance:* bear and forbear; sustain and abstain. Deny yourself and take up your cross daily. The more knowledge you have, the more renounce your own will; indulge yourself the less. The great boasters of knowledge turned the grace of God into wantonness; see that *your* knowledge be attended with Christian temperance, the voluntary abstaining from all pleasure which does not lead to God.

Godly Addition

[Add] to patience godliness. . .
brotherly kindness. . .love.
2 PETER 1:6–7, *Explanatory Notes*

Christian temperance extends to all things inward and outward: the due government of every thought as well as affection. It is using all outward, and restraining all inward, things that they may become a means of what is spiritual—a scaling-ladder to ascend to what is above. Intemperance is using things on earth, looking no higher, and getting no further. Only one who uses the creature so as to attain to more of the Creator is temperate and walking as Christ Himself also walked.

And to temperance, patience and to patience, godliness—its proper support: a continual sense of God's presence and providence; a filial fear of, and confidence in, Him. Otherwise, your patience may be pride, surliness, stoicism, but not Christianity.

And to godliness, brotherly kindness. No sullenness, sternness, moroseness: These are of the devil. Christian godliness is mild, sweet, serene, and tender; fervent in zeal and warm in charity. *And to brotherly kindness, love,* the pure and perfect love of God and of all mankind. *Brotherly kindness* seems to mean the love of Christians to one another.

These being added to your faith *and abounding*, increasing more and more—otherwise we fall short—*make you neither slothful nor unfruitful*, so that you are not faint or without fruit in the faith that works by love.

The Purpose of Christ's Coming

For this purpose the Son of God was manifested.
1 JOHN 3:8 NKJV

Many writers have painted the beauty of virtue and the deformity of vice. They have taken care to describe the happiness which attends virtue, and the misery which usually accompanies vice and always follows it. Yet, any changes effected in people by these means is seldom deep, universal, or durable. In a little while they vanish away.

If we would conquer vice, or steadily persevere in the practice of virtue, we must have better arms than these. Otherwise, we may *see* what is right; but we cannot *attain* it. The impotence of the human mind was painted by the Roman philo-sopher: "There is in every man, this weakness—thirst for glory. Nature points out the disease; *but nature shows us no remedy.*"

Though they sought for a remedy, they found none. For they sought where it never was and never will be found, in themselves: in reason, in philosophy. They did not seek it in God, in whom alone it is possible to find it. The best of them either sought virtue partly from God and partly from themselves, or sought it from those gods who were indeed but devils, not likely to make their seekers better than themselves. So dim was the light of the wisest men till "life and immortality were brought to light by the gospel" and "the Son of God was manifested to destroy the works of the devil!"

To Destroy the Devil's Work

*The reason the Son of God appeared
was to destroy the devil's work.*

1 JOHN 3:8 NIV

What these works of the devil are we learn from the words preceding and following the above text: "You know that He was manifested to take away our sins" (v. 5). "Whoever abides in Him does not sin. Whoever sins has neither seen Him nor known Him" (v. 6). One "who sins is of the devil, for the devil has sinned from the beginning" (v. 8). "Whoever has been born of God does not sin" (v. 9). From the whole of this it follows that "the works of the devil," here spoken of, are sin and the fruits of sin (NKJV).

We may learn more clearly of these "works of the devil" from the account God has left us in the first chapters of Genesis. To begin: The Lord God created man in His own image: His *natural* image and His *moral* image. In the *natural image*, Adam was a spirit endued with *understanding, a will* (with its various affections), *and liberty*. In the *moral image*, man was created "in righteousness and true holiness" (Ephesians 4:24 KJV).

His affections were rightly set to love, desire, and delight in what was good. As a free being, he chose what was good, according to his understanding, and was unspeakably happy, being assured that all his ways were good and acceptable to God. Yet, even with his understanding, his knowledge was limited, as he was a created being. And so, he was capable of mistaking, of being deceived.

How Evil Came into the World

The devil has sinned from the beginning.
1 JOHN 3:8 NASB

The liberty of man, in its very nature, included a power of choosing what was good and of refusing what was not. Without this liberty, both his will and his understanding would have been utterly useless. Yet as a created being, his knowledge was limited; thus, ignorance was inseparable from him. So it cannot be doubted, he might *mistake* evil for good. He was not infallible; therefore not impeccable.

After Lucifer concealed himself within the serpent in order to deceive Eve, he mingled truth with falsehood. "Has God said you may not eat of every tree of the garden?" Soon after, he persuaded her to disbelieve God, to suppose His threatening should not be fulfilled. She then lay open to the whole temptation: To *the desire of the flesh,* for the tree was "good for food." To *the desire of the eyes,* for it was "pleasant to the eyes." And to *the pride of life,* for it was "to be desired to make one wise," and consequently *honored.* So, *unbelief begot pride:* She thought herself capable of finding a better way to happiness than God had taught. *It begot self-will:* She determined to do her own will rather than the will of her Creator. *It begot foolish desires* and completed all by *outward sin:* She took of the fruit and ate; she gave to her husband, and he ate. In that moment, they *died!* The life of God was extinguished in the soul, and the body became susceptible to weakness, sickness, pain.

Before and After

God saw all that he had made, and it was very good.
GENESIS 1:31 NIV

Our first parent, Adam, came from the hand of God in His image, created in righteousness and true holiness. As his understanding, although limited, was without blemish, perfect in its kind in a created being, so were all his affections. They were rightly set and duly exercised on their proper objects. As a free being, he at first steadily chose whatever was good, according to the direction of his understanding. In so doing, he was inexpressibly happy, dwelling in God and God in him. He had an uninterrupted fellowship with the Father and the Son, through the eternal Spirit. He enjoyed the continual testimony of his conscience that all his ways were good and acceptable to God.

But when he took of the fruit and ate, this glory departed from him. He lost the whole moral image of God, righteousness, and true holiness. He was unholy; he was unhappy. He was full of sin, guilt, and tormenting fears. Being broken off from God, he looked upon Him as an angry judge, and was afraid. How much was his understanding darkened to think he could hide himself from the presence of the Lord among the trees of the garden!

Thus was his soul utterly dead to God! His body likewise began to die. It became prey to weakness, sickness, pain, and bodily death, leading to eternal death.

The Son of God Is Manifested

When the time had fully come, God sent his Son.
GALATIANS 4:4 NIV

We have seen that the works of the devil are sin and its fruits. How was the Son of God manifested for destroying them?

To the inhabitants of heaven, He was manifested as the only begotten Son of God, in glory equal with the Father before and at the foundation of the world (see Job 38:4–7). But how He was manifested to our first parents in paradise it is not easy to determine. It is generally supposed that He appeared to them in form as a man, and conversed with them face-to-face.

In like form, He is reasonably believed to have appeared to Enoch (who "walked with God"), to Abraham, Isaac, and Jacob on various occasions, and to Moses with whom He spoke mouth to mouth (see Numbers 12:8 KJV).

But all these were only types of that grand manifestation which came in the "fulness of the time" (Galatians 4:4 KJV). He was afterwards manifested to the shepherds, and to all in Jerusalem who waited for redemption. When He was of due age for executing His priestly office, He was manifested to Israel. He preached the kingdom of God in the towns and cities, manifested by numberless mighty signs and wonders and by His sinless life.

"Behold the Lamb of God, which taketh away the sin of the world" (see John 1:29 KJV) is His most glorious manifestation, when He bore our sins in His own body on the cross.

His Most Glorious Manifestation

"How is it that You will manifest Yourself to us, and not to the world?"

JOHN 14:22 NKJV

How wonderfully was He manifested both to angels and men when he was wounded for our transgressions! When He carried our sins in His own body on the cross. When, having made a full, perfect, and sufficient satisfaction for the sins of the world, He cried, "It is finished," bowed His head, and died!

He was further manifested in His resurrection from the dead; in His ascension into heaven; and in His pouring out the Holy Spirit on the day of Pentecost.

"That the LORD God might dwell among them" (Psalm 68:18 KJV) refers to a yet further manifestation of the Son of God, even His inward manifestation of Himself.

When He spoke of this to His disciples a little while before His death (John 14), one of them asked how He would manifest Himself to "us and not to the world." It is *by enabling us to believe in His name.*

He is inwardly manifested to us when we are enabled to say with confidence, "My Lord and my God!" Then each of us can boldly say, "The life which I now live. . .I live by faith in the Son of God, who loved me and gave Himself for me."

It is by thus manifesting himself *in our hearts* that He effectually "destroys the works of the devil."

Overturning Satan's Works

He. . .was manifest in these last times for you.
1 PETER 1:20 NKJV

Just as Satan began his first work in Eve by tainting her with unbelief, so the Son of God begins His work in us by *enabling us to believe in Him.* He both opens and enlightens our understanding. He commands light to shine out of darkness and takes away the veil which the god of this world had spread over our hearts.

Then we see not by a chain of reasoning, but by a kind of intuition, by a direct view, that "God was in Christ, reconciling the world to Himself," not imputing to me my former trespasses, enabling *me* to receive forgiveness of sins. The peace with God which follows particularly delivers us from the fear of death.

At the same time, the Son of God strikes at the root of the grand work of the devil—pride. The sinner humbles himself before the Lord, as it were in dust and ashes. Christ strikes at the root of *self-will.* The humbled sinner is enabled to say, "Not as I will, but as You will."

The Son of God destroys *the love of the world:* the *desire of the flesh, the desire of the eyes, and the pride of life;* and saves us from seeking or expecting to find happiness in any creature.

As Satan turned the heart of mankind from the Creator to the creature, so the Son of God destroys the works of the devil by turning men's and women's hearts back again from the creature to the Creator.

The Final Victory

We have this treasure in earthen vessels.

2 CORINTHIANS 4:7 NASB

The Son of God manifests Himself *in the hearts* of believers, turning their hearts back again to Him and destroying the works of the devil. He restores the guilty outcast from God to His favor, pardon, and peace. The burdened, miserable sinner in whom dwells no good thing is lifted to love and holiness, given inexpressible joy and real, substantial happiness.

But the Son of God does not destroy the whole work of the devil in us as long as we remain in this life. He does not yet destroy *bodily weakness,* sickness, pain, or a thousand infirmities incident to our humanity. He does not destroy all that *weakness of understanding,* which is the natural consequence of the soul's dwelling in a corruptible body. Both ignorance and error still belong to humanity. He entrusts us with only an exceedingly small share of knowledge in our present state, lest it should interfere with our humility and our dependency upon Him.

We are encompassed with these infirmities until the sentence is passed, "Dust thou art, and unto dust shalt thou return!" Then shall error, pain, and all bodily infirmities cease, destroyed by death. Death itself shall be destroyed at the resurrection of the dead, when the Son of God is manifested in the clouds of heaven! Then shall death be swallowed up in victory, and the Son of God destroy the last of the devil's works!

Nothing Else, Nothing Less

*He is also able to save to the uttermost
those who come to God through Him.*
HEBREWS 7:25 NKJV

Real religion is the restoration of a person by Him who bruises the serpent's head, to all that the old serpent deprived him of. A restoration, not only to the favor but likewise to the image of God. This implies not just deliverance from sin but the being filled with the fullness of God. Nothing *short of this* is Christian religion. Everything else, whether negative or external, is utterly wide of the mark. *This* runs through the Bible from the beginning to the end in one connected chain. The agreement of every part of it with every other is, properly, the analogy of faith.

Beware of taking *anything else* for religion. Do not imagine an outward form is religion. Or that honesty, justice, or whatever is called *morality* (excellent as it is) is religion. Least of all, do not dream that right opinion, often called faith, is religion.

O do not take *anything less than this fullness* for the religion of Jesus Christ. Do not take part of it for the whole! Take no less than the "faith that works by love," all inward and outward holiness. Do not be content with any religion which does not imply the destruction of all the works of the devil, that is, of all sin. Weakness of understanding and bodily infirmities will remain, but *sin* need not remain! Come boldly to the throne of grace, trusting in the mercy of God for full salvation!

God Will Do Greater Things

Do not be foolish,
but understand what the Lord's will is.

EPHESIANS 5:17 NIV

The inward kingdom of heaven, set up in the hearts of all who repent and believe the gospel, is righteousness, peace, and joy in the Holy Spirit. But these are only the first fruits. While these blessings are inconceivably great, yet we trust to see greater.

We trust to love the Lord our God not only as we do now, with a weak though sincere affection, but with all our heart, mind, soul, and strength. Indeed, we expect to be "made perfect in love" (1 John 4:18 NKJV). We look for power to rejoice always, pray without ceasing, and give thanks in everything. We believe the whole mind will be in us that was in Christ Jesus (see Philippians 2:5). And we expect to be cleansed from all our idols and saved from all our uncleannesses, inward or outward (see Ezekiel 36:29)—to be purified, as He is pure.

We look for such an increase in the experiential knowledge and love of God our Savior as will enable us always to walk in the light as He is in the light. We trust in His promise who cannot lie that the time will surely come when all we do shall be done to the glory of God.

The grand device of Satan is to destroy the first work of God in our souls, or at least to hinder its increase, by our expectation of that greater work. Yet there are ways to retort these fiery darts and rise the higher by what Satan intends for our falling.

Satan's Ignoble Design

We are not unaware of [Satan's] schemes.
2 CORINTHIANS 2:11 NIV

Satan endeavors to dampen our joy in the Lord by the consideration of our own vileness, sinfulness, and unworthiness. Added to this, he thrusts at us that there must be a far greater change than is yet, or we cannot see the Lord—that all sin must be done away in this life, or we cannot see God in glory.

Thus Satan undermines our joy in God for what He has already done, by a perverse presentation of what we have *not yet attained,* and the absolute necessity of attaining it. We are tempted to think lightly of the present gifts of God and to undervalue what we have already received, because of what we have not yet received.

You may cast this back upon Satan's head while, through the grace of God, you rejoice in confident hope that the sinfulness you sense within shall be done away. While you hold fast this hope, every evil temper you feel—though you hate it with a perfect hatred—may be a means, not of lessening your humble joy, but rather of increasing it.

For all the evil which remains will melt away before His face as wax melts in the fire. By this means, you may triumph in the Lord and rejoice in the God of your salvation. He who has done so much for you will yet do *so much greater* things than these.

Hold Fast Your Peace

We have peace with God
through our Lord Jesus Christ.
ROMANS 5:1 NIV

If Satan can dampen our joy in the Lord, he will soon attack our peace, also. He will suggest, "Are you fit to see God? He is of purer eyes than to behold iniquity. God is holy; you are unholy. How is it possible that you, unclean as you are, should be in a state of acceptance with God? How can you presume to think that all your sins are blotted out? How can this be until you are brought nearer to God, until you bear more resemblance to Him?"

Thus will he endeavor not only to shake your peace but even to overturn the very foundation of it. He will try to bring you back, by insensible degrees, to the point from which you first set out.

But, the more vehemently he assaults your peace with the suggestion that God is holy, and you are unholy, take the more care to hold fast that it is not by works of righteousness, or by your own righteousness, that you are accepted by God. Wear it as a bracelet upon your arm: "I am justified freely by His grace, through the redemption that is in Jesus." Value and esteem, more and more, that precious truth, "By grace you are saved through faith." So shall the sense of sinfulness you feel on the one hand, and of the holiness you expect on the other, both contribute to establish your peace and make it flow as a river.

God Is Never Late

With the Lord. . .
a thousand years are like a day.
2 PETER 3:8 NIV

If we hold fast, "Other foundation can no man lay than. . . Jesus Christ" and "I am justified freely by God's grace," still Satan urges, "But the tree is known by its fruits; have you the fruits of justification? Is that mind in you which was in Jesus Christ? Are you dead to sin and alive to righteousness?"

And then, comparing the small fruits we feel in our souls with the fullness of the promises, we shall be ready to conclude, "Surely God has not said that my sins are forgiven! Surely I have not received the remission of sins. What lot have I among those who are sanctified?"

But bind this about your neck; write it upon your heart: "I am accepted before God by the righteousness which is of God by faith." Admire more and more the free grace of God in so loving the world as to give His only begotten Son, that whoever believes in Him shall not perish but have everlasting life. So shall the peace of God flow on in an even stream, in spite of all those mountains of ungodliness. They shall become a plain in the day when the Lord comes to take full possession of your heart. The Lord is not lacking for time to accomplish the work that still needs to be done in your soul. And His time is the best time. Therefore, ask Him and trust in Him, for He cannot withhold from you anything that is good.

Hold Fast to God's Promises

*For a little while you may have had to suffer grief
in all kinds of trials.*
1 PETER 1:6 NIV

More especially in time of sickness and pain does Satan press with all his might, "Does not God say, 'Without holiness no one shall see the Lord?' You know holiness is the full image of God, and how far is this out of your sight! You cannot attain unto it. All these things you have suffered in vain. You are yet in your sins, and you must perish at the last."

If your eye is not steadily fixed on Him who has borne all your sins, Satan will again bring you under that fear of death in which you were once subject to bondage. By this means he impairs, if not wholly destroys, your peace as well as joy in the Lord. Now, the peace of God is a precious means of advancing the image of God in us. There is scarcely a greater help to holiness than this—a continual tranquility of spirit, the evenness of a mind fixed upon God, a calm repose in the blood of Jesus.

Without this, it is scarcely possible to grow in grace and in the vital knowledge of our Lord Jesus Christ. So, hold fast the beginning of your confidence steadfast to the end. You shall undoubtedly receive the promise of God, for time and for eternity. Be anxiously careful for nothing. Only make your requests known without doubt or fear but with thanksgiving to the One who has made these precious promises.

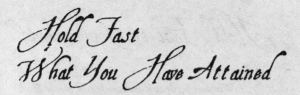

Hold Fast What You Have Attained

"The righteous will live by faith."
GALATIANS 3:11 NIV

Not content to strike at your peace and joy, Satan will level his assaults against your righteousness also. He will endeavor to shake, indeed to destroy, the holiness you have received by your very expectation of receiving more, of attaining all the image of God.

First, he strikes at our holiness by striking at our joy in the Lord. For joy in the Lord, like the peace of God, is a precious means of promoting every holy temper. It is a choice instrument of God by which He carries on much of His work in the believing soul.

Joy in the Lord is a considerable help to outward, as well as to inward, holiness. It strengthens us to go on in the work of faith and in the labor of love—to fight the good fight of faith and lay hold on eternal life. Joy in the Lord is peculiarly designed of God to be a balance both against inward and outward sufferings: to strengthen the hands that hang down and the feeble knees (see Hebrews 12:12). Consequently, whatever dampens our joy and clouds our peace proportionally obstructs our holiness, also.

Therefore, hold fast to "the life I now live, I live *by faith* in the Son of God who loved me and gave Himself for me." Let this be your glory and crown of rejoicing. See to it that no one take your crown.

Hold Fast to Your Faith

Without faith it is impossible to please God.
HEBREWS 11:6 NIV

Our wise adversary endeavors to make our conviction of the necessity of perfect love an occasion of shaking our peace by injecting doubts and fears that we shall never attain to this promised rest. At the same time, he endeavors to weaken, if not destroy, our faith. Indeed, faith and peace are inseparably connected so that they must remain or fall together.

So long as faith subsists, we remain in peace. Our heart stands fast while it believes in the Lord. But if we let go our faith, our filial confidence in a loving, pardoning God, our peace, is at an end, the very foundation on which it stood being overthrown.

Faith is the only foundation of holiness as well as of peace. Without this faith, without an abiding sense that Christ loved me and gave Himself for me, it is impossible that I should love God. For "we love Him, because He first loved us." And unless we love God, it is not possible to have any right affection toward God or people. It follows: Whatever weakens our faith does in the same degree obstruct our holiness.

The more you are tempted to give up your shield of faith, the more you have need to stir up the gift of God that is within you. Never let slip that you "have an advocate with the Father, Jesus Christ the righteous." Hold fast and press on in faith!

Hold Fast Your Confidence

"The word of the Lord endures forever."
1 PETER 1:25 NASB

It is far easier to conceive than to express the unspeakable violence with which Satan urges temptation on those who are hungering and thirsting after righteousness. They see in a strong, clear light, on one hand, the desperate wickedness of their own hearts. On the other hand is the unspotted holiness to which they are called in Christ Jesus.

Many times, there is no spirit left in them. They see the depth of their total corruption and alienation from God and the height of the glory of the Holy One, and are ready to give up both faith and hope. They are nearly ready to cast away that very confidence whereby they "can do all things with Christ strengthening" them. Yet through this alone will they receive the promise.

When this assault comes, hold fast, "I know that my Redeemer lives and shall stand at the latter day upon the earth." And "I now have redemption in His blood, even the forgiveness of sins."

Thus, being filled with all peace and joy in believing, press on in the peace and joy of faith to the renewal of your whole soul in the image of the One who created you. Meanwhile, cry continually to God that you will see the prize of your high calling, not as Satan represents it but in its native beauty. Not as something that must be or you will go to hell, but as what may be to lead you to heaven.

The Joy Set Before Us

Put on love, which is the bond of perfection.
COLOSSIANS 3:14 NKJV

Look upon perfect love, the promise of your renewal in the image of your Creator, as the most desirable gift in all the stores of the rich mercies of God. Beholding it in this true point of light, you will hunger after it more and more. With your whole soul athirst for God and for this glorious conformity to His likeness, press on until you attain.

But here another snare is laid for our feet. We do earnestly pant for that part of the promise which is to be accomplished in this life "for the glorious liberty of the children of God." Yet, we may be led unawares from the consideration of the glory which shall *hereafter* be revealed. We may be drawn away from the view of that incorruptible inheritance which is reserved *in heaven* for us. Our eye may insensibly be turned aside from that crown which the righteous judge has promised to give at that day to all who love His appearing.

Such would occasion us a great loss, for to walk in the continual sight of our goal is a needful help in our running the race that is set before us. It was so with Moses; it was the case with Christ (see Hebrews 11:25; 12:2). How much more needful for *us* is the view of that joy which is set before *us,* that we may endure whatever cross the wisdom of God lays upon us, and press on through holiness to glory.

Let God Be True

The one who calls you is faithful and he will do it.
1 THESSALONIANS 5:24 NIV

While our hearts are reaching toward the eternal crown of glory and to the glorious liberty which is preparatory to it, we may be in danger of falling into another snare of the devil wherein he labors to entangle the children of God.

We may take too much thought for tomorrow and neglect the improvement of today. We may so expect *perfect love* as not to use the love that God has already poured out into our hearts. Thus does Satan try to divide the gospel against itself and make one part of it overthrow the other.

Whenever our hearts are athirst for all the great and precious promises, and our souls break out in fervent desire, Satan does not lose the opportunity of tempting us to murmur against God: "Why is He so long in coming?" At least, Satan will work to excite some degree of fretfulness or impatience or even envy at those whom we believe to have attained the prize. From such tempers, Satan attempts to cause an evil report of the good way to prejudice the minds of unwary men and women against the glorious promises of God.

But none of this can make the promise of God of no effect. No; let God be true and every man a liar. The word of the Lord shall stand. "Faithful is He who calls you, who also will do it." Hold fast the hope of the gospel.

Press On!

Press toward the goal for the prize of the upward call of God in Christ Jesus.

PHILIPPIANS 3:14 NKJV

Press on to glory. Indeed, from the beginning, God has joined *pardon, holiness, and heaven.* And why should anyone put them apart? With your whole soul athirst for God and for the glorious conformity to His likeness, press on in the power of faith.

Let not one link of the golden chain be broken! Hold fast: "God for Christ's sake has forgiven me. He is now renewing me in His image. Shortly He will make me fit for Himself and take me to stand before His face. I, whom He has justified through the blood of His Son, being thoroughly sanctified by His Spirit, shall quickly ascend to the New Jerusalem, the city of the living God. Yet a little while and I shall come to the church of the firstborn, and to God, the judge of all, and to Jesus, the mediator of the new covenant.

"Soon will these shadows flee away and the day of eternity dawn upon me! Soon shall I drink of the river of water of life going out of the throne of God and of the Lamb! There all His servants shall praise Him and shall see His face, and His name shall be upon their foreheads. And no night shall be there; and they have no need of a candle or the light of the sun. For the Lord God enlightens them. And they shall reign forever and ever!"

In steadfast faith and hope, press on unto perfection!

Follow on in Faith

*Imitate those who through faith
and patience inherit the promises.*
HEBREWS 6:12 NKJV

Have you received a good hope of God's promise to be created anew in His image? Have you a strong consolation through grace that He will perform it? Be no more weary or faint in your mind, but follow on till you attain.

If you thus "taste of the good word and of the powers of the world to come," you will not murmur against God that you are not yet qualified for the inheritance of the saints. Instead of repining at your not being wholly delivered, you will praise God for thus far delivering you.

You will magnify God for what He has already done and take it as an "earnest," a down payment, of what He will do. You will not fret against Him because you are not yet renewed but bless Him that you shall be. Because now your salvation from all sin is "nearer than when you first believed."

Instead of uselessly tormenting yourself because the time is not fully come, you will calmly and quietly wait for it, knowing it "will come, and will not tarry."

You may yet cheerfully endure the burden of sin that still remains in you, *because it will not always remain.* Yet a little while, and it shall be entirely gone.

Wait the Lord's leisure; be strong, and He shall comfort your heart. Only put your trust in the Lord.

Press Through to Glory

Let us run. . . .the race. . .fixing our eyes on Jesus.
HEBREWS 12:1–2 NASB

Do you see any who appear (so far as man can judge, but God alone searches the hearts) to be partakers of their hope and already "made perfect in love"? Far from envying the grace of God in them, let that rejoice and comfort your heart. Glorify God for their sake! "If one member is honored" shall not "all the members rejoice with it"? Instead of jealousy or evil surmising concerning them, praise God for the consolation! Rejoice in having a fresh proof of the faithfulness of God in fulfilling all His promises. Stir yourself up all the more to lay hold of this for which Christ died.

To do such, redeem the time. Improve the present moment. Do not let the thought of receiving more grace tomorrow make you negligent of today. Sufficient for the day is the grace thereof. God is now pouring His benefits upon you; now approve yourself a faithful steward of His present grace.

Whatever may be tomorrow, give all diligence *today* to add to your faith courage, temperance, patience, brotherly kindness, and the fear of God, till you attain that pure and perfect love. Let these things be *now* in you and abound. In steadfast faith, in calm tranquility of spirit, in full assurance of hope, rejoicing evermore for what God has done, run the race set before you till, through perfect love, you enter into His glory!

No Anxious Care

"Consider the lilies of the field, how they grow."
MATTHEW 6:28 NKJV

The grass of the field (v. 30) is a general expression, including both herbs and flowers. *If God so clothe*—The word properly implies the putting on a complete dress that surrounds the body on all sides. It beautifully expresses that external membrane which (like the skin in a human body) at once adorns the tender fabric of the vegetable and guards it from the injuries of the weather.

Therefore take no thought—How kind are these precepts, the substance of which is only this: Do yourself no harm! Let us not be so ungrateful to Him, nor so injurious to ourselves, as to harass and oppress our minds with that burden of anxiety which He has so graciously taken off.

We will not, therefore, indulge these unnecessary, useless, mischievous cares. We will not borrow the anxieties and distresses of the morrow to aggravate those of the present day.

Rather, we will cheerfully repose ourselves on that heavenly Father who knows we have need of these things. He has given us the life which is more than meat, and the body which is more than raiment. And thus instructed in the philosophy of our heavenly Master, we will learn a lesson of faith and cheerfulness from every bird of the air and every flower of the field.

Be Anxious for Nothing

"It is your Father's good pleasure to give you the kingdom."
LUKE 12:32 NKJV

How much more, then, will it please our heavenly Father to give us food and raiment? And since you have such an inheritance, regard not your earthly possessions.

To the same effect, the apostle Paul wrote the Philippians (4:6 NKJV): *Be anxious for nothing, but in everything by prayer and supplication, with thanksgiving, let your requests be made known to God.*

If men are not gentle towards you, yet neither on this nor any other account, be not anxious, but pray. Carefulness and prayer cannot stand together. *In everything* great and small, *let your requests be made known;* they who by a preposterous shame or distrustful modesty cover, stifle, or keep in their desires, as if they were too small or too great, must be racked with care. But from them they are entirely delivered, who pour them out with a free and filial confidence.

To God—It is not always proper to disclose them to people. *By supplication*—which is the enlarging upon and pressing our petition. *With thanksgiving*—the surest mark of a soul free from care and of prayer joined with true resignation. This is always followed by peace. Peace and thanksgiving are joined together (Colossians 3:15). Thus *the morrow shall take care for itself*—Be careful for the morrow when it comes. Today, be free from care.

Justification and the New Birth

Having been justified by His grace we should
become heirs according to the hope of eternal life.
TITUS 3:7 NKJV

It is certain, on the one hand, that whoever is justified is also born of God; and, on the other, that whoever is born of God is also justified. Indeed, both these gifts of God are given to the believer in one and the same moment.

Yet, justification and the new birth are easily distinguished as being not the same but having widely different natures. Justification implies only a *relative,* the new birth a *real,* change. In justifying us, God does something *for* us; in begetting us again, He does the work *in* us.

Justification changes our outward relation to God, so that of enemies we become children. By the new birth, our *inmost souls* are changed, so that of sinners we become saints. The one restores us to the favor, the other to the image, of God. The one is the taking away the guilt, the other the taking away the power, of sin. So that, although they are joined together in point of time, yet are they of wholly distinct natures.

The not discerning the wide difference there is between being justified and being born again has been the cause of great confusion when trying to explain the great privilege of the children of God—to show how *whosoever is born of God doth not commit sin* (1 John 3:9 KJV).

Before Natural Birth

You have been born again. . .
through the living and abiding word of God.
1 PETER 1:23 NASB

From all the passages of Holy Scripture where the expression being "born of God" occurs, we may learn that it implies not barely the being baptized, or any outward change whatever. It is a vast inward change wrought in the soul by the operation of the Holy Spirit. It is a change in the whole manner of our existence; for from the moment we are born of God, we live in quite another manner than we did before. We are, as it were, in another world.

There is a near resemblance between the circumstances of the natural and of the spiritual birth. To consider the circumstances of the natural birth is the easiest way to understand the spiritual.

The child not yet born subsists but *feels, senses,* nothing, unless perhaps in a very dull and imperfect manner. He *hears* little, if at all. He *sees* nothing. There are faint stirrings of life, of motion, whereby he is distinguished from a mere mass of matter. But his senses, those avenues of the soul, are quite shut up, so that there is no interchange with the visible world.

It is not that the world is so very far away; no, it is quite near. But without senses, he has no avenue of communication. And there is a thick veil, so to speak, through which he can discern nothing. Just so it is with the soul not yet born again.

Before Spiritual Birth

"The Spirit gives birth to spirit."
JOHN 3:6 NIV

No sooner is a child born into the world than he exists in a different manner than before. He *feels* the air with which he is surrounded. It pours into him from every side, as fast as he alternately breathes it back to sustain the flame of life.

His *eyes* are open to receive the light. His *ears* are unclosed, and sounds rush in with endless diversity. Every sense is employed upon such objects as are peculiarly suitable to it.

So it is with one who is born of God. Before that great change is wrought by God, the individual does not *feel*, has no inward consciousness of, God's presence. He does not perceive the divine breath of life, without which he cannot subsist a moment. Nor is he sensible of any of the things of God; they make no impression upon his soul. The *eyes* of his understanding are closed, and darkness surrounds him on every side. He may have some faint dawnings of life, some small beginnings of spiritual motion. But as yet he has no spiritual senses capable of discerning spiritual objects.

He has scarce any knowledge of the other world, the invisible one. Not that it is far away; no, it is above, beneath, and on every side. Only the natural man does not discern it. He has no spiritual senses whereby we discern the things of God. A thick veil is interposed, and he knows not how to penetrate it.

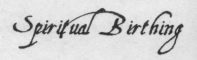

Spiritual Birthing

"So is everyone who is born of the Spirit."

JOHN 3:8 NASB

When one is born of God, born of the Spirit, how the manner of his existence is changed! His whole soul is now sensible of God, and he can say, by sure experience, "You are about my bed and about my path."

The Spirit or breath of God is immediately breathed into the newborn soul. The same *breath* which comes from also returns to God. As it is continually received by faith, so it is continually rendered back by love, prayer, praise, and thanksgiving. Love, prayer, and praise is the breath of every soul that is truly born of God. By these, spiritual life is not only sustained but increased day by day.

The *eyes* of his understanding are now open, seeing the One who is invisible. He clearly perceives the pardoning love of God toward him and all His exceeding great and precious promises. His *ears* are now opened, and the voice of God no longer calls in vain. He knows the voice of his shepherd—he hears and obeys the heavenly calling.

All his spiritual senses being now awakened, he has a clear communication with the invisible world. He now knows what the peace of God is: joy in the Holy Spirit and the love of God that is poured out in the hearts of those who believe. The veil is removed; there is nothing between the soul and the light, the knowledge and the love of God.

The Great Privilege of Those Who Are Born of God

Whosoever is born of God doth not commit sin.
1 JOHN 3:9 KJV

In what sense does the one who is born of God "not commit sin"?

One who is born of God, as has been just described, is one who continually receives into his soul the breath of life from God, the gracious influence of His Spirit, and continually renders it back. This one, thus born from above, believes and loves and by faith perceives the continual actings of God upon his spirit. By a kind of spiritual reaction, he returns the grace he receives in unceasing love, and praise, and prayer. The one thus born again not only does not commit sin, while he thus keeps himself, but so long as this "seed remains in him, he cannot sin, because he is born of God."

By sin, I here understand outward sin, according to the plain, common acceptation of the word: an actual, voluntary transgression of the law of God—the revealed, written law of God. Sin is the breaking of any commandment of God acknowledged to be such at the time it is transgressed.

But "whoever is born of God," while he abides in faith and love, and in the spirit of prayer and thanksgiving, not only *does not,* but *cannot,* thus commit sin. So long as *he thus believes in God through Christ, and loves Him, and is pouring out his heart before Him,* he cannot voluntarily transgress any command of God.

What Happened to David, Barnabas, and Peter?

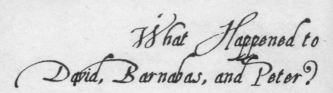

His praise shall continually be in my mouth.
PSALM 34:1 NASB

What appears to be an insuperable difficulty has induced many to deny the plain assertion of the apostle John and give up the privilege of the children of God. It is plain that the Spirit of God, in His Word, has given us infallible testimony concerning King David, who wrote the above words. And yet such a child of God could and did commit sin. Indeed, the horrid sins of adultery and murder.

Even after the Holy Spirit was more largely given at Pentecost, we have the melancholy instance of Barnabas. By the particular direction of the Holy Spirit, he was sent to accompany the apostle Paul as his colaborer among the Gentiles. Later, the contention was so sharp that Barnabas forsook the one to whom he had been joined so directly by the Holy Spirit.

And Peter, the first of the apostles, one of the three most highly favored by His Lord. When he came to Antioch, he was rebuked face-to-face by St. Paul because of his sin of dissembling. How can these cases be reconciled with the apostle's assertion?

What I have noted before is this: So long as "he that is born of God keepeth himself" (which he is able to do by the grace of God), "the wicked one toucheth him not." But if he *does not keep himself,* if he does not abide in the faith, he may commit sin as any other person.

The Case of David

"Turn to Me and be saved."
ISAIAH 45:22 NASB

To explain the perplexity by a particular case: David was born of God and saw God by faith, as his many psalms attest. He loved God in sincerity. He could truly say, "Whom have I in heaven but thee? and there is none upon earth that I desire beside thee" (Psalm 73:25 KJV). But there still remained in his heart that corruption of nature, which is the seed of all evil.

He was walking upon the roof of his house (2 Samuel 11:2), when he looked down and saw Bathsheba. He felt a temptation—a thought which tended to evil. The Spirit of God did not fail to convince him of this. He doubtless heard and knew the warning voice, but he yielded in some measure to the thought. The temptation began to prevail over him. Hereby his spirit was sullied; he saw God still, but it was more dimly than before. He loved God still, but not with the same strength and warmth of affection. Yet God checked him again, though His Spirit was grieved. His voice, though fainter and fainter, still whispered, "Sin lies at the door. Look unto Me and be saved."

But he would not hear. He looked again, not unto God but unto the forbidden object, till nature was superior to grace, and kindled lust in his soul. The eye of his mind was closed again, and God vanished out of his sight. Faith, the divine intercourse with God, and the love of God ceased together. David rushed on as a horse into the battle, and knowingly committed the outward sin.

Here It Is, Step by Step

Whether you turn to the right or to the left,
your ears will hear a voice behind you, saying,
"This is the way; walk in it."

ISAIAH 30:21 NIV

You see the unquestionable progress from grace to sin. Thus it goes on, from step to step: (1) The divine seed of loving, conquering faith remains in the one who is born of God. "He keeps himself" by the grace of God and "cannot commit sin." (2) A temptation arises; whether from the world, the flesh, or the devil, it matters not. (3) The Spirit of God gives him warning that sin is near and bids him more abundantly watch unto prayer. (4) He gives way, in some degree, to the temptation, which now begins to grow pleasing to him. (5) The Holy Spirit is grieved; his faith is weakened; and his love of God grows cold. (6) The Spirit reproves him more sharply, saying, "This is the way; walk in it." (7) He turns away from the painful voice of God and listens to the pleasing voice of the tempter. (8) Evil desire begins and spreads in his soul till faith and love vanish away.

He is then capable of committing outward sin, the power of the Lord being departed from him.

It is unquestionably true, that one who is born of God, keeping himself, does not, cannot commit sin. Yet if he *does not* "keep himself," he may commit all manner of sin with greediness.

The Case of Peter

He began to withdraw. . .
fearing the party of the circumcision.
GALATIANS 2:12 NASB

To explain this by another instance: The apostle Peter was full of faith and of the Holy Spirit. Hereby keeping himself, he had a conscience void of offense toward God and toward people.

Walking thus in simplicity and godly sincerity, he ate with the Gentile believers in Galatia because he knew that "what God had cleansed was not common or unclean"—until certain men came from James at Jerusalem.

When they were come, a temptation arose in his heart to fear those of the circumcision—those Jewish converts who were zealous for all the rites of the Mosaic law. A temptation to regard the favor and praise of these men more than the praise of God.

He was warned by the Spirit that sin was near, yet he yielded, in some degree, to the sinful fear of man, and his faith and love were proportionally weakened.

God reproved him again for giving place to the devil. Yet he would not hearken to the voice of his shepherd. He *gave himself up* to that slavish fear and thereby quenched the Spirit. Then God disappeared; faith and love being extinct, he committed the outward sin: *walking not uprightly,* not according to the truth of the gospel. He separated himself from his Christian brethren; by his evil example, the Gentile Christians were again entangled with that yoke of bondage from which God had set them free.

A Perplexing Question

Each one is tempted when,
by his own evil desire, he is dragged away and enticed.
JAMES 1:14 NIV

Many who are sincere of heart have been frequently perplexed by the question: "Does sin precede or follow the loss of faith? Does a child of God first commit sin, and thereby lose his faith? Or does he lose his faith first, before he can commit sin?"

I answer, Some sin of omission, at least, must necessarily precede the loss of faith—some inward sin. But the loss of faith must precede the committing outward sin.

The more any believer examines his own heart, the more he will be convinced of this: Faith, working by love, excludes both inward and outward sin from a soul watching unto prayer. Even then we are liable to temptation, particularly to the sin that does easily beset us.

If the loving eye of the soul be steadily fixed on God, the temptation soon vanishes away. But if not, we are, as the apostle James speaks (v. 14), *drawn out* of God by our *own desire* and *caught by the bait* of present or promised pleasures. Then that desire, conceived in us, brings forth sin (v. 15). And having, by inward sin, weakened and then destroyed our faith, we are cast headlong into the snare of the devil, so that we may commit any outward sin whatever.

Thou, therefore, watch always, that you may always hear and always obey the voice of God!

The Life of God in the Soul

"Be always on the watch,
and pray that you may be able to escape
all that is about to happen."
LUKE 21:36 NIV

The life of God in the soul of the believer immediately and necessarily implies a continual action of God upon the soul by the inspiration of God's Holy Spirit and a reaction of the soul upon God by an unceasing return of love, prayer, and praise.

From this, we may infer the absolute necessity of this continual reaction of the soul upon God in order to the continuance of the divine life in the soul. It plainly appears that God does not continue to act upon the soul unless the soul continues to react upon God.

It is easy to understand how these children of God, David, Barnabas, and Peter, might be moved from their steadfastness, and yet the great truth of God, declared by the apostle John, remain steadfast and unshaken. They did not keep themselves by the grace of God which was sufficient for each one. Each fell, step by step, first into negative, inward sin, not "stirring up the gift of God which was in him," not "watching unto prayer," not "pressing on to the mark of the prize for his high calling." He went into positive inward sin, inclining to wickedness in his heart, giving way to some evil desire or temper. Next, he lost his faith, his sight of a pardoning God, and, consequently, his love of God. Being then weak and like any other man, he was capable of committing even outward sin.

A Final Warning

Do not be conceited, but fear.
ROMANS 11:20 NASB

God goes before us with the blessings of His goodness. He first loves us and manifests Himself unto us. While we are yet afar off, He calls us to Himself and shines upon our hearts. But if we do not then love Him who first loved us nor hearken to His voice, turn our eye away from Him and not attend to the light which He pours in upon us, His Spirit will not always strive (Genesis 6:3). He will gradually withdraw and leave us to the darkness of our hearts. He will not continue to breathe into our soul, unless our soul breathes toward Him again, unless we unceasingly return to Him our love, praise, and prayer, the thoughts of our hearts, our words, and works: body, soul, and spirit in a holy, acceptable sacrifice (see Romans 12:1).

Let us learn to follow that direction of the great apostle, "Be not high-minded, but fear." Let us fear sin, more than death or hell. Let us have a jealous (though not painful) fear, lest we should lean to our own deceitful hearts. "Let him that standeth take heed lest he fall." Even he who now stands fast in the grace of God, in the faith that overcometh the world, may fall into inward sin and thereby "make shipwreck of his faith." How easily then will outward sin regain its dominion over him! Watch, therefore, that you may pray without ceasing, at all times, and in all places, pouring out your heart before Him! So shall you always believe, always love, and never commit sin!

Faith

Faith is the substance.
HEBREWS 11:1 KJV

Men and women generally understand *faith* to mean an extraordinary trust in God under the most difficult and trying circumstances (see 1 Corinthians 12:9; Hebrews 11). In the New Testament, it also means the gospel dispensation (see Galatians 3:23, 25), the fundamental truths of this gospel salvation delivered by God to remain unvaried forever (see Jude 3).

Faith in the full, general sense is a divine, supernatural sight of God, chiefly in respect of His mercy in Christ (see 1 Timothy 6:11). This faith is the foundation of righteousness, the support of godliness, the root of every grace of the Spirit. The *full assurance of faith* relates to present pardon. It is the highest degree of divine evidence that God is reconciled to *me* in the Son of His love. It is not an opinion or bare construction of Scripture. It is given by the immediate power of the Holy Spirit, which one can have for himself alone and for no one else.

When *faith* is in the midst of several Christian graces (see 1 Timothy 4:12), it generally means a particular branch, such as fidelity or faithfulness. St. Peter (see 2 Peter 1:5) uses *your faith* to mean the evidence of things not seen (see Hebrews 11:1), the knowledge of God and Christ, the root of all Christian graces. Yet it is certain that *faith* does not always imply *saving* faith (see Matthew 17:20). Many have had *such* a faith, and by it cast out devils; yet at last they will have their eternal portion with those evil spirits.

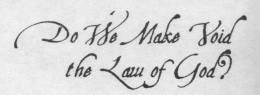

Do We Make Void the Law of God?

Do we then nullify the Law through faith?
May it never be!
ROMANS 3:31 NASB

There are three common ways in which people "make the law void through faith." *First, by not preaching it at all.* Under pretense of "preaching Christ" and magnifying the gospel, all the law is voided at one stroke. Yet in truth, this actually destroys both the law and the gospel. *Second, by teaching* (directly or indirectly) that *faith supercedes the necessity of holiness.* That holiness is less necessary, or a less degree is necessary, now than before Christ came, or that it is less necessary to us because we believe than otherwise it would have been. That Christian liberty is a liberty from any kind or degree of holiness. This perverts those great truths that we are now under the covenant of grace and not of works, and of being justified by faith without the works of the law. *Third, by making void the law in practice, though not in principle.* This is by living or acting as though faith was designed to excuse us from holiness. To allow ourselves in sin because we "are not under the law, but under grace" (Romans 6:14 KJV).

No, we do not establish the old ceremonial law; that is abolished forever. Nor the Mosaic dispensation; our Lord nailed that to His cross. Nor even the moral law, in the sense that keeping the commandments is the condition of our justification. Still, in the apostle's sense, we do *establish the law through faith.*

We Establish the Law by Our Doctrine

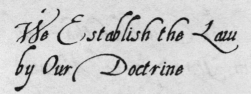

Do we then make void the law through faith?
Certainly not! On the contrary, we establish the law.
ROMANS 3:31 NKJV

We do not establish even the moral law as if the fulfilling of it were the condition of our justification. Yet it remains to determine how we may be able to say with the apostle, "We establish the law" through faith.

We establish it, first, *by our doctrine.* We endeavor to preach it in its whole extent, to explain and enforce every part of it as our great teacher did while upon earth.

We establish it by following St. Peter's advice: "If anyone speak, let him speak as the oracles of God." Speak as the holy men of old did, speaking and writing for our instruction as they were moved by the Holy Spirit. Speak as the apostles of our Lord did, by the direction of the same Spirit.

We establish it whenever we speak in His name by keeping back nothing from those who hear; by declaring, without any limitation, the whole counsel of God. To do this more effectively, we use great plainness of speech. We are not as those who *corrupt* the Word of God, as artful men do their bad wine (see 2 Corinthians 2:17). We do not *mix, adulterate, or soften* it to make it suit the taste of the hearers. We speak sincerity in the sight of God, as having no other aim than by manifestation of the truth to commend ourselves to everyone's conscience in the sight of God.

We Establish the Law in Its Spiritual Meaning

*"I did not shrink from declaring to you
the whole purpose of God."*

ACTS 20:27 NASB

We, *by our doctrine,* establish the law when we openly declare it to all men and women in the height, depth, length, and breadth of it. We establish the law when we declare every part of it, every commandment in it, not only in its full, literal sense but likewise *in its spiritual meaning.* Not only with regard to outward actions, which it either forbids or commands, but also with regard to the inward principle: the thoughts, desires, and intents of the heart.

We do this the more diligently because of its importance. If the tree is evil, if the dispositions and tempers of the heart are not right before God, all the fruit—every word and work— must be evil continually. But important as these things are, they are so little considered or understood that the law in its full spiritual meaning is, like the gospel, a mystery which was hid from ages and generations since the world began.

Indeed, the law of God, in its inward, spiritual meaning, is hid not only from pagans and from Jews. It is hid from what is called the Christian world, at least from a vast majority of them. The spiritual sense and purity of the commandments of God are still a mystery—to the Reformed Christians as well as to those in countries overspread with Romish Christianity.

The Hidden, Spiritual Sense

Even to this day when Moses is read,
a veil covers their hearts.
2 CORINTHIANS 3:15 NIV

The law in its spiritual meaning was utterly hid from the pagan world. With all their boasted wisdom, they neither found out God nor the law of God in the letter, much less in the spirit of it. Their foolish hearts were more and more darkened; while professing themselves wise, they became fools.

The spirituality of the law was almost equally hid from the bulk of the Jewish nation. They who were so ready to declare of others, " 'This crowd that does not know the law is accursed' " (John 7:49 NKJV) pronounced their own sentence. They were under the same curse, the same dreadful ignorance.

Witness our Lord's continual reproof of the wisest among them for their gross misinterpretations of it. Witness the supposition almost universally received among them that they needed only to make clean the outside of the cup. They thought outward exactness in paying tithe of mint, anise, and cummin would atone for inward unholiness—for the total neglect both of justice and mercy, of faith, and the love of God.

So hidden was the spiritual meaning that an eminent rabbi (falsely) commented thus on *If I incline unto iniquity with my heart, the Lord will not hear* (see Psalm 66:18): "If it be only in my heart, if I do not commit outward wickedness, the Lord will not regard it. He will not punish me unless I proceed to the outward act."

Declare the Whole Truth

*"Teaching them to obey everything
I have commanded you."*
MATTHEW 28:20 NIV

The "scribes and Pharisees" of the world—those with the form but not the power of religion—are generally wise and righteous in their own eyes. Even today, "hearing these things, they are offended," deeply offended, when we speak of religion of the heart. Particularly when we show that without this, it profits nothing, though we might give all our goods to feed the poor.

But offended they must be, for we must speak the truth as it is in Jesus. It is our part to deliver our own soul whether they will hear or whether they will not.

All that is written in the Book of God we are to declare, not as pleasing people, but the Lord. We are to declare not only the promises but also the threatenings. At the same time that we proclaim all the privileges which God has prepared for His children, we are to teach them all things whatsoever He has commanded.

We know that all these have their particular use. Some are for the awakening of those who are asleep. Some for instructing the ignorant; comforting the fainthearted; or for building up and perfecting the saints.

All Scripture is profitable for either doctrine, reproof, correction, or instruction. In the process of the work of God in his soul, the believer has need of every part of the Word that he may at length "be perfect, thoroughly furnished unto all good works" (see 2 Timothy 3:16–17, KJV).

A Whole Gospel

In accordance with the truth that is in Jesus.
EPHESIANS 4:21 NIV

It is our part to preach Christ *by our doctrine* by preaching all things He has revealed. We may, without blame, and with a special blessing from God, declare the love of our Lord Jesus Christ. We may speak in a more special manner of the Lord our righteousness. We may speak at length of the grace of God in Christ "reconciling the world to himself" (2 Corinthians 5:19 NKJV). We may, at proper opportunities, dwell upon His praise, as bearing our iniquities, as wounded for our transgressions, that by His stripes we may be healed.

But still, if we were to confine ourselves wholly to these, we should not be preaching Christ according to His Word. We are not clear before God *unless we proclaim Christ in all His offices.*

He is indeed our great High Priest, reconciling us to God by His blood, ever living to make intercession for us. But to preach Christ, as a workman who does not need to be ashamed, is to preach Him also as the prophet of the Lord, who by His Word and His Spirit is *with* us always guiding us into all truth. Indeed, He remains a King forever, giving laws to all whom He has bought with His blood. He restores to His image those He has first reinstated in His favor. He reigns in all believing hearts until He has subdued all things to Himself, utterly casting out all sin and bringing in everlasting righteousness.

Faith, the Handmaid of Love

> *If I. . .have not love, I am nothing.*
> 1 CORINTHIANS 13:2 NIV

We establish the law also when we so preach faith in Christ as *not to supercede but to produce holiness,* all manner of holiness, negative and positive, of the heart and of the life.

What should be frequently and deeply considered by all who would not "make void the law through faith" is this: We must continually declare that faith itself, even Christian faith—the faith of God's elect, the faith of the operation of God—is still only the handmaid of *love.*

As glorious and honorable as faith is, it is not the end of the commandment. God has given this honor to love alone. *Love is the end of all the commandments of God.*

Love is the end, the sole end, of every dispensation of God from the beginning of the world to the consummation of all things. And it will endure when heaven and earth flee away, for love alone "never faileth."

Faith will totally fail. It will be swallowed up in sight, in the everlasting vision of God. But even then, love—

In nature and its office still the same,
Lasting its lamp, and unconsumed in flame,
In deathless triumph shall for ever live,
And endless good diffuse, and endless praise receive.

Love Alone Is Eternal

God is love.
1 JOHN 4:16 NIV

Very excellent things are spoken of faith, and whoever is a partaker of it may well say, "Thanks be to God for His inexpressible gift!" Yet, it loses all its excellence when brought into a comparison with love. Indeed, all the glory of faith is that it ministers to love. Faith is the great temporary means which God has ordained to promote the eternal end: love.

Some magnify faith beyond all proportion so as to swallow up all other things. They totally misapprehend the nature of it so as to imagine that it stands in the place of love. Let these consider: As love will exist after faith, so did love exist long *before* faith. The angels who beheld the face of the Father from the moment of their creation had *no occasion* for faith. For faith in its general notion is the evidence of things not seen. Neither had they any *need* of faith in its more particular application—faith in the blood of Jesus. For He took not upon Himself the nature of angels, but only the seed of Abraham (see Hebrews 2:16).

There was, therefore, no place before the foundation of the world for faith, either in the general or the particular sense. But there was for love. Love existed from eternity, in God, the great ocean of love. Love had a place in all the children of God from the moment of their creation. From their gracious Creator, they received to exist and to love, at one and the same time.

Faith Was Added As a Means

The LORD God called to the man.
GENESIS 3:9 NIV

It is not certain that *faith*, even in the general sense of the word, had any place in paradise. It is highly probable, from the account we have in the book of Genesis, that Adam (before he rebelled against God) walked with Him by sight and not by faith.

For then his reason's eye was strong and clear,
And (as an eagle can behold the sun)
Might have beheld his Maker's face as near
As th' intellectual angels could have done.

He was then able to talk with God face-to-face, the One whose face we cannot now see and live. Consequently, Adam had no need of that faith whose work it is to supply the lack of sight.

On the other hand, it is absolutely certain that faith in its particular sense had then no place. For in that particular sense, it necessarily presupposes sin and the wrath of God declared against the sinner. Without these, there is no need of an atonement for sin in order to the sinner's reconciliation with God.

As there was no need of an atonement before the fall, so there was no place for faith in that atonement. For man was pure from every stain of sin; holy as God is holy.

And love, even then, filled his heart and reigned there without a rival. But when love was lost by sin, faith was added, not for its own sake, but as the means of reestablishing the law of love.

Faith Has Value before God

Love never fails.
1 CORINTHIANS 13:8 NIV

It was only when love was lost by sin in the Garden of Eden that faith was added. It was not added for its own sake, nor with any design that it should exist any longer than until it had answered the end for which it was ordained. Namely, to restore humanity to the love from which it had fallen. Faith, this evidence of things unseen, this confidence in redeeming love, could not possibly have any place until the promise was made that the Seed of the woman should bruise the serpent's head (see Genesis 3:15).

Faith, then, was originally designed of God to reestablish the law of love. Therefore, in speaking thus, we are not undervaluing faith, or robbing it of its due praise. On the contrary, we are showing its real worth, exalting it in its just proportion, and giving it that very place which the wisdom of God assigned it from the very beginning.

Faith is the grand *means* of restoring that holy love in which man was originally created. Although faith is of no value of itself (as neither is *any other means* whatever), yet it leads to the establishing anew the law of love in our hearts. In the present state of things, it is the only means under heaven for accomplishing this. On that account, it is an unspeakable blessing to us, and of unspeakable value before God.

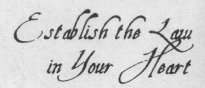

Establish the Law in Your Heart

Through Christ Jesus the law of the Spirit of life set me free.
ROMANS 8:2 NIV

The most important way of establishing the law is by establishing it in our own hearts and lives. Indeed, without this, what would all the rest avail?

We might establish it *by our doctrine* by preaching it in its whole extent, explaining and enforcing every part. We might open its most *spiritual meaning* and declare the mysteries of the kingdom. We might *preach Christ in all His offices* and *faith in Christ as opening all the treasures of His love.* And yet, if the law we preach is not established in our own hearts, we are of no more account before God than sounding brass or tinkling cymbals. Our preaching will be so far from profiting ourselves that it will only increase our damnation.

How may we establish the law in our own hearts to have full influence on our lives? *This can be done only by faith.* Faith alone effectually answers this end. So long as we walk by faith, not by sight, we go swiftly on in the way of holiness. Let the eye of the soul be constantly fixed, not on the things which are temporal, but on those which are eternal, and our affections are more and more loosened from earth and fixed on things above.

Faith is the most direct and effectual means of promoting righteousness and true holiness and establishing the holy and spiritual law in the hearts of those who believe.

Faith Establishes the Law of Love in Our Hearts

Love does no wrong to a neighbor;
therefore love is the fulfillment of the law.
ROMANS 13:10 NASB

Faith, in its more particular meaning, is confidence in a pardoning God. By faith, taken in this sense, we establish His law in our hearts in a most effectual manner. For there is no motive which so powerfully inclines us to love God as the sense of His love in Christ. Nothing like a piercing conviction of this enables us to give our hearts to the One who was given for us.

From this principle of grateful love to God arises love to our brother. Nor can we avoid loving our neighbor if we truly believe the love with which God has loved us. This love to others, grounded on faith and love to God, does no wrong to our neighbor.

Thus, as the apostle observes, it is the fulfilling of the entire negative law. For "You shall not commit adultery," "You shall not murder," "You shall not steal," "You shall not bear false witness," "You shall not covet," and every other commandment are all comprehended in the saying, "You shall love your neighbor as yourself" (see Romans 13:9 NKJV).

But love is not content with barely doing no wrong to a neighbor. Love continually incites us to do good, as we have time and opportunity. It excites us to do good in every possible kind and degree to all. It is, therefore, the fulfilling of the positive, as well as the negative, law of God.

Faith Works in the Heart by Love

In Christ Jesus. . .faith working through love.
GALATIANS 5:6 NKJV

Faith fulfills neither the negative nor the positive law as to the external only. Faith works *inwardly* by love to purify the heart, *cleansing it from all vile affections.* Everyone who has this faith purifies himself or herself even as God is pure (see 1 John 3:3). They purify themselves from every earthly, sensual desire; from all vile and inordinate (unruly, undue) affections; from the entire carnal mind. . . .

At the same time, if faith working by love has its perfect work, it fills the heart with all goodness, righteousness, and truth. It brings all heaven into the soul and causes the believer to walk in the light, even as God is in the light.

Let us thus endeavor to "establish the law" in ourselves. Not sinning "because we are under grace" but rather using all the power we receive thereby to fulfill all righteousness. Let us recall what light we received from God while His Spirit was convincing us of sin and beware we do not put out that light. Let nothing induce us to build again what we have destroyed. May we not resume anything, nor neglect anything, small or great, which we *then* clearly saw was not for the glory of God or the profit of our own soul.

To increase and perfect the light we had before, let us add the light of faith, looking on all things of earth as bubbles upon the water. Count nothing important or desirable, only what is "within the veil" where Jesus sits at the right hand of God.

Established to All Eternity!

Show this same diligence to the very end.
HEBREWS 6:11 NIV

We confirm a gift of God in our souls by a deeper sense of whatever He has shown us—a greater tenderness of conscience and a sharper sensibility of sin. We now walk with joy and not with fear. We look on pleasure, wealth, praise, all things of the earth, as worth nothing in the clear, steady light of eternal things.

Can *you* say, "You, Lord, are merciful to my unrighteousness; my sins You remember no more?" Then, for the time to come, see that you fly from sin as from the face of a serpent! For how exceeding sinful does it appear to you now!

On the other hand, in how amiable a light do you now see the holy and perfect will of God! *Now,* therefore, labor that it may be fulfilled in you, by you, and upon you! *Now* watch and pray that you may sin no more, that you see and shun the least transgression of His law!

When the sun shines into a dark place, you see the motes you could not see before. Now the Sun of Righteousness shines in your heart, and you see the sins you could not see before. *Now* be zealous to receive more light daily, more of the knowledge and love of God, more of the Spirit of Christ, more of His life, and of the power of His resurrection. *Now* use all you have already attained. So shall you daily increase in holy love till faith is swallowed up in sight and the law of love is established to all eternity!

Serving the Lord

"We will serve the LORD."
JOSHUA 24:15 NASB

Such a resolution is worthy of a white-haired saint with large experience of the goodness of the Lord to whom he had devoted himself! It is much to be wished that all those united in Christian fellowship would adopt this wise resolution. Then would the work of the Lord prosper, and His Word run and be glorified.

What does it mean to "serve the Lord" as a Christian, with the service of the heart, "worshipping Him in spirit and in truth?"

The first thing implied is *faith:* believing in the name of the Son of God. We cannot perform an acceptable service to God till we believe on Jesus Christ whom He has sent. The spiritual worship of God begins here.

As soon as one believes, he *loves God,* which is another thing implied in "serving the Lord." And if anyone truly loves God, he cannot but *love his brother* also. Gratitude to our Creator will surely produce benevolence to our fellow-creatures. If we love Him, we cannot help but love one another as Christ loved us.

One thing more is implied in "serving the Lord": *obeying Him;* steadily walking in all His ways; doing His will from our hearts. His servants hearken to His voice, diligently keep His commandments, carefully avoid what He has forbidden, and zealously do what He has enjoined—studying always to have a conscience void of offense toward God and man.

As for Me and My House

"As for me and my house,
we will serve the LORD."
JOSHUA 24:15 NASB

Every real Christian will say, "I and my house will serve the Lord." Who are included in the expression "my house"? The one in your house who claims your first and nearest attention is your *spouse,* seeing you are to love each other as Christ loved the Church. You are to use every possible means that he or she may be freed from every spot and walk unblamable in love.

Next to your spouse are your *children*—immortal spirits whom God has entrusted to your care for a time that you may train them up in all holiness and fit them for the enjoyment of God in eternity.

This is a glorious and important trust, seeing one soul is of more value than all the world beside. You are, therefore, to watch over every child with the utmost care, that when you are called to give an account of each to the Father of spirits, you may give your accounts with joy and not with grief.

Those you engage for longer or shorter periods of time, who voluntarily contract with you *for hire* are, in a measure, delivered into your hands. For that period of time, they are committed to your charge as one that must give an account. And it is not the will of your Master that these should go out of your hands before they receive from you something more valuable than silver or gold.

Restrain Them from Evil

"The Lord disciplines those he loves."
HEBREWS 12:6 NIV

What can we do that all our household may serve the Lord? May we not endeavor, first, to restrain them from all outward sin—from taking the name of God in vain and doing needless work on the Lord's Day? Those you hire may be restrained by argument or persuasion, but if they will not yield, they must be dismissed, be it ever so inconvenient.

Your spouse cannot be dismissed, except for adultery. In other cases, what can be done if *open sin is habitual?* All that can be done is done partly *by example,* partly *by argument or persuasion,* as dictated by Christian prudence. If evil ever can be overcome, it must be by good. We cannot beat the devil with his own weapons. If this evil cannot be overcome by good, we are called to suffer it. When God sees it to be best, He will remove it. Meantime, continue in earnest prayer; in due time, He will either take the temptation away or make it a blessing to your soul.

While your children are young, you may restrain them from evil *by advice, persuasion, and reproof,* and also *by correction.* Only remember, this means is to be used last—after all others have been tried and found ineffectual. All should be done with mildness and with kindness. Otherwise, your own spirit suffers loss, and the child reaps little advantage. Only do not think yourself wiser than God. He said, "Chasten. . .while there is hope, and let not thy soul spare for his crying" (Proverbs 19:18 KJV).

Instruct Them in Righteousness

"Those who are wise will instruct many."
DANIEL 11:33 NIV

We prepare our household to serve the Lord by *instructing* them. We take care to see that every person under our roof has all such knowledge necessary to salvation. It is our responsibility to see that our spouse and children are taught those things which belong to their eternal peace. Plan, especially for the Lord's Day, that all may attend the public services for instruction. And take care that they have time daily for reading, meditation, and prayer. Neither should any day pass without family prayer, seriously performed.

You should particularly endeavor to instruct your children early, plainly, frequently, patiently. *Whenever a child begins to speak,* you may be assured that reason has begun to work. From that time, lose no opportunity of speaking of the things of God.

But speak *plainly,* using such words as little children understand—such as they themselves use. Do this *frequently,* lifting up your heart to God that He would open their understanding and pour His light upon them.

But all this will not avail unless you *persevere* in it. Never leave off till you see the fruit of it. To do this, you will find the absolute need of being endued with power from on high. Without this, I am persuaded, none will have patience sufficient for the work.

Bring Forth Fruit with Patience

Cast your bread upon the waters,
for after many days you will find it again.
ECCLESIASTES 11:1 NIV

You have taught your children from their early infancy in the plainest manner you could, omitting no opportunity, and persevering in it. If you presently do not see fruit of your labor, you must not conclude that there will be none. The seed which has long remained in the ground may at last spring up into a plentiful harvest. Whatever the effect meantime, your reward is with the Most High.

Yet this is not all. Pious parents must take into account where their children are to be sent to *school.* The best thing is to send them to a private school, kept by a pious person, who endeavors to instruct a small number of children both in religion and learning.

When they have completed their schooling, you are doubtless thinking of *some business* for them. Before you determine anything in this matter, see that your eye is single. Is your view to please God? In what employment will they be most likely to love and serve God? *And do not regard if they get less money, provided they get more holiness.*

When your son or daughter is of age to marry, you will have great need of wisdom from above. Aim not at what the world calls a *good match* but simply at the glory of God and the real happiness of your children both in time and eternity.

Adorn the Gospel

*That they will adorn
the doctrine of God our Savior
in every respect.*
TITUS 2:10 NASB

It is undoubtedly true that if you are steadily determined to walk in this path—to endeavor that your household may thus *serve the Lord,* worshipping Him in spirit and in truth—you will have need to use all the grace, all the courage, all the wisdom which God has given you. For you will find such hindrances as only the mighty power of God can enable you to break through.

You will have all the *saints of the world* to grapple with, who think you carry things too far. You will have all the *powers of darkness* against you, employing both force and fraud. Above all is *the deceitfulness of your own heart* which, if you will hearken to it, will supply you with many reasons why you should be a little more conformable to the world.

But as you have begun, go on in the name of the Lord and in the power of His might. Set the smiling and the frowning world at defiance! Follow reason and the Word of God, not the customs and fashions of men.

Keep yourself pure. Whatever others do, let you and your household adorn the doctrine of God our Savior. Let you, your yokefellow, and your children be all on the Lord's side, sweetly drawing together in one yoke. Walk in all His commandments and ordinances, till every one of you shall receive his own reward, according to his own labor (1 Corinthians 3:8).

Self Denial

"If anyone wishes to come after Me,
let him deny himself."
LUKE 9:23 NKJV

It has been frequently imagined that the direction given here related chiefly, if not wholly, to the apostles. It is often thought to be given to the Christians in the first ages or to those in a state of persecution. But this is a grievous mistake. For although our blessed Lord is here directing His discourse more immediately to those who attended Him, yet in them He speaks to us—to all humanity—without any exception or limitation.

The very reason of the thing puts it beyond dispute that the duty here enjoined is not peculiar to the Christians of the early ages. It is of the most universal nature, respecting all times, all persons and all things—not only meats, drinks, and things pertaining to the senses.

The meaning is, "If anyone, of whatever rank, station, circumstances, in any nation, in any age of the world, will effectually come after Me, let him deny himself in all things. Let him take up his cross, of whatever kind—and that daily—and follow Me."

In the full extent of the expression, *denying ourselves and taking up our cross* is not *expedient* only, but *absolutely, indispensably necessary* either to our becoming *or continuing* His disciples. So necessary, that as far as we do not practice it, we are not His disciples. If we are not walking in the way of the cross, we are not following Him. We are not treading in His steps.

If Anyone Would Follow...

*"He must deny himself and take up
his cross daily and follow me."*
LUKE 9:23 NIV

An understanding of our Lord's meaning of these words is critical. In every stage of the spiritual life, there is a variety of hindrances to attaining grace or growing in it. Yet, all are resolvable into these general ones: Either we do not deny ourselves, or we do not take up our cross.

This is a point most opposed by numerous and powerful enemies. All our nature rises up in its own defense against this. Those who take nature rather than grace for their guide abhor the very sound of it. The great enemy of our souls well knows its importance and moves every stone against it.

Even those who have in some measure shaken off the yoke of the devil and experienced a real work of grace in their hearts are not friends to this grand doctrine of Christianity. Although it is peculiarly insisted on by their Master, some are as deeply ignorant of it as if there were not one word about it in the Bible.

Others are further off still, having unawares imbibed strong prejudices against it. They represent self-denial and taking up our cross in the most odious colors. They call it *seeking salvation by works* or *seeking to establish our own righteousness.* You are in constant danger of being wheedled, harassed, or ridiculed out of this important gospel doctrine. Let fervent prayer, then, go before, accompany, and follow what you are about to read.

The Will of God Is Our Rule

It is He who has made us, and not we ourselves.
PSALM 100:3 NASB

The will of God is the supreme, unalterable rule for every intelligent being, equally binding every angel in heaven and every individual upon earth. This is the natural, necessary result of the relation between creatures and their Creator.

But if the will of God be our one rule of action in everything, great and small, it follows that we are not to do our own will in anything. This is the nature of self-denial: *the denying or refusing to follow our own will* from a conviction that the will of God is the only rule of action to us. And we see the reason: *because we are creatures; He is our Creator.*

This reason for self-denial holds with regard to the angels and to man, innocent and holy, as he came from the hands of his Creator. A further reason arises from the condition in which all individuals are since the fall. We are all now shaped in wickedness, conceived in sin. Our nature is altogether corrupt in every power and faculty. Our will, equally depraved with the rest, is wholly bent to indulge our natural corruption.

On the other hand, it is the will of God that we resist and counteract that corruption, not at some times or in some things only, but at all times and in all things. This is a further ground for constant and universal self-denial.

Thy Will Be Done

"Choose for yourselves today."
JOSHUA 24:15 NASB

The will of God is a path leading *straight to God*. The will of man, which once ran parallel to it, is now another path, not only different from it, but in our present state, directly contrary to it. It leads *from* God. If we walk in the one, we must necessarily quit the other. We cannot walk in both. Indeed, *one of faint heart and feeble hands may go in two ways,* one after the other. But he cannot, at one and the same time, follow his own will and follow the will of God. He must choose one or the other—denying God's will to follow his own; or denying himself to follow the will of God.

Now, it is undoubtedly pleasing, for the time, to follow our own will by indulging the corruption of our nature. But by following our own will in anything, we strengthen the perverseness of it. By indulging it, we continually increase the corruption of our nature. So, by food agreeable to the palate, we often increase a bodily disease. It gratifies the taste, but it inflames the disorder. It brings pleasure, but it also brings death.

To deny ourselves is to deny our own will where it does not fall in with the will of God, however pleasing our will may be. It is to deny ourselves any pleasure that does not arise from or lead to God, though it be a flowery path—to refuse what we know to be deadly poison, though agreeable to our taste.

Embrace the Cross

"What. . .if he gains the whole world
and forfeits his soul?"
MATTHEW 16:26 NASB

Everyone who would follow Christ, who would be His real disciple, must not only deny himself but also take up his cross. A cross is anything contrary to our will, anything displeasing to our nature. So that taking up our cross goes a little further than denying ourselves. It rises a little higher and is a more difficult task to our natures—it being easier to forgo pleasure than to embrace pain.

Now, in running the race that is set before us according to the will of God, there is often a cross lying in our way, something which is not only not joyous but grievous. Something which is contrary to our will, displeasing to our nature.

What then is to be done? The choice is plain. Either we take up the cross, or we must turn aside from the way of God.

In order to the healing of that corruption, that evil disease which everyone of us brings into the world, it is often needful to pluck out, as it were, a right eye, to cut off a right hand. When the desire or affection is deeply rooted in the soul, the tearing away is often like the piercing of a sword. The Lord then sits upon the soul as a refiner's fire to burn up all the dross. This is a cross indeed, essentially painful in its very nature. The soul cannot pass through the fire without pain.

A Token of His Love

"What can a man give in exchange for his soul?"
MATTHEW 16:26 NIV

The means to heal a sin-sick soul of a foolish desire, an inordinate, unruly affection, are often painful, not in the nature of the thing but from the nature of the disease. Our Lord said to the rich young man, "Go sell what you have and give to the poor," as well knowing this was the only means of healing his covetousness. But the very thought of it gave the young man so much pain that "he went away sorrowful." He chose rather to part with his hope of heaven than with his possessions on earth. This was a burden he could not consent to lift, a cross he would not take up. And in one kind or another, every follower of Christ will surely have need to "take up his cross daily."

"Taking up" differs a little from "bearing" a cross. We are said to "bear our cross" when we endure with meekness and resignation what is laid upon us without our choice. We do not properly "take up our cross" except when we voluntarily suffer what is in our power to avoid. When we willingly embrace the will of God, though contrary to our own. When we choose what is painful because it is the will of our wise and gracious Creator.

We are well-advised to take up, as well as to bear, our cross. It is, in one sense, common to all Christians, seeing all temptations are "common to man." In another sense, it is our peculiar cross, prepared for and given to us by God as a token of His love, for our advance in holiness.

For Our Eternal Profit

"Whoever loses his life for me will find it."
MATTHEW 16:25 NIV

Consider the cross lying in your path with all its circumstances. It has a quality specific to you. It is prepared by God for *you*. It is given by God to *you*. And He gives it to you *as a token of His love*. If you receive it as such, it is ordered by Him for your good. After using such means to remove the pressure as Christian wisdom directs, lie as clay in the potter's hand. It is for your good, both with regard to the quality of it, its quantity and degree, its duration, and every other circumstance.

In all this, we may easily conceive our blessed Lord to act as the physician of our souls. He does not act for His pleasure, merely, but for our profit, that we may be partakers of His holiness. If, in searching our wounds, He puts us to pain, it is only to heal them. He cuts away what is putrefied or unsound to preserve the sound part. And if we would choose the loss of a (physical) limb rather than the whole body should perish, how much more should we choose, figuratively, to cut off a right hand rather than the whole soul should be cast into hell!

We see plainly, then, the nature and ground of taking up our cross. It does not imply *disciplining ourselves,* as some speak, but embracing the will of God, though contrary to our own. Choosing wholesome though bitter medicines. Freely accepting temporary pain in whatever kind or degree as is necessary to eternal pleasure.

Still Unawakened

"Whoever wishes to save his life will lose it."
MATTHEW 16:25 NASB

It is always owing to the lack of either self-denial or of taking up one's cross that anyone does not thoroughly follow Christ, is not fully His disciple.

It is true, this may be partly owing, in some cases, to the lack of the means of grace: of hearing the true Word of God spoken with power. Or the lack of the sacraments, or of Christian fellowship.

But where none of these is lacking, the great hindrance of our receiving or growing in grace is always the lack of denying ourselves, or of taking up our cross. A few instances will make this plain.

One hears the Word which is able to save the soul. He or she is well pleased with what they hear. They acknowledge the truth and are a little affected by it. Yet they remain "dead in trespasses and sins," senseless and unawakened.

Why is this? Because they will not part with their bosom sin, although they now know it is an abomination to the Lord. They came to hear, full of lust and unholy desire and will not part with them. Therefore, no deep impression is made upon the soul.

The foolish hearts are still hardened. That is, they are senseless and unawakened, because they will not deny themselves.

A Fatal Insensibility

A little slumber,
a little folding of the hands to sleep—
PROVERBS 6:10 NKJV

Suppose one begins to awake out of spiritual sleep, and the eyes are a little opened. Why are they so quickly closed again? Why do individuals again sink into the sleep of death?

Because they again yield to their bosom sin. They drink again of the pleasing poison. Therefore, it is impossible that a lasting impression could be made upon the heart. They relapse into their fatal insensibility, because they will not deny themselves.

But this is not the case with all. We have many instances of those who, when once awakened, sleep no more. The impressions once received do not wear away. They are not only deep, but lasting. Yet, many of these have not found what they seek. They mourn and yet are not comforted.

Now, why is this? It is because they do not bring forth fruit in keeping with repentance. They do not, according to the grace they have received, cease from evil and do good (see Isaiah 1:16–17). They do not cease from their easily besetting sin: the sin of their constitution, their education, or their profession. Or they omit doing the good they may (and know they ought to) do because of some disagreeable circumstances attending it. That is, they do not attain faith, because they will not deny themselves or take up their cross.

Lack of Perseverance

Be on the alert with all perseverance.
EPHESIANS 6:18 NASB

But here is one who did receive the heavenly gift. He did taste of the powers of the world to come. He saw the light of the glory of God in the face of Jesus Christ. The peace that passes all understanding did rule his heart and mind. The love of God was poured into his heart by the Holy Spirit which was given to him.

Yet he or she is now weak as any other person. They again relish the things of earth. They have more taste for the things which are seen than for those which are not seen. The eye of the understanding is closed again, so that they cannot see Him who is invisible. Their love is grown cold. The peace of God no longer rules the heart.

And no marvel. For they have again given place to the devil and grieved the Holy Spirit of God. They have turned again unto folly, to some pleasing sin if not in outward act, yet in heart. They have given place to pride, or anger, or desire, to self-will, or stubbornness.

Or they did not stir up the grace of God which was in them. They gave way to spiritual sloth. They would not be at the pains of praying always and watching with perseverance.

They made shipwreck of the faith for lack of self-denial and taking up their cross daily.

Deny Self to Obey the Lord

Fervent in spirit. . .
devoted to prayer.
ROMANS 12:11–12 NASB

Here is one who has not made shipwreck of the faith. He still has a measure of the Spirit of adoption, which continues to witness with his spirit that he is a child of God. However, he is not going on to perfection. He is not, as once, hungering and thirsting after righteousness, panting after the whole image and full enjoyment of God as the hart pants after the water brooks (Psalm 42:1). Rather, he is weary and faint in his mind, and, as it were, hovering between life and death.

And why is he thus? Because he has forgotten the Word of God which says that *by works faith is made perfect* (James 2:22). He does not use all diligence in working the works of God. He does not continue instant in prayer—private as well as public. He has slacked off communing at the Lord's Table, or in hearing the Word, in meditation, fasting, and religious conference. If he does not wholly neglect some of these means of grace, at least he does not use them with all his might.

Why does he not now continue in prayer? Because in times of dryness it is pain and grief to him. He does not continue in hearing the Word at all opportunities because sleep is sweet, or it is cold or rainy. So his faith is not made perfect, neither can he grow in grace, because he will not deny himself and take up his cross.

Serve the Lord by Serving Others

" 'I was sick, and you visited Me. . .
in prison, and you came to Me.' "
MATTHEW 25:36 NASB

Another cause of not growing in grace, of not being made perfect in faith, is another manner in which those who still have the Spirit of adoption do not deny themselves. They are not zealous of doing *works of charity* or mercy. They are not merciful to the extent of their power, with the full ability which God gives. They do not fervently serve the Lord by doing good to people, in every way and in every degree possible, to their souls as well as bodies.

But why do they not continue in works of mercy? Because they cannot feed the hungry or clothe the naked unless they retrench the expenses of their own apparel or use cheaper or less pleasing food. Beside which, visiting the sick or those that are in prison is attended with many disagreeable circumstances.

And so are most works of *spiritual mercy:* reproof in particular (see Leviticus 19:17). They *would* reprove their neighbor, but sometimes shame, sometimes fear, comes between. For they may expose themselves, not only to ridicule, but to heavier inconveniences, too. Upon these and like considerations, they omit one or more, if not all, works of mercy as well as piety.

And so their faith is not made perfect and they, likewise, do not grow in grace, because they will not deny themselves and take up their daily cross.

Are You Fully Following?

> *"We must go through many hardships
> to enter the kingdom of God."*
> ACTS 14:22 NIV

As the preceding considerations make manifest, it is always owing to the lack either of self-denial or taking up the cross that anyone does not thoroughly follow the Lord and is not fully a disciple of Christ.

It is owing to this that one who is dead in sin does not awake though the trumpet is blown. That another who begins to awake yet has no deep or lasting conviction. That one who is deeply and lastingly convinced of sin does not attain remission of sins. That some who have received this heavenly gift do not retain it but make shipwreck of the faith. And that others, who do not draw back, are yet weary and faint in their minds and do not reach the mark of the prize of the high calling of God.

How easily may we thus learn that those who directly or indirectly oppose the doctrine of self-denial and the daily cross know neither the Scripture nor the power of God. They are ignorant of a hundred particular texts and the general tenor of the Word of God. How unacquainted must they be with true, genuine Christian experience which the Holy Spirit works in the soul!

To have a conscience void of offense, it is not enough that a minister of the gospel not oppose the doctrine of self-denial. He must press it with all his might, to all his hearers, at all times, and in the clearest manner possible.

Practice Self-Denial to the End

Endure hardship with us
like a good soldier of Christ Jesus.
2 TIMOTHY 2:3 NIV

We may learn yet another thing from these considerations—the real cause why *whole bodies of people* who were once burning and shining lights have now lost both their light and heat. If they did not hate and oppose this precious gospel doctrine, they at least lightly esteemed it. If they did not boldly say, "We trample all self-denial underfoot; we devote it to destruction," yet they neither valued it according to its high importance, nor took any pains in practicing it.

One has said that the *mystic* writers teach self-denial. No! The *inspired* writers! And God teaches it to every soul who is willing to hear His voice.

May each of you who read this apply it to your own soul. Meditate upon it when you are in secret. Ponder it in your heart. Take care not only to understand it thoroughly but to remember it to your life's end. Cry unto the strong for strength, that you may no sooner understand, than enter upon the practice of it!

Delay not but practice it immediately, from this very hour. Practice it universally, on every one of the thousand occasions which occur in all circumstances of life! Practice it daily, without intermission, from the first hour you set your hand to the plough. Endure thus to the end, till your spirit returns to God!

Live Wholly to God

We preach Christ crucified. . .
Christ the power of God and the wisdom of God.
1 CORINTHIANS 1:23–24 NASB

Many there are who have retained the profession of Christianity but have *lived away the substance* of their religion. No sooner are any truths proposed which distinguish the Spirit of Christ from the spirit of the world than the preacher is esteemed as one who sets forth new, strange doctrines. Like the men of Athens, his hearers cry out, "You bring strange things to our ears. We would know what these things mean." Yet, he is only preaching "Jesus and the resurrection," with the necessary consequences of it: *If Christ be risen, you ought to die unto the world and live wholly unto God.*

This is a hard saying to the natural man who is alive to the world and dead to God. He will not readily be persuaded to receive these truths as from God unless they be so qualified in the interpretation as to have neither use nor significancy left.

He does not receive the words of the Spirit of God taken in their plain and obvious meaning. They are foolishness to him. Neither indeed can he know them, because they are spiritually discerned. They are perceivable only by that spiritual sense which in him was never yet awakened. For lack of this, he rejects, as idle fancies, truths which are the wisdom and the power of God.

The Circumcision of the Heart

Circumcision is that which is of the heart,
by the Spirit, not by the letter.
ROMANS 2:29 NASB

One of those important truths that can be only spiritually discerned is that *circumcision is of the heart,* in the spirit and not in the letter. The distinguishing mark of a true follower of Christ—one in a state of acceptance with God—is not outward circumcision or baptism, or *any* outward form. It is a right state of soul, a mind and spirit renewed after Him who created it.

That it is spiritually discerned the apostle intimates in the next words, "Whose praise is not of men, but of God." As if he had said, "Do not expect, whoever you are who thus follows your Master, that the world of men who do not follow Him will say, 'Well done, good and faithful servant.'

"Know that the circumcision of the heart, the seal of your calling, is foolishness with the world. Be content to wait for your applause until the day of the Lord's appearing. In that day, you will have praise from God in the great assembly of men and angels."

Of what does that circumcision of the heart consist which receives the praise of God? In general, we may observe, it is that habitual disposition of soul which, in the Scriptures, is termed holiness. It directly implies being cleansed from sin and being endued with those virtues which were in Christ Jesus, renewed in the spirit of our minds so as to be perfect as our Father in heaven is perfect.

Start with Humility

"Blessed are the poor in spirit,
for theirs is the kingdom of heaven."
MATTHEW 5:3 NASB

More particularly, *circumcision of the heart implies humility, faith, hope, and charity.*

Humility is a right judgment of ourselves. It cleanses our minds from high conceits of our own perfections. It cuts off that undue opinion of our own abilities and attainments which are the genuine fruit of a corrupted nature.

Such lowliness of mind disposes those who possess it to embrace, with a ready mind, that *faith* which alone is able to make them whole. Faith is the best guide of the blind. But it must be such a faith as is mighty through God to the overturning all of that wisdom of the world which is foolishness with God.

The circumcision of the heart next implies a strong consolation through *hope.* By this, the children of God have a good assurance that, through His grace, they now do the things which are acceptable in His sight. It gives them a joyous prospect of that crown of glory which is reserved in heaven for them.

Perhaps you, by a deep humility, a steadfast faith, and a lively hope, have in good measure cleansed your heart from its inbred pollution. Yet one thing is lacking. If you would be perfect, to all these, add charity; add *love* and you have the circumcision of the heart.

A Right Judgment of Ourselves

He. . .gives grace to the humble.
PROVERBS 3:34 NIV

To be still more particular: *Humility,* the right and proper judgment of ourselves, entirely cuts off that vain thought, "I am rich and wise and have need of nothing." It convinces us that we are by nature "wretched, miserable, poor, blind, and naked" (Revelation 3:17 NKJV). It convinces us that in our best estate, we are, of ourselves, all sin and vanity. We see that confusion, ignorance, and error reign over our understanding; unreasonable, earthly, sensual, devilish passions usurp authority over our will. In a word, that there is no whole part in our soul, that all the foundations of our nature are out of course.

At the same time, we are convinced that we are not sufficient of ourselves to help ourselves. That, without the Spirit of God, we can do nothing but add sin to sin. That it is He alone who works in us by His almighty power, either to will or to do that which is good. For it is as impossible for us even to think a good thought, without the supernatural assistance of His Spirit, as to create ourselves or to renew our whole souls in righteousness and true holiness.

A sure effect of our having formed this right judgment of the sinfulness and helplessness of our nature is a disregard of the honor which comes from other people—usually paid to some supposed excellency in *us.* One who knows himself knows he does not deserve it.

Faith, the Healing Medicine

With humility comes wisdom.
PROVERBS 11:2 NIV

One who has humility of heart, and thus knows himself truly, neither desires nor values the applause which he knows he does not deserve. By comparing what is said, either for or against him, with what he feels in his own heart, he has reason to think that the world, as well as the god of this world, was a liar from the beginning. And even as to those who are not of the world, who serve his great Master, yet he does not rest upon their approbation. He is assured, that whatever God wills, he can never lack instruments to perform. For He is able, even of the stones, to raise up servants to do His pleasure.

This is the lowliness of mind, learned of Christ, by those who follow His example and tread in His steps. This knowledge of their disease, by which they are more and more cleansed from one part of it, pride and vanity, disposes them to embrace with a willing mind the second thing implied in the circumcision of the heart: *that faith* which is the one medicine given under heaven to heal their sickness.

This faith is the best guide of the blind, the surest light of those who are in darkness, the most perfect instructor of the foolish. But it must be such a faith as is mighty through God to pulling down strongholds, overturning the false maxims of earth, its evil customs and habits, and everything that exalts itself against the knowledge of God.

A Victorious Faith

*This is the victory that overcometh the world,
even our faith.*
1 JOHN 5:4 KJV

Such a faith as is mighty through God casts "down imaginations" and brings "every thought into captivity to the obedience of Christ" (2 Corinthians 10:5 KJV, NKJV). And all things are possible to one who *thus* believes. The eyes of the understanding are enlightened. He sees his calling—to glorify God, who has bought him with so high a price. To glorify God in his body and in his spirit, which are now God's by redemption as well as by creation. He feels the exceeding greatness of God's power; that as He raised up Christ from the dead, so He is able to quicken us, dead in sin, by His Spirit which dwells in us.

And "this is the victory that overcomes the world, even our faith." That faith is not only an unshaken assent to all that God has revealed in Scripture—in particular those important words, "Jesus Christ came into the world to save sinners" and "He bore our sins in His own body on the tree." It is likewise the revelation of Christ *in our hearts*—a divine conviction of His free, unmerited love to me a sinner—a sure confidence in His pardoning mercy wrought inwardly by the Holy Spirit—a confidence whereby every believer is enabled to bear witness: "I know that my Redeemer lives, and that Jesus Christ the righteous is the atoning sacrifice for my sins. He has reconciled even me to God, and I have redemption through His blood, even the forgiveness of sins."

A Lively Expectation

*He has given us
new birth into a living hope.*
1 PETER 1:3 NIV

The faith mighty through God for the revelation of Christ in the heart evidences both redemption and the power of Him that inspires that faith. He delivers His children from the yoke of sin and purges their consciences from dead works. He strengthens them so that they are no longer constrained to obey sin in its desires. Instead of yielding to it, they now yield themselves entirely unto God, as those now alive from the dead.

Those who are by faith born of God have also *strong consolation through hope,* the next thing which circumcision of the heart implies—the testimony of their own spirits with the Holy Spirit which witnesses in their hearts that they are the children of God. Indeed, it is the same Spirit who works in them that clear and cheerful confidence that their hearts are upright toward God. That good assurance that they are now in the path that leads to life and shall, by the mercy of God, endure in it to the end.

It is He who gives them a lively expectation of receiving all good things at God's hand—a joyous prospect of that crown of glory which is reserved in heaven for them. By this anchor, a Christian is kept steady in the midst of the waves of this troublesome world and preserved from striking upon either of those fatal rocks—presumption or despair. And thus he is a good soldier of Christ.

Living Hope, a Motive to Purity

Everyone who has this hope fixed on Him purifies himself, just as He is pure.
1 JOHN 3:3 NASB

The one who has a living hope from God is thereby kept steady in his course of life. He is neither discouraged by the misconceived severity of his Lord, nor does he despise the riches of His goodness. He neither apprehends the difficulties of the race set before him to be greater than he has strength to conquer, nor expects them to be so little as to yield in the conquest till he has put forth all his strength. The experience he already has in the Christian warfare assures him that he cannot gain any advantage except by pursuing the same course as the apostle: "I run. . .I fight. . .I keep my body under subjection, lest. . .I should become a castaway" (see 1 Corinthians 9:26–27 KJV).

By the same discipline, every good soldier of Christ accustoms himself to endure hardship. Confirmed and strengthened by this, he will be able to renounce not only the works of darkness, but every appetite and every affection which is not subject to the law of God. For everyone who has this hope, says St. John, purifies himself, even as God is pure. It is the Christian's daily care, by the grace of God in Christ and through the blood of the covenant, to purge the innermost recesses of his soul from the lusts that before possessed and defiled it. He well knows that his body is the temple of God, and he ought not admit anything into the house where the Spirit of holiness condescends to dwell.

To All These, Add Love

Love is the fulfillment of the law.
ROMANS 13:10 NIV

Whoever you are—if to a deep humility and a steadfast faith you have joined a lively hope, you have in good measure cleansed your heart from its inbred pollutions. Yet you lack one thing. If you will be perfect, to all these add charity. Add love, and you have the circumcision of the heart.

"Love is the fulfilling of the law; the end of the commandment." Very excellent things are spoken of love. It is the essence, the spirit, the life, of all virtue. It is not only the first and greatest command, but it is all the commandments in one. Whatever things are just, whatever things are pure, whatever things are amiable or honorable—if there is any virtue, any praise, they are all comprised in this one word: love. In this is perfection, glory, and happiness. The royal law of heaven and earth is this, "You shall love the Lord your God with all your heart, all your soul, all your mind, and all your strength."

Not that this forbids us to love anything besides God. It implies that we love our brother, also. Nor does it forbid us (as some have strangely imagined) to take pleasure in anything but God. To suppose this is to suppose that the fountain of holiness is directly the author of sin, since He has inseparably connected pleasure to the use of that which is necessary to sustain the life He has given us. So this can never be the meaning of His command.

Love Above All

" 'Love the Lord your God with all your
heart. . .soul. . .mind and. . .strength.' "
MARK 12:30 NIV

The real sense of these words is this: The one perfect good
shall be your one ultimate end. One thing shall you desire for
its own sake—the fulfillment of Him who is all in all. One
happiness shall you propose to your soul: union with Him
that made it, having fellowship with the Father and the Son,
and joined to the Lord in one Spirit.

One design you are to pursue to the end of time—the
enjoyment of God in time and eternity. Desire other things so
far as they tend to this. Love the creature as it leads to the
Creator. But in every step you take, let this be the glorious
point that terminates your view. Let every affection, thought,
word, and work be subordinate to this. Whatever you desire or
fear, seek or shun, think, speak, or do, let it be in order to your
happiness in God, the sole end as well as source of your being.

Have no ultimate end but God. Thus our Lord: "One thing
is needful" and if your eye be singly fixed on this one thing, your
whole body shall be full of light. Thus St. Paul: "This one thing
I do, I press toward the mark, for the prize of the high calling in
Christ Jesus." Thus St. James, "Cleanse your hands. . .purify
your hearts." Thus St. John: "Love not the world. . .for it is not
of the Father" but the mark of those who will not have Him to
reign over them.

Obtaining the Praise of God

And his praise is not from men, but from God.
ROMANS 2:29 NASB

There are some plain reflections by which any may judge whether they are of the world or of God. First, no one is entitled to the praise of God unless his heart is circumcised by humility. In his own eyes, he is little and vile, deeply convinced of the inbred corruption of his nature—prone to all evil, averse to all good. He continually feels in his inmost soul that without the Spirit of God resting upon him he can neither think, desire, speak, nor act anything good or well pleasing in the sight of God.

No one, I say, has a title to the praise of God till he feels his lack of God. Not till he seeks the honor which comes of God only and neither desires nor pursues that which comes from people—only so far as it tends to the honor which comes from God.

A truth which naturally follows is that no one shall obtain the honor which comes from God unless his heart is circumcised by faith, even a faith of the operation of God. Unless he lives and walks by faith, refusing to be any longer led by his senses, appetites, or passions, or even by that blind guide, natural reason. Only when faith directs every step, as seeing Him that is invisible, looking at the things which are eternal—when faith governs all his desires, designs, and thoughts, all his actions and conversations—then only can he obtain the praise which comes from God alone.

No Other Foundation

No man can lay a foundation other than. . .Jesus Christ.
1 CORINTHIANS 3:11 NASB

Our religion is not grounded on the eternal *fitness* of things; the intrinsic *excellence* of virtue and the *beauty* of actions flowing from it; nor on the *reasons* of good and evil, and the *relations* of beings to each other. The gospel knows *no other foundation of good works than faith*, or of faith than Christ.

It clearly informs us that we are not His disciples while we deny Him to be the author, or His Spirit the inspirer and perfecter, both of our faith and our works. "If anyone does not have the Spirit of Christ, he is not His" (Romans 8:9 NKJV). He alone can quicken those who are dead to God—can breathe into them the breath of Christian life—and go before, accompany, and follow them with His grace, so as to bring their good desires to good effect. As many as are thus led by the Spirit of God are the sons of God (v. 14). This is God's short and plain account of true religion and virtue. *Other foundation can no man lay.*

From this we learn that none are truly led by the Spirit unless that Spirit bears witness with their spirits that they are children of God; unless they see the prize and the crown before them and rejoice in hope of the glory of God.

God Himself teaches us to balance the toil of "light afflictions" with the joy set before us, the living hope of our inheritance, incorruptible, undefiled, that does not fade away.

To Follow Your Master

> *"If your right hand causes you to sin,*
> *cut it off and throw it away."*
> MATTHEW 5:30 NIV

Do you find in yourself the joyful assurance that you fulfill the terms and shall obtain the promises of this covenant? If not, beware that you do not quarrel with the covenant itself. Nor blaspheme the terms of it, complaining they are too severe, that no one ever did live up to them. For what is this but to reproach God as if He were a hard master, requiring of His servants more than He enables them to perform? As if He had mocked the helpless works of His hands by binding them to impossibilities, by commanding them to overcome where neither their strength nor His grace was sufficient for them!

On the contrary extreme are those who hope to fulfill the commands of God without taking any pains at all. Vain hope! that a child of Adam should expect to see the kingdom of Christ and of God without striving, without *agonizing,* first to enter in at the small, narrow gate. Vain hope that one who was conceived and born in sin, whose inward parts are wickedness, should entertain a thought of being purified as his Lord is pure unless he tread in Christ's steps and take up his cross daily, even "casting his right hand" or his "right eye" from him. Vain hope that he should ever dream of shaking off his old opinions, passions, tempers, of being sanctified throughout, in spirit, soul, and body, without a constant and continued course of general self-denial!

The One Essential

I discipline my body. . .lest,
when I have preached to others,
I myself should become disqualified.
1 CORINTHIANS 9:27 NKJV

From the apostle's words, we can infer no less than constant, continual self-denial. St. Paul lived in "infirmities, in reproaches, in necessities, in persecutions, in distresses" for Christ's sake. He was full of signs and wonders and mighty deeds. He had been caught up into the third heaven. Yet he reckoned, as one has strongly expressed it, that all his virtues would be insecure, and even his salvation in danger, without this constant self-denial.

"So run I, not as uncertainly; so fight I, not as one that beateth the air." By this, he plainly teaches us that one who does *not* thus run, who does *not* deny himself daily, does run uncertainly, and fights to as little purpose as one who beats the air.

To as little purpose likewise does one talk of fighting the fight of faith whose heart is not circumcised by love. He vainly hopes to attain the crown of incorruption. For *love* cuts off the lust of the flesh, the lust of the eye, and the pride of life. It engages the whole person, body, soul, and spirit, in the ardent pursuit of that crown of righteousness. Love is so essential to a child of God that without it the living are counted dead before God. Though I know all languages, have all knowledge, and many other gifts including all faith, even "give my body to be burned, and have not love, it profits me *nothing!*"

The Sum of the Perfect Law

If I. . .have not love, I am nothing.
1 CORINTHIANS 13:2 NIV

These words are the sum of the perfect law, the true circumcision of the heart. Let the spirit, with the whole train of its affections, return to the God who gave it. He would not have other sacrifices from us, but the living sacrifice of the heart He has chosen. Let it be continually offered up to God through Christ, in flames of holy love. Let no creature be permitted to share with Him, for He is a jealous God. He will not divide His throne with another; He will reign there without a rival. Let no design, no desire be admitted there but what has Him for its ultimate object.

This is the way in which those children of God once walked, who speak thus: "Desire not to live but to praise His name. Let all your thoughts, words, and works tend to His glory. Set your heart firm on Him, and on other things only as they are in and from Him. Let your soul be filled with so entire a love of Him that you may love nothing but for His sake." "Have a pure intention of heart, a steadfast regard to His glory in all your actions." "Fix your eye upon the blessed hope of your calling, and make all things of the world minister to it."

When, in every motion of our heart, in every word of our tongue, in every work of our hands, we pursue nothing but in relation to Him and in subordination to His pleasure, then, and not till then, is that mind in us which was also in Christ Jesus.

Evil-Speaking

Speak evil of no one.
TITUS 3:2 NKJV

"Speak evil of no man," says the great apostle, as plain a command as "You shall do no murder." But who, even among Christians, regards this command? Indeed, how few are there who understand it?

Evil-speaking is not, as some suppose, the same with lying or slandering. All one says may be as true as the Bible, yet the saying of it is evil-speaking. For evil-speaking is neither more nor less than speaking evil of an absent person; relating something evil which was really done or said by one that is not present when it is related. Suppose, having seen a man drunk, or heard him curse or swear, I tell this when he is absent. It is evil-speaking.

This is also, by an extremely proper name, termed "backbiting." Nor is there any material difference between this and what we usually style "talebearing." If the tale be delivered in a soft and quiet manner (perhaps with expressions of goodwill to the person, and of hope that things may not be quite so bad), then we call it "whispering."

But in whatever manner it is done, the thing is the same—the same in substance if not in circumstance. Still it is evil-speaking. If we relate to another the fault of a third person when he or she is not present to answer for themselves, the command, "Speak evil of no man" is trampled underfoot.

A Difficult Sin to Avoid

Set a guard. . .over my mouth;
keep watch over the door of my lips.
PSALM 141:3 NASB

How common is the sin of evil-speaking among high and low, rich and poor, wise and foolish, learned and unlearned! How few can testify before God that they are clear in this matter!

The very commonness of this sin makes it difficult to be avoided. We are encompassed with it on every side. Almost all humanity seems in conspiracy against us! Their example steals upon us, so that we insensibly slide into the imitation of it.

Besides, it is recommended from within as well as from without. There is scarcely a wrong temper in the minds of men and women which may not occasionally be gratified by evil-speaking and thus incline us to it. It gratifies our pride to relate faults of others whereof we think ourselves not guilty. Anger, resentment, and all unkind tempers are indulged by speaking against those with whom we are displeased. By reciting the sins of others, people often indulge their own foolish and hurtful desires.

Evil-speaking is the more difficult to avoid because it frequently attacks us in disguise. We speak thus out of a noble, (it is well if we do not say) holy indignation against these vile creatures! We commit sin from mere hatred of sin! We serve the devil out of pure zeal for God! "So do the passions" (as one speaks) "all justify themselves," and palm sin upon us under the veil of holiness!

Christ's Cure of Evil-Speaking

*"If your brother sins,
go and show him his fault in private."*
MATTHEW 18:15 NASB

Unquestionably there is a way to avoid the snare and not fall into evil-speaking. Our blessed Lord has marked out a plain way for His followers. None who warily and steadily walk in this path will ever fall into evil-speaking. This rule is either an infallible preventive or a certain cure.

In the preceding verses (vv. 7–9), our Lord had said that unspeakable misery will arise from the fountain of *offenses* (offenses being all things whereby anyone is turned out of, or hindered in, the ways of God). Such is the wickedness, folly, and weakness of mankind; but miserable is the one by whom the offense comes. Wherefore, if the most dear enjoyment, the most beloved, useful person, turn you out of God's way or hinder you, cut them off and cast them from you.

But how can we avoid *giving offense* to some and *being offended* by others? Especially, suppose they are quite in the wrong and we see it? Our Lord here teaches us how: He lays down a sure method of avoiding both offenses and evil-speaking. If your brother sins against you, tell him in private. If he listens, you have gained your brother. If not, take with you one or two more, as witnesses. If he refuses to hear them, tell it to the church. If he refuses to hear the church, let him be to you as a heathen, to whom you still owe earnest, tender goodwill, but not familiarity.

Between the Two of You Alone

*"If your brother sins against you,
go and tell him his fault
between you and him alone."*

MATTHEW 18:15 NKJV

The most literal way of following this first rule above is the best. If you yourself see or hear a fellow Christian commit undeniable sin—so that it is impossible for you to doubt the fact, then your part is plain. Take the first opportunity of going to him and tell him of his fault between the two of you.

Great care must be taken that this is done in a *right spirit* and a right manner. The success of a reproof greatly depends on the spirit in which it is given. Pray earnestly that it may be done in a lowly spirit and a meek one. For a person cannot otherwise be restored than in a spirit of meekness (see Galatians 6:1).

See also that *the manner* in which you speak is according to the gospel of Christ. Avoid everything in look, gesture, tone of voice that savors of pride or self-sufficiency; anything dogmatic or arrogant; anything approaching disdain, overbearing, or contempt. With equal care, avoid all appearance of anger; railing accusation; any shadow of ill-will, bitterness, or sourness of expression. Use the air and language of sweetness as well as gentleness, that all may appear to flow from love in your heart. Yet this sweetness need not hinder your speaking in the most serious and solemn manner. As far as possible, use the very words of the holy Word of God, as under the eye of Him who is coming to judge the living and the dead.

In the Spirit of Gentleness

Restore him gently.
GALATIANS 6:1 NIV

If any good is done by what is spoken, it is God who does it. Pray that He would guard your heart, enlighten your mind, and direct your tongue to such words as He may please to bless. If one opposes the truth, yet he cannot be brought to the knowledge of it, but by gentleness. Still speak in a spirit of tender love, "which many waters cannot quench." If love is not conquered, it conquers all things. Who can tell the force of love?

> *Love can bow down the stubborn neck,*
> *The stone to flesh convert;*
> *Soften, and melt, and pierce, and break*
> *An adamantine heart.*

If you do not have access to speak to the person, you may do it by a messenger, a common friend in whose prudence and uprightness you can thoroughly confide. To speak in your own person is far better; but this way is better than none. Only beware you do not feign lack of opportunity in order to shun the cross.

If you can neither speak yourself nor find a confidential messenger, it only remains to write. There may be some circumstances which make this the most advisable way. When the person has a warm, impetuous temper, the message may be so introduced and softened in writing as to make it far more tolerable. Many will read the very same words which they could not bear to hear. By adding your name, it is almost the same as speaking in person.

Take This Step First

"Go and show him his fault,
just between the two of you."
MATTHEW 18:15 NIV

It should be well observed, not only that this is a step which our Lord absolutely commands us to take, but that He commands us to take this step first, before we attempt any other. No alternative is allowed, no choice of anything else: this is the way; walk in it. It is true, He enjoins us—if need require—to take two other steps. But they are to be taken *after* this step, and *neither of them before* it. Much less are we to take any other step, either before or beside this. To do *anything else,* or *not to do this,* is, therefore, equally inexcusable.

Do not think to excuse yourself for taking an entirely different step by saying, "I did not speak to anyone, till I was so burdened that I could not refrain." No wonder you were burdened, unless your conscience was seared. For you were under the guilt of sin, of not obeying a plain commandment of God. You ought immediately to have gone and told your brother of his fault between you and him alone. If you did not, how should you be other than burdened? And what a way you have found to unburden yourself! God reproves you for a sin of omission, for not telling your brother of his fault. And you comfort yourself under His reproof by telling your brother's fault to another person! Ease bought by sin is a dear purchase! I trust in God, you will have no ease till you go to your brother and tell him and no one else.

One Cautious Exception

> "Go and tell him his fault
> between you and him alone."
> MATTHEW 18:15 NKJV

I know of only one exception to this rule. There may be a peculiar case wherein it is necessary to accuse the guilty, though absent, in order to preserve the innocent. For instance: You are acquainted with the design which a person has against the property or life of another. Now, the circumstances may be such that there is no other way of hindering that design from taking effect but the making it known, without delay, to the one against whom it is laid. In this case, therefore, this rule is set aside, as is that of the apostle, "Speak evil of no man." It is lawful, indeed our bounden duty, to speak evil of an absent person in order to prevent his doing evil to others and himself at the same time.

But remember, meanwhile, that all evil-speaking is, in its own nature, deadly poison. Therefore, if you are sometimes constrained to use it as a medicine, yet use it with fear and trembling. Remember, it is so dangerous a medicine that nothing but absolute necessity can excuse your using it at all.

Accordingly, use it as seldom as possible; never but when there is such a necessity. And even then use as little of it as is possible—only so much as is necessary for the end proposed.

At all other times, "go and tell him his fault between you and him alone."

If He Will Not Listen...

> *"Take one or two more with you, so that. . .*
> *every fact may be confirmed."*
> MATTHEW 18:16 NASB

But what if he will not hear? if he repay evil for good? if he be enraged rather than convinced? What if he hear to no purpose, and go on in the evil of his way? We must expect this will frequently be the case; the mildest and tenderest reproofs will have no effect. (But the blessing we wished for another will return into our own hearts.) And what are we to do then?

Our Lord has given us a clear and full direction: Then "take with you one or two more." This is the *second* step. It may be observed with regard to this as well as to the preceding rule: Our Lord gives us no choice, leaves us no alternative. He expressly commands us to do this, neither sooner nor later, but *after* we have taken the first step, *before* we have taken the third.

Take one or two whom you know to be of a loving spirit, lovers of God and of their neighbor. See they are of a lowly spirit and clothed with humility. Let them also be meek and gentle, patient and long-suffering; not apt to return evil for evil or railing for railing, but contrariwise blessing. Let them be of understanding, endued with wisdom from above; and unbiased, free from partiality, free from prejudice of any kind.

Care should be taken that the persons and their characters are well known to the individual. Let those who are acceptable to him be chosen preferable to any others.

Love Dictates the Proceeding

Serve one another in love.
GALATIANS 5:13 NIV

You are taking one or two others with you to speak with a brother who would not "hear" you. Love will dictate the manner in which you will proceed according to the nature of the case. Nor can any one manner be prescribed for all cases. But, in general, before they enter upon the thing itself, let them mildly and affectionately declare that they have no anger or prejudice toward him, and that it is merely from a principle of goodwill they now come or at all concern themselves with his affairs. To make this the more apparent, they might then calmly attend to your repetition of your former conversation with him and to what he said in his own defense before they attempt to determine anything. After this, they would be better able to judge in what manner to proceed "that by the mouth of two or three witnesses every word might be confirmed." That whatever you have said might have its full force by the additional weight of their authority.

In order to this, they may: (1) briefly repeat what you spoke and what he answered; (2) enlarge upon, open, and confirm the reasons you had given; (3) give weight to your reproof, showing how just, how kind, how seasonable it was; and, lastly, enforce the advices and persuasions you had given. And they may, if need should require hereafter, bear witness of what was spoken.

Tell It to the Church

> *"If he refuses to listen to [the witnesses],*
> *tell it to the church."*
> MATTHEW 18:17 NIV

That we may be thoroughly instructed in this weighty affair, our Lord has given us this still further direction. This is the third step. The question is, how this word "the church" is to be understood, but its very nature will determine this beyond all reasonable doubt. You cannot tell it to the entire body of individuals (worldwide) termed the Church. Nor would it answer any Christian end if you could. This, therefore, is not the meaning of the word.

It would not answer any valuable end to tell the faults of a particular member to the church—all the congregations or societies—united together in your town or city. It remains that you tell it to the elder or elders, those who are overseers, of the church—of that flock of Christ to which you both belong—who watch over your and his soul "as they that must give an account."

And this should be done, if it conveniently can, in the presence of the person concerned—plainly, but with all the tenderness and love that the nature of the thing will admit. It properly belongs to their office to determine concerning the behavior of those under their care, and to rebuke, according to the demerit of the offense, "with all authority." When, therefore, you have told them, you have done all which the Word of God or the law of love requires of you. You are now not partaker of his sin. But if he perish, his blood is on his own head.

Who Is on the Lord's Side?

*"If he refuses to listen even to the church,
treat him as you would a pagan."*
MATTHEW 18:17 NIV

Let it be observed that telling a brother's fault to the church,
but nothing else, is the *third* step which we are to take. And we
are to take it in its order *after* the first two. Not before the second; much less before the first, unless in some very particular
circumstance. Indeed, in one case, the second step may coin-
cide with this one, and may be, in a sense, one and the same.
The elders of the church may be so connected with the offending brother that they may set aside the necessity, and supply
the place, of the one or two witnesses. So that it may suffice to
tell it to them after you have told it to him alone.

When you have done this, you have delivered your own
soul. If he will not hear the church, if he persists in his sin, "let
him be to you as a heathen." You are under no obligation to
think of him any more, only when you commend him to God
in prayer. You need not speak of him any more, but leave him
to his own Master. Indeed, you still owe him, as to all other
unbelievers, earnest, tender goodwill. You owe him courtesy,
and as occasion offers, the kindnesses of humanity. But have
no friendship, no familiarity with him, no other interchange
than with an open sinner.

Who will rise up with me and take God's part against evil-
speaking? By the grace of God, will you be one who is not carried away by the torrent?

How to Prevent Evil-Speaking

The words of a talebearer are as wounds,
and they go down into the innermost parts.

PROVERBS 18:8 KJV

Are you determined to "speak evil of no man"? Then learn one lesson well: *"Hear* evil of no man." If there were no hearers, there would be no speakers, of evil. And is not the receiver (of stolen goods) as bad as the thief? If, then, any begin to speak evil in your hearing, check them immediately. Refuse to hear. Let him or her use ever so soft a manner, so mild an accent, ever so many professions of goodwill for the one he is stabbing in the dark.

Resolutely refuse to hear, though the whisperer complain of being burdened till he speak. *Burdened!* O foolish one, do you bear your cursed secret as a woman travails with child? Go and be delivered of your burden in the way the Lord has ordained. First, go and tell your brother of his fault, between the two of you alone. Next, take with you one or two common friends and tell him in their presence. If neither of these steps takes effect, then, "tell it to the church."

But at the peril of your soul, tell it to no one else, either before or after, unless in the one exempt case when it is absolutely needful to preserve the innocent. For why should you burden another as well as yourself by making him or her a partaker of your sin? Be strong, by the grace of God, and set an example to the Christian world!

A Final Challenge

"That the world may believe that You sent Me."
JOHN 17:21 NASB

O that all who bear the name of Christ would put away evil-speaking, talebearing, and whispering. Let none of them proceed out of your mouth! See that you speak evil of no one; of the absent, speak nothing but good.

If you would be distinguished, let it be by this mark: "They censure no one behind his back." What a blessed effect of this self-denial would we quickly feel in our hearts! How our peace would flow like a river! How the love of God would abound in our own souls while we thus confirm our love to our brothers and sisters! And what effect it would have on all that are united in the name of the Lord Jesus! How brotherly love would continually increase when this grand hindrance of it was removed!

Nor is this all. What an effect might this have even on the wild, unthinking world! How soon they would see in us what they could not find among all the thousands of their own, and cry, "See how these Christians love one another!"

By this chiefly would God convince the world and prepare them also for His kingdom. As we may learn from those remarkable words in our Lord's last, solemn prayer: "I pray for those who will believe in Me, that they may be one. . .that the world may believe that You sent Me." *Lord, hasten the time that we thus love one another in deed and in truth, even as Christ has loved us!*

The Wilderness State

"Therefore you now have sorrow."
JOHN 16:22 NKJV

After God delivered Israel, bringing them out of the land of bondage, they did not immediately enter into the land which He had promised to their fathers. They wandered in the wilderness and were variously tempted and distressed. In like manner, after God has delivered those who fear Him from the bondage of sin and Satan, after being justified freely by His grace through the redemption that is in Jesus, yet not many immediately enter into that rest which remains for the people of God. The greater part wander, more or less, out of the good way into which He had brought them. They come into a waste and a howling desert where they are variously tempted and tormented. In allusion to the case of the Israelites, some have termed this a "wilderness state."

It properly consists in the loss of that faith, that satisfactory conviction, the divine evidence of things not seen, which God once wrought in their hearts. Hence proceeds the loss of love which rises and falls in the same proportion with true, living faith. Loss of joy in the Holy Spirit follows, for if the loving consciousness of pardon is no more, the joy resulting from it cannot remain. With loss of faith, love, and joy, there is joined the loss of that peace which passes all understanding. That sweet tranquility of mind is gone; loss of peace is accompanied with loss of power over sin. The glory is departed, even the kingdom of God which was in the heart.

Causes of the Wilderness State

He does not afflict willingly
or grieve the sons of men.
LAMENTATIONS 3:33 NASB

Of the various causes of the wilderness state, I *dare not* rank the bare, arbitrary, sovereign will of God, for He rejoices in the prosperity of His servants and delights not to afflict or grieve the children of men. His invariable will is our sanctification, attended with peace and joy in the Holy Spirit. He never desires to withdraw His gifts from us (see Romans 11:29); He never deserts us, as some speak. It is *we who desert Him.*

The most usual cause of inward darkness is *sin* of some kind, *either of commission or omission.* This may be observed to darken the soul in a moment, especially if it is a known, a willful, or presumptuous sin. But light is more frequently lost by giving way to sins of omission. This does not *immediately* quench the Spirit, but gradually and slowly.

The neglect of private prayer, or the hurrying over it, is perhaps the most frequent sin of omission. This lack cannot be supplied by any other means whatever; the life of God in the soul will surely decay and gradually die away.

Another neglect which brings darkness to the soul of a believer is not rebuking a "neighbour" when we see him in a fault but we "suffer sin upon him" (Leviticus 19:17 KJV). By neglecting to reprove him, we make his sin our own. We become accountable for it. By thus grieving the Spirit of God, we lose the light of His countenance.

Inward Sin Causes Darkness

The kindness of God leads you to repentance.
ROMANS 2:4 NASB

The light of God's countenance upon us may be lost by giving way to *inward sin*. For example, pride. How natural it is for one filled with peace and joy to think more highly of himself than he ought to think! But seeing God resists the proud, this must certainly obscure, if not destroy, the light of God in the soul.

The same effect may be produced by giving place to anger, even though it is colored with the name of zeal for the glory of God. Indeed, all zeal, save the flame of love, is the flame of wrath. In proportion as wrath prevails, love and joy in the Holy Spirit decrease—particularly in the case of anger at those who are united with us by civil or religious ties. We lose the sweet influences of the Holy Spirit and become an easy prey to any enemy that assaults us.

We may be endangered by foolish desire or inordinate affection—seeking happiness in anything or anyone other than God. We likewise give the god of this world an advantage over us if we do not stir up the gift of God in us. There need be no more than *not to fight,* to give way to spiritual sloth. This as surely destroys the light of God, if not so swiftly, as murder or adultery.

Often the *cause* of darkness may lie days, weeks, or months before. That God *now* withdraws His light and peace is not proof of His severity but of His long-suffering and tender mercies, for He designs to bring us to repentance.

Ignorance and Temptation

My people are destroyed for lack of knowledge.
HOSEA 4:6 NASB

Another cause of this darkness of soul is *ignorance,* which is of various kinds. If people do not know the Scriptures, if they imagine there are passages which teach that all believers *must* sometimes be in darkness, their ignorance will naturally bring upon them the darkness which they expect.

Ignorance of the work of God in the soul is frequently an occasion of darkness. Many people have been taught that we are not always to walk in *luminous faith,* that we are to rise higher: Leave these *sensible comforts* and live by *naked faith.* Naked indeed, if it is stripped of love, peace, and joy in the Holy Spirit!

A third general cause is *temptation.* When the Lord first shines on our heads, temptation frequently flees away. All is calm within and perhaps without. But in a short time, the floods arise anew. The evil which yet remains in the heart will move afresh. Anger and many other roots of bitterness will endeavor to spring up, and Satan will be casting in his fiery darts. When so various assaults are made at once, perhaps with the utmost violence, it is not strange that heaviness and perhaps darkness should occur, especially if they were not expected. The force of inward temptations is heightened if we had thought too highly of ourselves, particularly when we *reason* with the enemy, instead of instantly casting ourselves in simple faith upon God, who alone knows how to deliver His own out of temptation.

The Cure of Darkness of Soul

> O LORD. . .
> *examine my heart and my mind.*
> PSALM 26:2 NIV

To suppose that the cure is the same in all cases is a great and fatal mistake but an extremely common one. The cure of spiritual, as well as bodily, diseases must be as various as the causes of them. The first thing, then, is to determine the cause; this will naturally point out the cure.

For instance: Is it sin which occasions darkness? What sin? Does your conscience accuse you of committing any sin whereby you grieve the Holy Spirit? How can you expect His light and peace should return until you put the thing from you and receive His pardon? Or perhaps it is some sin of omission: Do you reprove those who sin in your sight? Do you walk in the means God has given: public, family, private prayer? If you habitually neglect these known duties, make haste to be no more "disobedient to the heavenly calling." Till the sin, whether of commission or omission, be removed, all comfort is false and deceitful. Look for no peace within till you are at peace with God, which cannot be without fruits suitable to repentance.

Or is there some inward sin which springs up to trouble you? Have you thought more highly of yourself than you ought to think? Have you gloried in anything other than Jesus Christ? Have you ascribed your successes to your own strength, wisdom, or courage? If so, you see the way you are to take: Humble yourself under the hand of God that, in due time, He may exalt you.

Suit the Cure to the Cause

Examine yourselves. . .test yourselves.
2 CORINTHIANS 13:5 NIV

Have you forced God to depart from you by giving place to anger? Have you fretted because of the ungodly or been envious against evildoers? Have you been offended against your brothers or sisters in the Lord, looking at a real or imagined sin—so as to sin against the law of love by estranging your heart from them? Look to the Lord that you may renew your strength—that all this sharpness and coldness be done away and love, peace, and joy return, together with a tenderhearted, forgiving spirit.

Have you given way to any foolish desire? to any kind or degree of inordinate, unruly, misplaced affection? How then can the love of God have place in your heart till you put away your idols? It is vain to hope for recovery of His light till you "pluck out the right eye" and cast it from you. Cast out every idol from His sanctuary, and the glory of the Lord shall soon appear.

Perhaps it is the lack of striving, spiritual sloth, that keeps your soul in darkness. You go on in the same even track of outward duties and are content to abide there. Do you wonder that your soul is dead? O stir yourself up before the Lord. Shake yourself from the dust. Wrestle with God for the mighty blessing. Pour out your soul in prayer! Continue with all perseverance! Watch! Awake out of sleep and keep awake, that you not be more and more alienated from the light and life of God.

Consider the Cause

I thought about the former days.
PSALM 77:5 NIV

Are you presently experiencing darkness within your soul? Upon the fullest and most impartial examination of yourself, you cannot discern that you at present give way to spiritual sloth or any other inward or outward sin. Consider your former tempers, words, actions. Have these been right before the Lord? Commune with Him in private "and be still." Desire Him to try the ground of your heart and bring to your remembrance whatever has at any time offended the eyes of His glory. If the guilt of unrepented sin remain on your soul, it can only be that you will remain in darkness till, having been renewed by repentance, you are again washed by faith in the fountain opened for sin and uncleanness.

Entirely different will be the manner of cure if the cause of the disease is not sin but ignorance. It may be ignorance of the meaning of Scriptures, perhaps caused by hearing those who are ignorant in this respect. In this case, such ignorance must be removed before we can remove the darkness arising from it. The true meaning of misunderstood texts must be shown, for there are several Scriptures which have been pressed into the service of proving that all believers *must* walk in darkness. Examine these closely to determine to whom the words are spoken, and the particular circumstances surrounding their utterance. For God requires His children to walk by faith, but *walking in darkness* is no part of God's design.

Ignorance of Scripture

"My people go into exile
for their lack of knowledge."
ISAIAH 5:13 NASB

One Scripture which is misunderstood is Isaiah 50:10 (NKJV): *"Who among you fears the LORD? . . .walks in darkness and has no light?"* But it does not appear from the text or the context that this person ever had light. And we advise one who is still dark of soul, having never seen the light of God's countenance, to trust in the name of the Lord and wait upon God.

Another text is Hosea 2:14 (NKJV): *"I will allure her, will bring her into the wilderness, and speak comfort to her."* It has been inferred that God will bring every believer into the wilderness, a state of deadness and darkness. But this text does not speak of *individual* believers. It manifestly refers to *the Jewish nation.*

A third is John 16:22 (NKJV); Jesus says: *"You now have sorrow; but I will see you again and your heart will rejoice, and your joy no one will take from you."* The context shows that our Lord was speaking privately to His apostles about His coming death and resurrection, not about God's dealings with believers in general.

Lastly, 1 Peter 4:12 (NKJV): *Beloved, do not think it strange concerning the fiery trial which is to try you.* Literally, the text reads: "Wonder not at the burning which is among you, which is for your trial." This refers to martyrdom and sufferings connected with it, and, like the others, is foreign to the point that all believers *must* "walk in darkness."

The Peace of God Refines the Soul

The peace of God. . .
will guard your hearts and your minds.
PHILIPPIANS 4:7 NASB

The question arises, "But is not darkness much more profitable for the soul than light? Is not the work of God in the heart more swiftly and effectually carried on during a state of inward suffering—by anguish, pain, distress, and spiritual martyrdoms than by continual peace?" So the *mystics* teach. But the *Scripture nowhere* says that the absence of God best perfects His work in the heart! Rather, His presence and a clear communion with the Father and the Son: A strong consciousness of this will do more in an hour than His absence in an age. Joy in the Holy Spirit will far more effectually purify the soul than the lack of it. And the peace of God is the best means of refining the soul from the dross of earthly affections. Away then with the idle notion that the peace of God and joy in the Holy Spirit are obstructive of righteousness.

So long as people dream thus they may well walk in darkness. The effect cannot cease till the cause is removed. Yet we must not imagine it will immediately cease even then. When either sin or ignorance has caused darkness, one or the other may be removed, and yet the light which was obstructed may not immediately return. As it is the free gift of God, He may restore it sooner or later, as it pleases Him. Even in natural things, a wound is not immediately healed when the dart that caused it is removed.

Expect Temptation

*The Lord knows how to rescue
the godly from temptation.*
2 PETER 2:9 NASB

If darkness is occasioned by manifold, heavy, and unexpected temptations, the best way of removing and preventing this is to teach believers always to expect temptation. They dwell in an evil world, among wicked, subtle, malicious spirits, and have a heart capable of evil. They must be convinced that the whole work of sanctification is not, as they may have imagined, wrought at once. When they first believe, they are as newborn babes who are to gradually grow up. They may expect many storms before they come to the full stature of Christ.

Above all, let them be instructed, when the storm is upon them, not to reason with the devil but to pray. Let them pour out their souls before God and show Him of their trouble. And these are the persons unto whom, chiefly, we are to apply the great and precious promises. Not to the ignorant, till the ignorance is removed. Much less to an impenitent sinner.

To the tempted we may declare the loving-kindness of God. Dwell upon His faithfulness and the virtue of that blood shed for us to cleanse us from all sin. God will bear witness to His Word and bring them out of trouble. He will say, "Arise, shine; for your light has come! And the glory of the Lord is risen upon you."

Indeed, that light, if you walk humbly and closely with God, will shine more and more unto the perfect day (see Proverbs 4:18).

Heaviness of Soul

Ye are in heaviness.
1 PETER 1:6 KJV

There is a near relationship between the darkness of mind in the wilderness state and heaviness of soul, which is more common among believers. The resemblance is so great that they are frequently confounded together. But they are not equivalent terms; far, far from it. The difference is so wide and essential, as all the children of God need to understand, to prevent them sliding out of heaviness into darkness.

The manner of persons to whom the apostle Peter wrote the above words were believers at that time. He expressly says (v. 5) *you are kept by the power of God through faith unto salvation.* Again (v. 7), he mentions *the trial of their faith;* and yet again (v. 9), he speaks of their *receiving the end of their faith, the salvation of their souls.* So, though they were in heaviness, they were possessed of living faith. Their heaviness did not destroy their faith. Neither did it destroy their peace, which is inseparable from true, living faith. The apostle prays (v. 2) not that *grace and peace* may be *given* them, but that it may be *multiplied.*

They were also full of a *living hope.* For he speaks (v. 3) of their living hope of their inheritance that fadeth not away. In spite of their heaviness, they still retained a hope full of immortality. And they still *rejoiced* (v. 8) *with joy unspeakable and full of glory.* Their heaviness, then, was also consistent both with living hope and inexpressible joy!

Kept by the Power of God

[You] who through faith are shielded by God's power.
1 PETER 1:5 NIV

In the midst of their heaviness, these people still enjoyed the *love of God.* "Whom," says the apostle, "having not seen, you love" (v. 8). Though you have not yet seen Him face-to-face, He is your God, your love, the desire of your eyes, and your exceeding great reward.

Once more: Though they were heavy, yet they were *holy;* they retained the same power over sin. Being redeemed by the blood of Christ, they were kept from sin "by the power of God." So that, upon the whole, their heaviness well consisted with faith, with hope, with love of God and man, with the peace of God, with joy in the Holy Spirit, with inward and outward holiness. It did no way impair, much less destroy, any part of the work of God in their hearts. It did not at all interfere with that "sanctification of the Spirit" which is the root of all true obedience. Neither did it interfere with the happiness which must needs result from grace and peace reigning in the heart.

From this we may easily learn what kind of heaviness they were in. The constant, literal meaning of the word in the original is *made sorry, grieved.* This being observed, there is no ambiguity, nor any difficulty in understanding the expression. These persons were *grieved.* Their heaviness was neither more nor less than *sorrow or grief*—a passion with which everyone is well acquainted.

Inward Affliction

You may have had to suffer grief
in all kinds of trials.
1 PETER 1:6 NIV

It is probable the King James translators rendered the word *heaviness* rather than *sorrow* or *grief* to denote two things. First the degree, and next the continuance of it. It does seem that here is not a slight degree of *grief*, but such as makes a strong impression upon, and sinks deep into, the soul. Neither does it appear to be a transient *sorrow*, such as passes away in an hour. But rather such as, having taken fast hold of the heart, is not presently shaken off, but continues for some time. A settled temper, rather than a passion—even in those who have a living faith in Christ and the genuine love of God in their hearts.

Even in these, this heaviness may sometimes be so deep as to overshadow the whole soul, coloring all the affections. It may likewise have an influence over the body, pressing it down, and weakening it more and more. And yet, all this may consist with a measure of that faith which still works by love.

This may well be termed a "fiery trial." Though not the same as the apostle speaks of in the fourth chapter, yet many of the expressions used there may be applied to this inward affliction. They cannot be properly applied to those in darkness, who do not, cannot rejoice. Neither is it true that the Spirit of glory and of God rests upon them. But He frequently does on those in heaviness, who, though sorrowful, are always rejoicing.

A Bodily Affliction

No one said a word to [Job],
because they saw how great his suffering was.
JOB 2:13 NIV

What are the causes of such sorrow or heaviness in a true believer? The apostle tells us clearly, *You are in heaviness through manifold temptations.* Manifold: many in number and of many kinds. They may be varied and diversified a thousand ways by the change or addition of numberless circumstances. This very diversity and variety make it more difficult to guard against them.

Among these, we rank all *bodily disorders*, particularly acute diseases and violent pain. Perhaps one person in a thousand has a constitution so as not to feel pain like others. But, in general, pain is misery, often overturning patience. Even where the grace of God enables them to possess their souls in patience, there is much inward heaviness, the soul sympathizing with the body.

All diseases of long continuance, though less painful, are apt to produce the same effect. This is especially so with those termed *nervous disorders*. And faith does not overturn the course of nature. Natural causes still produce natural effects. Faith no more hinders the *sinking of the spirits* in an hysteric illness than it does the rising of the pulse in a fever.

Again, when *calamity and poverty* come as a whirlwind, is this a little temptation? What shall they do who have not food and lodging and nothing for their little ones? I am astonished that it occasions no more than heaviness even in those who believe!

Death Causes Sorrow

Grief in all kinds of trials.
1 PETER 1:6 NIV

Next to the calamity of poverty we may place the *death* of those who were near and dear to us. Perhaps of a tender parent, not yet declined in years. Of a beloved child just rising into life and clasping about our heart. Of a friend who was as our own soul—the best gift of heaven next to the grace of God.

A thousand circumstances may enhance the distress. Perhaps the child or friend died in our embrace. Perhaps, was snatched away when we looked not for it. In all these cases, we not only may, but ought to, be affected: It is the design of God that we should. He would have our affections regulated, not extinguished. There may be sorrow without sin. A still deeper sorrow may we feel for those who are dead while they live— because of the unkindness, ingratitude, apostasy of those united to us in the closest ties. Who can express what a lover of souls may feel for a friend, a brother dead to God? Or any near relation rushing into sin in spite of all arguments and persuasions? The anguish may be heightened by the consideration that he or she once ran well in the way of life.

In all this, our adversary will press his opportunity. He will labor to inject unbelieving, blasphemous, or repining thoughts; to stir up the heart against God and renew our natural enmity against Him. And if we begin to reason with Satan, more and more heaviness, if not utter darkness, will ensue.

A Just and Merciful God

*He does not willingly bring affliction or grief
to the children of men.*
LAMENTATIONS 3:33 NIV

Our great adversary is always walking about seeking whom he may devour (see 1 Peter 5:8). When a soul is in heaviness, he uses all his power and skill to gain an advantage over the one already cast down. He will not be sparing of his fiery darts, those most likely to find an entrance, to fix most deeply in the heart, by their suitableness to the temptation that assaults the heart.

He labors to inject unbelieving, blasphemous thoughts against God, suggesting that He does not regard or govern the earth. Or that He does not govern it by the rules of justice and mercy. If we try to fight Satan with his own weapons, begin to reason with him, more and more heaviness ensues, if not utter darkness.

It has been supposed that another cause of heaviness is God's withdrawing Himself from the soul because it is His sovereign will. *This I absolutely deny!* Certainly, He will withdraw if we grieve His Holy Spirit either by outward or inward sin; either by doing evil or neglecting to do good; by giving way to pride, anger, spiritual sloth, foolish desire, or inordinate affection. But that He ever does so *merely because He pleases is repugnant* to the nature of God, utterly beneath His majesty and wisdom. There is no text in all the Bible which gives any color for such a supposition! It is inconsistent with both His justice and His mercy, and with the experience of all His children.

"If Need Be..."

In this you greatly rejoice,
though now for a little while
you may have had to suffer.
1 PETER 1:6 NIV

One more cause of heaviness is found in (so-called) *mystic* authors. One has written, "I found myself in a forlorn condition, altogether poor, wretched, and miserable. The proper source of this grief is the knowledge of ourselves by which we. . . see ourselves most opposite to Him; that our inmost soul is entirely corrupted, depraved, full of all kind of evil and malignity. . . ." From this, it has been *inferred* that the knowledge of ourselves, without which we should perish everlastingly, must (even after we have attained justifying faith) occasion the deepest heaviness.

But in a preceding paragraph, this author had said she "felt God's love." It may be so; yet it does not appear that this was justification. It is more probable it was the drawings of the Father; so that which followed was no other than conviction of sin, which in the nature of things must precede justifying faith.

There will be a far deeper, clearer, fuller knowledge of our inbred sin, our total corruption by nature, after justification than before. But *this need not occasion darkness, nor must it bring even heaviness.* Were it so, the apostle would not have used "if need be." God may increase the knowledge of Himself and the experience of His love in proportion as He increases the knowledge of ourselves, so that instead of a desert and misery, there is love, peace, and joy, springing up into everlasting life.

To Increase Our Faith

"These have come so that your faith. . .
may be proved genuine."
1 PETER 1:7 NIV

For what ends, what purposes, does God permit heaviness to befall so many of His children? The apostle gives us a plain and direct answer: that the trial of their faith, "being much more precious than gold that perishes, though it is tested by fire, may be found to praise, honor, and glory at the revelation of Jesus Christ."

There may be an allusion to this in the fourth chapter, although there it primarily relates to quite another thing, as I have already observed. *Do not think it strange concerning the fiery trial which is to try you. . .but rejoice to the extent that you partake of Christ's sufferings, that when His glory is revealed, you may also be glad with exceeding joy* (vv. 12–13 NKJV).

Hence, we learn that the first and great end of God's permitting the temptations which bring heaviness on His children is the trial of their faith, which is tried by these, even as gold is by the fire. Now we know gold tried in the fire is purified, is separated from its dross. And so is faith in the fire of temptation. The more it is tried, the more it is purified. And not only purified, but also strengthened, confirmed, increased abundantly, by so many proofs of the wisdom and power, the love and faithfulness of God. This, then—*to increase our faith*—is one gracious end of God's permitting those manifold temptations.

To Enlarge Our Hope, Joy, Love

Even though you do not see him now, you. . .
are filled with an inexpressible and glorious joy.

1 PETER 1:8 NIV

Manifold temptations serve to try, to purify, to confirm and *to increase our living hope,* whereunto "the God and Father of our Lord Jesus Christ has begotten us again of His abundant mercy." Indeed, our hope increases in the same proportion as our faith. On this foundation it stands: Believing in His name, living by faith in the Son of God, we hope for, have a confident expectation of, the glory that shall be revealed. Consequently, whatever strengthens our faith increases our hope, also.

At the same time, it increases our joy in the Lord, which must attend a hope full of immortality. In this view, the apostle exhorts believers, "Rejoice that you partake of Christ's sufferings." On this very account, happy are you, "for the Spirit of glory and of God rests upon you." And by this you are enabled, in the midst of sufferings to "rejoice with joy unspeakable and full of glory."

We rejoice the more because the trials that increase our faith and hope increase our love, also—both our gratitude to God for all His mercies, and our goodwill to all mankind. The more deeply sensible we are of the loving-kindness of God our Savior, the more is our heart inflamed with love to Him who first loved us. And this—*the increase of our love*—is another end of the temptations permitted to come upon the believer.

To Advance Us in Holiness

*Our light and momentary troubles are
achieving for us an eternal glory
that far outweighs them all.*
2 CORINTHIANS 4:17 NIV

Another purpose of manifold temptations among the children of God is *their advance in holiness*—holiness of heart, and of life. The latter naturally results from the former, for a good tree will bring forth good fruit. And all inward holiness is the immediate fruit of the faith that works by love. By this, the blessed Spirit purifies the heart from pride, self-will, passion, love of the world, foolish and hurtful desires, vile and vain affections. Beside that, through the operation of His Spirit, sanctified afflictions tend directly to holiness. They humble, more and more, and abase the soul before God. They calm and make meek our turbulent spirit, tame the fierceness of our nature, soften our obstinacy and self-will, crucify us to the world, and bring us to expect all our strength from, and to seek all our happiness in, God.

All these are so that our faith, love, and holiness *may be found,* if they do not yet appear, unto *praise* from God Himself, *honor* from men and angels, and *glory* assigned by the great judge to all that have endured to the end, when every man is rewarded according to his works; according to the work which God wrought in his heart, and the outward works which he has wrought for God; and according to what he has suffered. So that these light afflictions, which are only for a moment, work out for us a far more exceeding and eternal weight of glory!

Serene in the Storm

*"He is my refuge and my fortress;
My God, in Him I will trust."*

PSALM 91:2 NKJV

Others may often receive an advantage from seeing the behavior of a believer under affliction. We find by experience, example frequently makes a deeper impression upon us than precept. Such examples have a strong influence on those who are partakers of like precious faith. And what examples have a stronger influence, even on them who have not known God, than that of a soul calm and serene in the midst of storms! Sorrowful, yet always rejoicing; meekly accepting whatever is the will of God, however grievous to nature. Saying, in sickness and pain, "The cup which my Father has given me, shall I not drink it?" To say, in loss or in want, "The Lord gave; the Lord has taken away; blessed be the name of the Lord!"

We need not be solicitous how to *avoid,* so much as how to *be improved by,* heaviness. Our great care should be so to behave ourselves under it, so to wait upon the Lord in it that it may fully answer all the design of His love in permitting it to come upon us. That it may be a means of increasing our faith, of confirming our hope, and of perfecting us in all holiness.

Whenever heaviness comes, let us have an eye to those gracious ends for which it is permitted and use all diligence that we may not make void the counsel of God against ourselves.

Distinguish the Difference

Your testimonies are very sure;
Holiness adorns Your house, O LORD, forever.
PSALM 93:5 NKJV

How wide is the difference between darkness of soul and heaviness! Nevertheless, these two are generally confounded with each other, even by experienced Christians! Darkness, or the wilderness state, implies a total loss of *joy* in the Holy Spirit. Heaviness does not. In the midst of heaviness, we may rejoice with inexpressible joy! Those in darkness have lost *the peace of God.* Those in heaviness have not. So far from it, that at the very time peace as well as grace may be multiplied to them. In darkness, *the love of God* is waxed cold, if not utterly extinguished. In heaviness, it retains its full force, or rather, increases daily.

In darkness, *faith* itself, if not totally lost, is, however, grievously decayed. The evidence and conviction of things not seen, particularly of the pardoning love of God, is not so clear or strong as in time past. And trust in Him is proportionally weakened. Those in heaviness, though they see Him not, yet have a clear, unshaken evidence of that love whereby all their sins are blotted out.

So that, as long as we can distinguish faith from unbelief, hope from despair, peace from war, the love of God from the love of the world, we may infallibly distinguish heaviness from darkness!

Heaviness Is Not Always Needful

> *Though now for a little while, if need be,*
> *you have been grieved by various trials.*
>
> 1 PETER 1:6 NKJV

We may learn from the Scripture that there *may* be need of heaviness. But there can be no need of darkness. There may be need of our being in heaviness "for a season"—for a little while —for the purposes already mentioned. Such heaviness is a natural result of manifold temptations which are needful to try and to increase our faith, to confirm and enlarge our hope, to purify our heart from all unholy tempers, and to perfect us in love. By consequence, these manifold temptations are needful *to brighten our crown and add to our eternal weight of glory!*

But we cannot say that darkness is needful in order to any of these ends. It is in no way conducive to them. The loss of faith, hope, love is surely neither conducive to holiness nor to the increase of that reward in heaven which will be in proportion to our holiness on earth.

From the apostle's manner of speaking, we may gather that even heaviness is not *always* needful. *Now for a little while, if need be. . .* So it is not needful *for all persons,* nor for any person *at all times.* God is able, has both power and wisdom, to work when He pleases, the same work of grace in any soul, by other means. So that some individuals go on in strength, with scarcely any heaviness at all. But these cases are indeed rare.

To Accomplish God's Purpose

"I have tested you in the furnace of affliction."
ISAIAH 48:10 NASB

As having an absolute power over the heart of man, God moves all the springs of the heart at His pleasure. In some instances, He causes those whom it pleases Him to go on from strength to strength, even till they "perfect holiness," with scarcely any heaviness at all. But these cases are rare. God generally sees good to try acceptable men and women in the furnace of affliction.

Therefore, manifold temptations and heaviness, more or less, are usually the portion of His dearest children. Indeed, almost all the children of God experience this, in a higher or lower degree.

We ought, doubtless, to watch and pray and use our utmost endeavors to avoid falling into darkness. But we need not care so much how to *avoid* heaviness as how to *improve* ourselves when it comes. Let us be careful to wait upon the Lord so that heaviness may accomplish the end for which He has permitted it—that our faith may be increased, our hope confirmed, unholy tempers purged away, and our love perfected.

Let us earnestly work together with Him, by the grace which He is continually giving us, in "purifying ourselves from all pollution, both of flesh and of spirit." And by daily growing in the grace of our Lord Jesus Christ, till we are received into His everlasting kingdom!

Your Father Knows

> *"Your Father knows what you need*
> *before you ask Him."*
> MATTHEW 6:8 NASB

In His words just before those above cited, our Lord had been advising against *vain repetition*. Repeating any words without meaning them is certainly vain repetition. Therefore, we should be extremely careful in all our prayers to mean what we say and to say only what we mean from the bottom of our hearts. The vain and heathenish repetitions which we are here warned against are most dangerous, yet very common. This is a principal cause why so many who still profess religion are a disgrace to it. Indeed, all the words in the world are not equivalent to one holy desire. And the very best prayers are but vain repetitions if they are not the language of the heart.

And *your Father knows what things you have need of.* We do not pray to inform God of our wants. Omniscient as He is, He cannot be informed of anything which He did not know before. And He is always willing to relieve our needs. The chief thing lacking is a suitable disposition on our part to receive His grace and blessing. Consequently, one great purpose of prayer is to produce such a disposition in us, to exercise our dependence on God, to increase our desire of the things we ask for, and to make us so sensible of our needs that we never cease wrestling till we have prevailed for the blessing (see Genesis 32:24–30).

This Is the Way

"Pray, then, in this way."
MATTHEW 6:9 NASB

He who best knew what we ought to pray for and how we ought to pray, what matter of desire, what manner of address would most please Himself and best become us, has here dictated to us a most perfect and universal form of prayer. It comprehends all our real wants, expresses all our lawful desires—a complete directory and full exercise of all our devotions. He here directs us to pray *thus*—for these things; sometimes, in these words. At least in this manner: short, close, full.

This prayer consists of three parts—the preface, the petitions, and the conclusion. The preface, *Our Father who art in heaven,* lays a general foundation for prayer. It comprises what we must first know of God before we can pray in confidence of being heard. It likewise points out to us the faith, humility, and love of God and man with which we are to approach God in prayer.

Our Father—who art good and gracious to all, our Creator, our preserver; the Father of our Lord and of us in Him, Your children by adoption and grace. Not *my* Father only, but the Father of the universe, of angels and human beings. *Who art in heaven*—filling heaven and earth and beholding all things in heaven and earth; knowing every creature and all their works, and every possible event from everlasting to everlasting. The Almighty Lord and ruler of all, superintending and disposing all things.

Daily Bread: Food and Grace

> "Give us today our daily bread."
> MATTHEW 6:11 NIV

The second portion of this prayer consists of six *petitions*, four of which we here consider: *Hallowed be Thy name*—May You, O Father, be truly known by all intelligent beings and with affections suitable to that knowledge! May You be duly honored, loved, feared, by all in heaven and in earth, by all angels and all men!

Thy kingdom come—May Your kingdom come quickly and swallow up all the kingdoms of the earth! May all people receive You, O Christ, for their King and truly believe in Your name. May they be filled with righteousness, peace, joy, holiness, and happiness till they are removed into Your kingdom of glory to reign with You forever.

Thy will be done on earth, as it is in heaven—May all inhabitants of the earth do Your will as willingly as the holy angels! May these do it continually even as they, without any interruption of their willing service. And, as perfectly as they! O Spirit of grace, through the blood of the everlasting covenant, make them perfect in every good work to do Your will, and work in them all that is well pleasing in Your sight!

Give us, O Father (for we claim nothing of right; only of Your free mercy) *today* (for we take no thought for tomorrow) *our daily bread*—all things needful for our souls and bodies, not only the meat that perishes, but the sacramental bread, and Your grace, the food which endures to everlasting life.

Thine Is the Kingdom

*"The kingdom and the power
and the glory, forever. Amen."*
MATTHEW 6:13 NASB

Two final petitions: *And forgive us our debts, as we also forgive
our debtors*—Give us, O Lord, redemption in Your blood, the
forgiveness of sins. As You enable us freely and fully to forgive,
so forgive us all our trespasses.

And lead us not into temptation, but deliver us from evil—
Whenever we are tempted, O Lord who helps our infirmities,
do not allow us to be overcome or suffer loss by it, but make a
way for us to escape so that we may be more than conquerors,
through Your love, over all sin and the consequences of it.

The principal desire of a Christian's heart is the glory of
God (vv. 9–10); and all one wants for himself or others is the
"daily bread" of soul and body, pardon of sin, and deliverance
from the power of it and of the devil (vv. 11–13). There is
nothing besides that a Christian can wish for. Therefore, this
prayer comprehends all his or her desires. Eternal life is the certain consequence, or rather completion, of holiness.

The conclusion: *For Thine is the kingdom*—The sovereign
right of all things that are or ever were created. *The power*—
The executive power, whereby You govern all things in Your
everlasting kingdom. *And the glory*—The praise due from
every creature for Your power, all Your wondrous works, and
the mightiness of Your kingdom, which endures through all
ages, even *forever. Amen.*

"Be Ye Perfect..."

"You are to be perfect,
as your heavenly Father is perfect."
MATTHEW 5:48 NASB

There is scarcely any expression in the Holy Scripture which has given more offense than the word *perfect*. The very sound of it is an abomination to many. And whoever *preaches perfection* (as the phrase is)—that is, asserts that it is attainable in this life—runs great hazard of being accounted worse than a heathen or a cheat.

Hence, some have advised wholly to lay aside the use of those expressions, "because they have given so great offense." But are they not found in the Word of God? If so, by what authority can any messenger of God lay them aside, even though all men and women should be offended?

We have not so learned Christ. Neither may we thus give place to the devil. Whatever God has spoken, that we will speak, whether men will hear or whether they will not. We know that then alone can any minister of Christ be "pure from the blood of all men." Only when he has "not shunned to declare" to them the whole "counsel of God" (Acts 20:26–27 KJV).

We may not, therefore, lay these expressions aside. They are the words of God and not of man. But we may and ought to explain the meaning of them—so that those who are sincere of heart may not err to the right hand or left. That they may not miss the mark of the prize of their high calling.

Not Perfectly Perfect, Yet

Not that I. . .have already become perfect.
PHILIPPIANS 3:12 NASB

Explaining the meaning of these expressions regarding *perfection* is needful; the more so, because, in the verse above cited, the apostle speaks of himself as not perfect. And yet immediately after, in the fifteenth verse, he speaks of himself and many others *as perfect:* "Let us therefore, as many as be perfect, be thus minded" (KJV).

To remove the difficulty arising from this seeming contradiction, to give light to those pressing forward to the mark, and that those who are lame be not turned out of the way, I shall endeavor to show in what sense Christians *are not,* and in what sense they *are, perfect.*

They are not perfect in knowledge; that is, they are not free from *ignorance.* Nor, secondly, from *mistake*—an almost unavoidable consequence of ignorance. It is true, the children of God do not mistake as to the things essential to salvation. But in things unessential to salvation they do err, and that frequently.

Thirdly, they are not so perfect as to be free from *infirmities.* But let us take care to understand this aright. By it I mean not only those properly termed *bodily infirmities,* but all those inward and outward imperfections which are *not of a moral nature*—such as slowness of understanding, and a poor memory.

Nor can we expect, in this life, to be wholly free from *temptation.* Such perfection does not belong to this earth.

Not Free from Ignorance

For who has known the mind of the Lord?
ROMANS 11:34 NASB

From both experience and Scripture it appears that Christians are *not so* perfect in this life as to be free from ignorance. They may know many things relating to the present world. They know, of the world to come, the general truths which God has revealed. They know things that the natural, unconverted, person does not know—that manner of love with which the Father has loved them that they should be called the children of God. They know the mighty working of His Spirit in their hearts, the wisdom of His providence directing their paths and causing all things to work together for their good. They know how to keep a conscience void of offense toward God and toward others.

But innumerable are the things which they do not know. Touching the Almighty Himself, they cannot search Him out to perfection, nor any one attribute or circumstance of the divine nature. It is not for them to know the times and the seasons when God will work His great works on the earth; nor when the heavens shall pass away, and the elements melt with a fervent heat.

They do not know the reasons of many of His present dispensations with humanity. With regard to His dealings with themselves, they often know little or nothing. How little do they know of His visible works. Or how He unites the parts of this vast universe by a secret chain which cannot be broken! So great is the ignorance, so very little the knowledge, of even the best of men and women.

Not Free from Mistake

*Teach a righteous man
and he will increase his learning.*
PROVERBS 9:9 NASB

No one is so perfect in this life as to be free from ignorance. Nor, secondly, from mistake, which is almost an unavoidable consequence of ignorance. Those who know but in part are ever liable to err touching the things they know not. True, as to the things essential to salvation, the children of God do not err. They do not put darkness for light or light for darkness. Nor do they seek death in the error of their ways, for they are taught of God. And the way which He teaches them, the way of holiness, is so plain that the wayfaring man, though a fool, need not err therein (see Isaiah 35:8). But in things nonessential to salvation, they frequently do err.

The best and wisest are frequently mistaken even with regard to facts or to the circumstances, believing them to have been different than they were. Hence arise still further mistakes.

Thus they judge not according to truth, because of their error regarding the facts or circumstances. Hence, also, they may judge not according to truth in regard to the characters of men and women. Not only by supposing good ones to be better, or wicked ones to be worse, than they are. But also by believing to be good those who are very wicked. Or perhaps believing some to have been, or to be, wicked, who were, or are, holy and unreprovable.

Still Liable to Err

Little children, let no one deceive you.
1 JOHN 3:7 NKJV

As careful as they are to avoid it, the best of men are liable to mistake even with regard to the Holy Scriptures. They do mistake daily, especially with regard to those parts which less immediately relate to practice. Hence, even the children of God are not agreed as to the interpretation of many places in the Holy Word. Nor is their difference of opinion any proof that they are not the children of God on either side. But it is a proof that we are no more to expect any living person to be infallible than to be omniscient.

It has been objected that St. John says to his brothers and sisters in the faith, *You have an anointing from the Holy One, and you know all things* (1 John 2:20 NKJV). The answer is plain: "You know all things needful for your souls' health." That St. John never designed to extend this further, that he could not speak it in an absolute sense, is clear. Otherwise, he would describe the disciple as being above his Master, seeing Christ Himself, as man, did not know all things. ("Of that. . . hour," said Jesus, "no one knows. . .but only the Father"— Mark 13:32 NKJV.) It is clear from the apostle's own words (1 John 2:26 NKJV): "These things I have written to you concerning those who try to deceive you," and his often-repeated caution, "Let no man deceive you" (1 John 3:7 KJV). This had been altogether needless had not the very ones who had that anointing from the Holy One been liable not only to ignorance, but also to mistake.

Not Free from Infirmities

*"Yet man is born to trouble as surely as
sparks fly upward."*
JOB 5:7 NIV

Christians are *not so* perfect as to be free either from ignorance
or error. Nor, thirdly, from infirmities. Only let us take care to
understand this word aright. Let us not give that soft title to
known sins, as some do. So, one man tells us, "Every man has
his infirmity, and mine is drunkenness." Another has the
"infirmity" of uncleanness; another of taking God's holy name
in vain. Yet another has the "infirmity" of returning reviling for
reviling. It is plain that all who thus speak—if they do not
repent—shall, with their infirmities, go quickly into hell!

By this term I mean not only those which are properly
termed *bodily infirmities* but all those inward or outward
imperfections which are not of a moral nature. Such are weakness or slowness of understanding, dullness or confusedness of
apprehension, incoherence of thought, irregular quickness, or
heaviness of imagination. Such also is the lack of a ready or
retentive memory.

Such, in another kind, are those which are commonly, in
some measure, consequent upon these. Namely, slowness of
speech, impropriety of language, ungracefulness of pronuncia-
tion—or a thousand nameless defects in either conversation or
behavior which are found in the best of us, in a larger or smaller
proportion. And from these no one can hope to be perfectly
freed till the spirit returns to God who gave it.

Not Free from Temptation

[Jesus] was in the desert forty days,
being tempted by Satan.
MARK 1:13 NIV

Until our spirits return to God, Christians cannot expect to be wholly free from temptation. Such perfection does not belong to this life. It is true, there are those who have been "given up" to work all uncleanness, who scarce perceive the temptations which they do not resist. Therefore, they seem to be without temptation. There are also many whom the wise enemy of souls sees fast asleep in the dead form of godliness. These he will not tempt to gross sin, lest they should awake before they drop into everlasting burnings.

I know there are children of God who, being now justified freely, having found redemption in the blood of Christ, feel no temptation for the present. God has said to their enemies, " 'Do not touch My anointed ones, and do My prophets no harm' " (see 1 Chronicles 16:22 NKJV). And for this season, it may be for weeks or months, He causes them to ride on high places. He bears them as on eagles' wings above all the fiery darts of the wicked one. But this state will not last always, as we may learn from considering the life of our Lord. The Son of God Himself, in the days of His flesh, was tempted even to the end of His life. Therefore, so let His servant expect to be, for it is enough that he be as his Master (see Matthew 10:24–25).

Stages in the Christian Life

I write to you, little children. . .
fathers. . .young men.
1 JOHN 2:12–13 NKJV

Christian perfection does not imply, as some seem to have imagined, an exemption either from ignorance, mistake, infirmities, or temptation. Indeed, it is only another term for *holiness.* Thus, everyone that is holy is, in the scriptural sense, perfect. Yet, we may observe that neither in this respect is there any absolute perfection on earth. *There is no perfection of degrees*—none which does not admit of a continual increase. How much soever anyone has attained, or in how high a degree soever he or she is perfect, they still have need to *grow in grace* and daily advance in the knowledge and love of God our Savior.

In what sense, then, *are* Christians perfect? First, it should be premised that there are several stages in Christian life, as in natural. Some of the children of God are but newborn babes; others have attained more maturity.

Accordingly, in his First Epistle (vv. 12–14 NKJV), St. John applies himself severally to those he terms *little children,* those he styles *young men,* and those he entitles *fathers.* "Little children. . .your sins are forgiven you. . . young men. . .you have overcome the wicked one. . .fathers. . .you have known Him who is from the beginning." These "fathers" knew the Father, Son, and Holy Spirit in their inmost souls, "perfect men," grown up "to the measure of the stature of the fullness of Christ" (Ephesians 4:13).

Not to Commit Sin

To the law and to the testimony!
If they do not speak according to this word,
they have no light of dawn.

ISAIAH 8:20 NIV

"I write to you little children," says St. John, "because your sins are forgiven." Because thus far you have attained; being justified freely, you have peace with God through Jesus Christ. "I write to you, young men, because you have overcome the wicked one" or as he afterwards adds, "because you are strong, and the word of God abides in you." You have quenched the fiery darts of the wicked one, the doubts and fears which disturbed your first peace. And the witness of God that your sins are forgiven now abides in your heart. "I write to you, fathers, because you have known Him who is from the beginning"— known the Father, the Son, and the Holy Spirit in your inmost soul. You are "perfect men," being grown up to the measure of the stature of the fullness of Christ.

It is of fathers that I now speak chiefly, for these only are perfect Christians. But even babes in Christ are in such a sense perfect, or born of God (an expression also taken in various senses) as, first, *not to commit sin*. If anyone doubt of this privilege of the children of God, the question is not to be decided by abstract reasonings which may be drawn out endlessly, leaving the point just as it was. Nor is it to be determined by the experience of this or that person. To the law and the testimony we appeal. By His Word will we abide, and that alone.

Free from Outward Sin

We died to sin;
how can we live in it any longer?
ROMANS 6:2 NIV

The experience of individuals determines nothing, either way. "Let God be true and every man a liar." By His Word we abide; by that alone we ought to be judged. Now the Word of God plainly declares that even those who are justified—born again in the lowest sense—do not continue in sin, cannot live any longer in it (Romans 6:1–2). They are planted together in the likeness of the death of Christ (v. 5). Their old man is crucified with Him, the body of sin being destroyed; henceforth, they do not serve sin. Being dead with Christ, they are free from sin (vv. 6–7). They are dead to sin and alive to God (v. 11). Sin has no more dominion over them who are not under the law but under grace. These, being *free from sin,* are become the servants of righteousness (vv. 14, 18).

The very least which can be inferred from these words is that the persons spoken of here, namely, all real Christians, believers in Christ, are made *free from outward sin.* The same freedom, which St. Paul expresses in a variety of phrases, St. Peter expresses in one: *"He who has suffered in the flesh has ceased from sin"* (1 Peter 4:1–2 NKJV)—no longer living to the desires of men but to the will of God. This *ceasing from sin,* interpreted in the lowest sense—as regarding only the outward behavior—must denote ceasing from the outward act, from any outward transgression, from *committing sin.*

What St. John Says

We know that anyone born of God
does not continue to sin.

1 JOHN 5:18 NIV

Most express of all Scriptures on this subject are the well-known words of St. John in the third chapter of his First Epistle, verse eight, etc.: *He who sins is of the devil, for the devil has sinned from the beginning. For this purpose the Son of God was manifested, that He might destroy the works of the devil. Whoever has been born of God does not sin, for His seed remains in him; and he cannot sin, because he has been born of God.* And those words from chapter five, verse eighteen: *We know that whoever is born of God does not sin; but he who has been born of God keeps himself, and the wicked one does not touch him* (NKJV).

Indeed, it is said this means only that he does not sin *willfully;* or he does not commit sin *habitually;* or *not as other men do;* or *not as he did before.* But by whom is this said? by St. John? No! There is no such word in the text; nor in the whole chapter; nor in all his Epistle; nor in any part of his writings whatever. Why, then, the best way to answer a bold assertion is simply to deny it. And if anyone can prove it from the Word of God, let him bring forth his strong reasons.

And a *sort* of reason has been frequently brought to support these strange assertions, drawn from examples recorded in the Word of God. They cite Abraham, Moses, and David, "the man after God's own heart." And these we will consider directly.

Greater than John the Baptist

"Yet he who is least in the kingdom of heaven
is greater than [John the Baptist]."
MATTHEW 11:11 NIV

"What!" say some, "did not Abraham commit sin—prevaricating and denying his wife? Did not Moses commit sin, when he provoked God at the waters of strife? Indeed, to produce one for all, did not even David, the man after God's own heart, commit sin in the matter of Uriah the Hittite, even murder and adultery?"

It is most sure he did. All this is true. But what would you infer from it? It may be granted, first, that David, in the general course of his life, was one of the holiest men among the Jews. Secondly, that the holiest men among the Jews did sometimes commit sin. But if you would infer from this that all Christians do and *must* commit sin as long as they live—this consequence we utterly deny. It will never follow from these premises.

Consider the declaration of our Lord, above cited. "Among those born of women, there has not risen a greater than John the Baptist. Notwithstanding, *he that is least in the kingdom of heaven is greater than he.*" I fear there are some who have imagined "the kingdom of heaven" to mean the kingdom of glory, as if the Son of God had just revealed that the least glorified saint in heaven is greater than anyone on earth! No; the kingdom of heaven here mentioned is the kingdom of God on earth to which all true believers in Christ belong! We cannot measure their privileges by those which had been once given to the Jews.

A More Glorious Ministry

*How much more glorious is the ministry
that brings righteousness!*
2 CORINTHIANS 3:9 NIV

By saying that John the Baptist was the greatest "born of women" and that the least in the kingdom of heaven is greater than John, our Lord declares two things: First, that before His coming in the flesh, among all the children of men there had been no one greater than John the Baptist. It evidently follows that neither Abraham, Moses, nor David, nor any Jew was greater than John. Our Lord, secondly, declares that one who is least in the kingdom of God (in that kingdom which He came to set up on earth) is greater than John. Not a greater prophet— as some have interpreted the word, for this is obviously false in fact. But greater in the grace of God and the knowledge of our Lord Jesus Christ. Therefore, *we cannot measure the privileges of real Christians by those formerly given to the Jews.*

Their ministration, or dispensation, we allow, was glorious. But ours *exceeds in glory* (see 2 Corinthians 3:7–11). So that whoever would bring down the Christian dispensation to the Jewish standard, whoever gleans up the examples of weakness recorded in the Law and the Prophets and thence infers that they who have "put on Christ" are endued with no greater strength, do greatly err, neither knowing the Scriptures nor the power of God.

Many have twisted various Scriptures to "prove" the same error. But a close examination shows the truth to be otherwise.

Until the Son of God Appeared

*The reason the Son of God appeared was
to destroy the devil's work.*
1 JOHN 3:8 NIV

"Does not the Scripture," some ask, "say expressly, *Even a just
man sins seven times a day?*" I answer, No. The Scripture says
no such thing. We do read, "A just man falleth seven times,
and riseth up again" (Proverbs 24:16 KJV). The words "a day"
are not in the text; further, there is no mention of *falling into
sin.* What is mentioned is *falling into temporal affliction,* as
appears from the next words: "But the wicked shall fall into
mischief." As if he had said, *God will deliver the just out of trouble, but when you fall, there shall be none to deliver you.*

"But," they say, "Solomon asserts: *There is no man that
sinneth not,* and *There is not a just man upon earth that does
good and sins not.*" I answer, Without doubt it was thus in the
days of Solomon. Indeed, it was so from Adam to Moses,
from Moses to Solomon, and from Solomon to Christ. From
the day sin entered the world, there was not a just man who
did good and did not sin, *until the Son of God was manifested
to take away our sins.*

Now, the heir, as long as he is a child, is no different from
a servant (see Galatians 4:1). So were all the holy men of old
under the Jewish dispensation. But when the fullness of time
had come, God sent forth His Son that they might receive the
adoption of sons—that grace manifested by the appearing of
our Savior. And since the gospel was given, *he that is born of
God does not sin.*

When Pentecost Was Fully Come

Our Savior Christ Jesus. . .
abolished death and brought life and
immortality to light through the gospel.
2 TIMOTHY 1:10 NASB

It is of great importance to carefully observe the wide difference there is between the Jewish and the Christian dispensation. The ground of this the apostle John assigns in the seventh chapter of his Gospel (vv. 38–39). He relates those words of our blessed Lord, " 'He who believes in Me, as the Scripture has said, out of his heart will flow rivers of living water.' " He immediately adds, "This He spoke concerning the Spirit, whom those believing in Him would [afterwards] receive; for the Holy Spirit was not yet given, because Jesus was not yet glorified" (NKJV).

Now the apostle cannot mean here—as some have taught—that the miracle-working power of the Holy Spirit was not yet given. For this *was* given; our Lord had given it to all the apostles when He first sent them to preach the gospel. He gave them power over unclean spirits to cast them out, power to heal the sick, and power to raise the dead. But the Holy Spirit was not yet given in His *sanctifying graces,* as He was after Jesus was glorified. It was then that Christ ascended up on high and led captivity captive, receiving gifts for even the rebellious—that the Lord God might dwell among them (see Psalm 68:18). And when the day of Pentecost was fully come, those who had waited for the promise of the Father were made more than conquerors over sin by the Holy Spirit then given unto them.

The Great Salvation

*Fix your hope completely on the grace to be brought
to you at the revelation of Jesus Christ.*
1 PETER 1:13 NASB

That the great salvation from sin was not given until Jesus was glorified, St. Peter also testifies. He speaks of his brethren in the flesh as *now* receiving the goal of their faith, the salvation of their souls, and adds (vv. 10–12 NKJV): *Of this salvation the prophets have inquired and searched carefully, who prophesied of the grace* (the gracious dispensation) *that would come to you, searching what, or what manner of time, the Spirit of Christ who was in them was indicating when He testified beforehand the sufferings of Christ and the glories* (the glorious salvation) *that would follow. To them it was revealed that, not to themselves, but to us they were ministering the things which now have been reported to you through those who have preached the gospel to you by the Holy Spirit sent from heaven;* namely, at the day of Pentecost and so to all generations, into the hearts of all true believers. On the ground of the grace brought to them by the revelation of Jesus Christ, the apostle adds this strong exhortation, "Prepare your minds for action. . . like the Holy One who called you, be holy yourselves also in all your behavior" (vv. 13, 15 NASB).

Those who have duly considered these things must allow that privileges of Christians are in no way to be measured by Old Testament accounts of those under the Jewish covenant. The fullness of time is *now* come; the Holy Spirit *is* given; the great salvation of God *is brought to men* by the revelation of Jesus Christ, the Son of God, in the flesh.

Unsound Inferences

Whoever abides in Him does not sin.
1 JOHN 3:6 NKJV

With the revelation of Jesus Christ (in the flesh), the kingdom of heaven is now set up on earth. Therefore, if any would prove that the apostle's words, above, are not to be understood in the plain, obvious meaning, it is from the New Testament they must bring proofs.

The first thing usually offered is taken from the apostles. "Did not," it is said, "even the greatest of them commit sin? St. Paul by his sharp contention with Barnabas, and St. Peter by his dissimulation at Antioch?" Well, suppose both Peter and Paul *did* then commit sin; what would you infer from such? That all the other apostles committed sin sometimes? There is no shadow of proof in this. Or would you infer that all the other Christians of the apostolic age committed sin? Worse and worse. This is such an inference as is not sensible. Or will you argue that if two of the apostles did once commit sin, then all other Christians, in all ages, do and will commit sin as long as they live? Alas! A child of common understanding would be ashamed of such reasoning. Least of all can you reasonably infer that anyone *must* commit sin at all. God forbid we should thus speak! No *necessity* of sinning was laid upon them. The grace of God was sufficient for them, as for us at this day. With the temptation which fell on them, there was yet a way to escape, just as for us. So that, whoever is tempted to any sin need not yield, for no one is tempted above what he or she is able to bear (see 1 Corinthians 10:13).

In What Do We Delight?

For Christ's sake, I delight in weaknesses. . . .
For when I am weak, then I am strong.
2 CORINTHIANS 12:10 NIV

This argument for continuing in sin is often offered: "But St. Paul besought the Lord three times and yet could not escape from his temptation." Consider his words, literally translated: *There was given to me a thorn to the flesh, an angel* (or messenger) *of Satan, to buffet me. Touching this, I besought the Lord thrice that it might depart from me. And he said unto me, My grace is sufficient for thee: For my strength is made perfect in weakness. Most gladly therefore will I rather glory in my weaknesses, that the strength of Christ may rest upon me. Therefore I take pleasure in weaknesses—for when I am weak, then am I strong.*

First, it does not appear that this thorn *occasioned* St. Paul to commit sin, much less laid him under any *necessity* to do so. So, from this it cannot be proved that any Christian *must* commit sin.

Secondly, the ancient fathers inform us St. Paul's thorn in the flesh was bodily pain. St. Cyprian expresses it: "Many and grievous torments of the flesh and of the body."

Thirdly, to this agree the apostle's own words: "A thorn to the flesh to smite, beat, or buffet me."

Fourthly, whatever it was, it could no more be inward stirrings than outward expressions of pride, anger, or lust. For would the apostle actually *glory* in any of these sins?

Believers Do Not Glory in Sin!

I will boast all the more gladly
about my weaknesses,
so that Christ's power may rest on me.
2 CORINTHIANS 12:9 NIV

That St. Paul's thorn in the flesh was not either inward or outward sin is manifest beyond all possible exception by the words above cited. He gloried in his weakness, that the strength of Christ might rest upon him. What! Did he glory in pride, or anger, or lust? Was it through *these* weaknesses that the strength of Christ rested on him? He goes on, that "when I am weak *in body* then I am strong *in spirit.*" Will anyone dare to say, "When I am weak by pride or lust, then I am strong in spirit"? Of any who find the strength of Christ resting upon them I ask, "Can you glory in anger or pride or lust? Can you take pleasure in *these* infirmities? Do *these* weaknesses make you strong? Would you not rather do anything to escape them?" Judge, then, yourselves, whether the apostle could glory and take pleasure in them!

Lastly, this thorn was given to him more than fourteen years before he wrote the epistle, which was many years before the end of his life. So that, from any spiritual weakness (if such *had* been), we could *by no means infer* that he was never made strong, that Paul the aged, the father in Christ, still labored under the same weakness.

From all this, it appears that this instance of St. Paul is quite foreign to our present question and does in no way clash with the assertion of St. John, "He that is born of God does not sin."

The Perfect Man

If anyone is never at fault. . .
he is a perfect man.
JAMES 3:2 NIV

Some people believe St. James contradicts St. John's assertion
that one who is born of God does not sin. His words are: "In
many things we offend all" (v. 2 KJV). "Is not," they say,
"offending the same as committing sin?" In this place, I allow it
is. I allow the persons here spoken of did commit sin, many
sins. But *who* are the ones spoken of? Why, those teachers
whom God had not sent *who presumed* to be teachers (v. 1;
probably the same vain men who taught the *faith without
works,* which is so sharply reproved in the preceding chapter).
Not the apostle himself, nor any real Christian.

Use of the word *we* is a figure of speech, common in
other, as well as the inspired, writers. The apostle could not
possibly include himself or any other true believer, as appears
from the same word in verse nine. With the tongue, "bless *we*
God and curse *we* men; out of the same mouth proceed blessing and cursing." True, but not out of the mouth of the apostle, nor of anyone who is in Christ a new creature. And from
the words, "knowing that *we* shall receive the greater condemnation. . .for in many things *we* offend all." *We!* Who? Not the
apostles nor any true believer, for "there is no condemnation
to those who walk not after the flesh but after the Spirit."
There immediately follows the mention of one who *does not
offend.* He is thereby contradistinguished from the one who
did offend and is pronounced *a perfect man.*

God Cleanses from Sin

If we claim to be without sin,
we deceive ourselves and the truth is not in us.
1 JOHN 1:8 NIV

How shall we reconcile St. John with himself? In one place he declares, *Whoever is born of God does not sin,* and *We know that one born of God does not sin* (3:6, 9). And yet in another place, he writes the words above cited and *If we say that we have not sinned, we make Him a liar, and His word is not in us* (1:10 NKJV).

As great a difficulty as this may first appear, it vanishes away if we observe, first, that the tenth verse fixes the sense of the eighth: *If we say we have no sin* in the former, being explained by *If we say we have not sinned* in the latter verse. Secondly, the point in the present question is not whether we have or have not sinned *before* now. And neither of these verses asserts that we do sin or commit sin *now.*

Thirdly, the ninth verse explains both the eighth and the tenth: *If we confess our sins, he is faithful and just to forgive us our sins, and to cleanse us from all unrighteousness.* As if he had said, "The blood of Jesus cleanses us from all sin; but let no one say I need it not; that I have no sin to be cleansed from. If we say we have no sin, that we have not sinned, we deceive ourselves, and make God a liar. But *if we confess our sins, he is faithful and just* not only *to forgive us our sins,* but also *to cleanse us from all unrighteousness"* that we may *go and sin no more.*

Thus Far Perfect

I write this to you so that you will not sin.
1 JOHN 2:1 NIV

St. John is well consistent with himself as well as with the other holy writers. Let us place all his assertions in one view: He declares, *first,* the blood of Jesus cleanses us from all sin. *Secondly,* no one can say, "I have not sinned; I have no sin to be cleansed from." *Thirdly,* God is ready both to forgive our past sins and to save us *from them* for the time to come. *Fourthly,* these things I write to you that you will not sin. But if anyone should sin (or *have sinned* as the word might be rendered) he need not continue in sin, seeing we have an advocate with the Father, Jesus Christ the righteous. Thus far all is clear.

But lest any doubt should remain, the apostle resumes this subject in the third chapter, explaining his own meaning. *Let no one deceive you* (as though I had given any encouragement to those who continue in sin). *He who practices righteousness is righteous. . . . He who sins is of the devil. . . . For this purpose the Son of God was manifested, that He might destroy the works of the devil. Whoever has been born of God does not sin. . . in this the children of God and the children of the devil are manifest* (vv. 7–10 NKJV).

The point, which till then might possibly have left some doubt in weak minds, is purposely settled by the last of the inspired writers, and decided in the clearest manner. In conformity to this, and to the whole tenor of the New Testament, we fix the conclusion: *A Christian is so far perfect as not to commit sin.*

As the Tree, so Is the Fruit

"Out of the heart. . .proceed the evil thoughts."
MARK 7:21 NASB

The glorious privilege of every Christian, though only a *babe in Christ,* is the freedom from *committing* sin. But it is only of those who are *strong in the Lord* (those who "have known Him who is from the beginning") that it can be affirmed they are in such a sense perfect as to be *freed from evil thoughts and evil or sinful tempers.*

First, from evil or sinful thoughts. Only let it be observed that thoughts concerning evil are not always evil thoughts. A thought concerning sin and a sinful thought are widely different. So our blessed Lord Himself doubtless thought of, or understood, the thing spoken by the devil when he said, "All these things I will give you if you will fall down and worship me." Yet He had no evil or sinful thought; nor, indeed, was He capable of any. It follows that neither have real Christians, for "everyone that is perfect shall be as his master" (Luke 6:40 KJV). Therefore, if He was free from evil or sinful thoughts, so are they likewise.

From where would evil thoughts proceed in the servant who is *as his Master?* Out of the heart (if at all) come evil thoughts. If the heart is no longer evil, then evil thoughts can no longer proceed out of it. If the tree were corrupt, so would be the fruit. But the tree is good; the fruit is good also; our Lord Himself bearing witness: "A good tree cannot bear bad fruit; and a bad tree cannot bear good fruit" (Matthew 7:17–18 NIV).

Be As Your Master

We demolish arguments. . .
and we take captive every thought
to make it obedient to Christ.
2 CORINTHIANS 10:5 NIV

From his own experience, St. Paul asserts the happy privilege of real Christians. "The weapons of our warfare are not carnal, but mighty in God. . .for casting down *reasonings*" (for so the original word signifies; all the arguments of pride and unbelief against the declarations, promises, and gifts of God), "and every high thing that exalts itself against the knowledge of God, bringing every thought into captivity to the obedience of Christ."

As Christians indeed are freed from evil thoughts, so are they, *secondly, from evil tempers,* as evidenced from the declaration of our Lord Himself: "The disciple is not above his master: but everyone that is perfect *shall be as his master*" (Luke 6:40 KJV).

Our Lord had just previously been delivering some of the sublimest doctrines of Christianity—some of the most grievous to flesh and blood. *I say unto you, Love your enemies, do good to those who hate you. . .and to him who strikes you on the one cheek, offer the other also.* Now He well knew the world would not receive these. He therefore immediately adds, "Can the blind lead the blind? shall they not both fall into the ditch? The disciple is not above his master: but every one that is perfect shall be as his master" (vv. 39–40 KJV). As if He was assuring them He would fulfill His word. The Master was free from all sinful tempers; so, therefore, is His disciple, every real Christian.

Free from Pride and Self-Will

> *"I have been crucified with Christ;*
> *and it is no longer I who live,*
> *but Christ lives in me."*
>
> GALATIANS 2:20 NASB

Every real Christian can, with St. Paul, say these (above) words, words that manifestly describe a deliverance from inward as well as from outward sin. This is expressed (KJV) both negatively: *I live not*—my evil nature, the body of sin, is destroyed—and positively: *Christ liveth in me*—therefore, all that is holy, just, and good. Indeed, both *Christ liveth in me* and *I live not* are inseparably connected. For what communion has light with darkness or Christ with Belial? (See 2 Corinthians 6:14–15.)

The One who lives in true believers has "purified their hearts by faith." Insomuch that everyone who has Christ in him the hope of glory purifies himself even as Christ is pure (1 John 3:3). He is purified from *pride,* for Christ was lowly of heart. He is pure from *self-will* or desire, for Christ desired to do only the will of His Father and to finish His work. And he is pure from *anger,* in the common sense of the word, for Christ was meek and gentle, patient, and long-suffering.

I say *in the common sense of the word,* for all anger is not evil. We read of the Lord Himself (see Mark 3:5) that He looked around with anger. But with what kind of anger? The next words show: being *grieved for the hardness of their hearts.* He had anger at the sin, at the same time, grief and sorrowful love for the offenders. Go, you that are perfect, and do likewise.

At the Time Present

Because in this world we are like him.
1 JOHN 4:17 NIV

Jesus does save His people from their sins (see Matthew 1:21). And not only from outward sins, but also from the sins of their hearts: from evil thoughts and from evil tempers. "True," say some, "we shall thus be saved from our sins; but not till death. Not in this world."

But how are we to reconcile this with the express words of St. John (above)? "Herein is our love made perfect, that we may have boldness in the day of judgment: because as he is, so are we *in this world*" (KJV). The apostle here, beyond all contradiction, speaks of himself and other living Christians—as though he had foreseen this very evasion and set himself to overturn it from the foundation. Of these he flatly affirms, that not only at or after death, but *in this world,* they are as their Master.

Exactly agreeable to this are his words in the first chapter of this Epistle (vv. 5, 9 NKJV). "God is light and in Him is no darkness at all. . . . If we walk in the light. . . we have fellowship with one another, and the blood of Jesus Christ His Son cleanses us from all sin." And again, "If we confess our sins, He is faithful and just to forgive us our sins and to cleanse us from all unrighteousness." It is evident; the apostle here also speaks of a deliverance accomplished *in this world.* For he says not the blood of Christ *will cleanse* at the hour of death, but that it *cleanses,* at the time present, *us,* living Christians, *from all sin.*

From All Unrighteousness

If we walk in the Light
as He Himself is in the light. . .
the blood of Jesus His Son cleanses us from all sin.
1 JOHN 1:7 NASB

It is evident that if *any* sin remain, we are not cleansed from *all* sin. If *any* unrighteousness remain in the soul, it is not cleansed from *all* unrighteousness. Neither let any sinner against his or her own soul say that this relates to justification only, or the cleansing us from the guilt of sin. First, because this is confounding together what the apostle clearly distinguishes. He mentions first, *to forgive us our sins;* and then, *to cleanse us from all unrighteousness.*

Secondly, because this is asserting justification by works in the strongest sense possible. It is making all inward as well as outward holiness necessarily *previous* to justification. For *if* the cleansing here spoken of is no other than the cleansing from the guilt of sin, then we are not cleansed from guilt, that is, not justified, unless on condition of "walking in the light, as He is in the light." It remains, then, that Christians are saved in this world from all sin, from all unrighteousness. They are *now* in such a sense perfect as *not to commit sin, and to be freed from evil thoughts and evil tempers.*

Thus has the Lord fulfilled the things He spoke by His holy prophets since the world began, by Moses in particular: *[I] will circumcise your heart. . .to love the LORD your God with all your heart and with all your soul* (Deuteronomy 30:6 NKJV).

From All Your Filthiness; from All Your Idols

Create in me a clean heart, O God;
and renew a right spirit within me.
PSALM 51:10 KJV

The Lord gave also by His prophet Ezekiel this most remarkable promise: " *'Then I will sprinkle clean water on you, and you shall be clean; I will cleanse you from all your filthiness and from all your idols. I will give you a new heart and put a new spirit within you. . . . I will deliver you from all your uncleannesses. . . .' Thus says the Lord GOD. . .'I [will] cleanse you from all your iniquities. . . . I, the LORD, have spoken it, and I will do it'* " (Ezekiel 36:25–36, selected NKJV).

Having therefore these promises, both in the law and the prophets, and having the prophetic word confirmed to us in the gospel by our blessed Lord and His apostles, "let us cleanse ourselves from all filthiness of the flesh and spirit, perfecting holiness in the fear of God" (2 Corinthians 7:1 NKJV). And let us fear, lest so many promises being made of entering into His rest, of ceasing from our own works, any of us should come short of that rest (see Hebrews 4:1).

This one thing let us do: Forgetting those things that are behind, and reaching forward unto those things which are before, let us press toward the mark, for the prize of the high calling of God in Christ Jesus (see Philippians 3:14). May we cry unto Him day and night, till we also are delivered from the bondage of corruption, into the glorious liberty of the sons of God.

We are Only Stewards

"There was a certain rich man who had a steward."
LUKE 16:1 NKJV

The relation which man bears to God, as creature to the Creator, is exhibited to us in the Word of God under various representations. But no character more exactly agrees with the present state of man than that of steward. Our blessed Lord frequently represents him as such, and there is a peculiar propriety in the representation. This exactly expresses our situation in the present world, specifying what kind of servant we are to God, and what kind of service our divine master expects from us.

We are indebted to God for all we have. Although a debtor is obliged to return what he has received, yet, until the time of payment comes, he is at liberty to use it as he pleases. But it is not so with a steward; he is not at liberty to use what is lodged in his hands as *he* pleases, but as *his master* pleases. For he is not the proprietor of those things but barely entrusted with them to dispose of as his master orders.

Now this is exactly the case of everyone with relation to God. We are not at liberty to use what He has lodged in our hands as *we* please, but as *He* pleases who alone is the possessor of heaven and earth, and the Lord of every creature. He entrusts us with them on the express condition that we use them only *as our Master's goods,* and according to the particular directions He has given us in His Word.

According to His Will

The Lord said,
"Who then is the faithful and sensible steward?"
LUKE 12:42 NASB

On the condition that these are His goods and that we use them according to His directions, God has entrusted us with our souls, our bodies, our possessions, and whatever other talents we have received. To impress this weighty truth on our hearts, we must come to particulars.

God has entrusted each of us with *our soul*, an immortal spirit made in His image. Likewise the powers and faculties of the soul—understanding, imagination, memory, will, and a train of affections, either included in the soul or closely dependent upon it: love and hatred, joy and sorrow, respecting present good and evil; desire and aversion, hope and fear, respecting what is to come.

Now, of all these, we are only stewards. God has entrusted us with these powers and faculties, not that we may employ them according to our own will, but according to His. In doing His will, we most effectually secure our own happiness, seeing it is only in doing His will that we can be happy, either in time or in eternity. Thus we are to use our understanding, our imagination, our memory, wholly to the glory of Him that gave them. Thus our will is to be regulated as He directs. We are to love and hate, rejoice and grieve, desire and shun, hope and fear, according to the rule which is prescribed by Him whose we are and whom we are to serve in all things.

Committed to Our Trust

You are not your own;
you were bought at a price.
Therefore honor God with your body.
1 CORINTHIANS 6:19–20 NIV

God has entrusted us with our *bodies* as well as our souls. He has entrusted us with an exquisitely wrought machine and all the powers and members of it. We have the organs of sense—sight, hearing, and the rest. But none of these are our own. None of these are lent to us in such a sense as to leave us at liberty to use them as we please even for a season! No! We have received them on the terms that we employ them all in the very manner which He appoints.

It is on the same terms that He imparted to us that most excellent talent of speech. It is given to be employed in glorifying God. It follows that there is not a word of our tongue for which we are not accountable to Him.

To Him we are equally accountable for the use of our hands, our feet, and all the members of our body. These talents are committed to our trust, until the time appointed of the Father, for us to use as stewards, not as proprietors—that we should give them as "instruments of righteousness unto God" (Romans 6:13 KJV).

Likewise has God entrusted us with a portion of *worldly goods*—with food to eat, raiment to put on, and a place to lay our heads—with not only the necessities but the conveniences of life. And all to be used as He has commanded us.

Only for a Time

He commanded his house steward.
GENESIS 44:1 NASB

There are *several talents* God has entrusted us with that are not properly under any of the preceding heads. Such is bodily strength, health, a pleasing person, an agreeable speech. Such also are learning and knowledge, in their various degrees, with all the other advantages of education. Such is the influence which we have over others, whether by their love or esteem for us; or by power—power to do them good or hurt, to help or hinder them in the circumstances of life.

Add to these, that invaluable *talent of time* with which God entrusts us from moment to moment. Add, also, that on which all the rest depend and without which they would all be curses, not blessings—*the grace of God,* the power of the Holy Spirit which alone works in us all that is acceptable in His sight.

But it is not forever, nor indeed for any considerable time, that we are the stewards of the Lord, the possessor of heaven and earth. We have this trust reposed in us only during the short, uncertain space that we sojourn here on earth, only so long as this fleeting breath is in our nostrils. The hour is swiftly approaching, it is just at hand, when we "can be no longer stewards"!

The moment the body returns to the dust and the spirit to God who gave it, we are stewards no more. The days of our stewardship are ended.

How Did We Employ His Goods?

> *"Give an account of your stewardship,*
> *for you can no longer be steward."*
>
> LUKE 16:2 NKJV

Being no longer stewards, it remains that we give an account of our stewardship. The moment a soul drops the body and stands naked before God, it cannot but know what its portion will be to all eternity. But the time when we are to give this account is when the great white throne comes down from heaven, and He that sits thereon, from whose face the heavens and the earth flee away (see Revelation 20:11). The dead, small and great, will stand before God, and the books will be opened—the book of Scripture, to those who were entrusted with it; the book of conscience, to all humanity.

The judge will then inquire, "How did you employ *your soul?* How did you employ *the body* with which I entrusted you? How did you employ *the worldly goods* which I lodged in your hands? Did you employ *your health and strength* in a vigorous pursuit of that better part which none can take away from you? Above all, were you *a good steward of my grace,* going before, accompanying, and following you? Did you duly observe and carefully improve all the influences of My Spirit? every good desire? every measure of light? all His sharp and gentle reproofs? When you were made partaker of this Spirit, did you stand fast in that liberty, all your thoughts, words, and actions in one flame of love, a holy sacrifice? Then, well done; enter into the joy of your Lord!"

How Did We Employ Our Souls?

" 'This very night your soul is required of you.' "
LUKE 12:20 NASB

To come to particulars: God, the judge of all, will ask, "How did you employ *your soul?* I entrusted you with an immortal spirit endowed with various powers and faculties—with understanding, imagination, memory, will, affections. I gave you full and express directions how all these were to be employed. Did you employ your understanding according to those directions? Namely, in the knowledge of yourself and Me? My nature and My attributes? My works? My Word? Did you employ your memory in treasuring up what would be for My glory, your salvation, and the advantage of others? Did you store up what you had learned from My Word and your experiences of My wisdom, truth, power, and mercy? Was your imagination employed in awakening your pursuit of wisdom and holiness?

"Did you follow My directions with regard to *your will?* Was it swallowed up in Mine, so as never to oppose but always run parallel with it? Your affections—did you give Me your heart? Did you not love the world, the things of the world? Was I the object of your love? Was all your desire unto Me? Was I the joy of your heart, the delight of your soul? Did you sorrow only for what grieved My Spirit? Did you fear and hate nothing but sin? Were your thoughts employed according to My will on what was pure, what was holy? on whatever was conducive to My glory, and to peace and goodwill among men?"

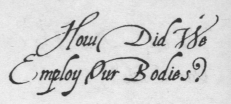

How Did We Employ Our Bodies?

You have been bought with a price: therefore glorify God in your body.
1 CORINTHIANS 6:20 NASB

To be particular still: Your Lord will ask you, "How did you employ *the body* with which I entrusted you? I gave you a tongue to praise Me. Did you use it to the purpose for which it was given? Did you employ it, not in evil or idle speaking or uncharitable and unprofitable conversations, but in such as was good, necessary, or useful either to yourself or others? such as always tended, directly or indirectly, to render grace to the hearers?

"I gave you, together with your other senses, those grand avenues of knowledge: sight and hearing. Were these employed to the excellent purposes for which they were bestowed upon you? in bringing you more instruction in righteousness and true holiness?

"I gave you hands and feet and various other bodily members to perform the works prepared for you. Were they employed in doing the will of Him who sent you into the world, merely to work out your own salvation? not in doing the will of the flesh, your evil nature, or your mind—those things to which your reason or fancy led you? Did you present *all your members*, not to sin as instruments of unrighteousness, but to Me alone, through the Son of My love, as instruments of righteousness?"

How Did We Employ Our Worldly Goods?

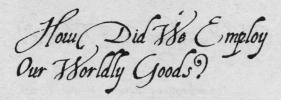

Whatever you do, do all to the glory of God.
1 CORINTHIANS 10:31 NASB

The Lord and judge of all will next inquire, "How did you employ *the worldly goods* I lodged in your hands? Did you use your food, not to seek or place your happiness in it, but to preserve the body in health, in strength and vigor, a fit instrument for your soul? Did you use clothing, not to nourish pride or vanity, much less to tempt others to sin, but to conveniently and decently defend yourself from the injuries of the weather? Did you prepare and use your house and all other conveniences with a single eye to My glory, studying to please, not yourself, but Me?"

Once more: "In what manner did you employ *that talent, money?* not in gratifying the desire of the flesh, of the eye or the pride of life? not in vain expenses, not hoarding it up to leave behind? but first supplying your needs and your family's and restoring the remainder to Me through the poor, whom I had appointed to receive it? I gave you the right to be supplied first, and the blessedness of giving rather than receiving. Were you accordingly a general benefactor to others? feeding the hungry, clothing the naked, comforting the sick, assisting the stranger, relieving the afflicted according to their various necessities—eyes to the blind and feet to the lame? a father to the fatherless, and a husband to the widow? And did you labor to improve all outward works of mercy as means of saving souls from death?"

What About Our Talents?

"To one he gave five talents, to another, two, and to another, one, each according to his own ability."
MATTHEW 25:15 NASB

Your Lord will further inquire, "Have you been a wise and faithful steward with *the talents of a mixed nature* which I lent you? Did you employ your health and strength, not in folly or sin, not in pleasures which perished with the using, not in making provision for the flesh to fulfill the desires of it but in a vigorous pursuit of that better part which none could take away from you? Did you employ what was pleasing in your person or speech, whatever advantages you had by education, learning, and knowledge, for promoting virtue in the world and enlarging My kingdom? Did you employ your share of power or influence over others, by the love and esteem they had, for the increase of their wisdom and holiness? Did you employ *the talent of time* with wariness and circumspection, as duly weighing the value of every moment and knowing all were numbered in eternity?

"Above all, were you a good steward of My grace? How did you profit by the spirit of bondage and fear which was previous to the Spirit of adoption? And when you were made a partaker of this Spirit, crying in your heart, *Abba, Father,* did you stand fast in the liberty in which I made you free? Did you from that time present your soul and body, all your thoughts, words and actions, in one flame of love, glorifying Me with your body and your spirit? If so, well done! Enter into the joy of your Lord!"

Have We Been Faithful in All?

"The Son of Man. . .
will reward each person according to
what he has done."
MATTHEW 16:27 NIV

After the account has been rendered, what will remain, either to the faithful or to the unfaithful steward? *Nothing but the execution of that sentence* which has been passed by the righteous judge, fixing you in a state which admits of no change through everlasting ages—rewarded all eternity according to your works.

From these plain considerations *we may learn, first,* how important is this short, uncertain day of life! How deeply it concerns every one of us to let none of these run to waste, but to improve them to the noblest purposes as long as the breath of God is in our nostrils!

We learn, *secondly,* that there is no employment of our time, no action or conversation, that is purely indifferent. These either *are* or *are not* employed according to His will. If they are so employed, all is good; if they are not, all is evil. Again, it is His will that we should continually grow in grace and in the living knowledge of our Lord Jesus Christ. Every thought, word, and work whereby this knowledge is increased and by which we grow in grace is good; if not, it is truly and properly evil.

We learn, *thirdly,* there are no works of supererogation. *We can never do more* than our duty. Seeing *everything* is from Him, everything is His due. If we pay Him less than all, we cannot be faithful stewards.

To the Utmost of Our Power

> Each will receive his own reward
> according to his own labor.
>
> 1 CORINTHIANS 3:8 NASB

Considering the above words, we cannot be *wise* stewards unless we labor to the utmost of our power. We must put forth *all* our strength, not leaving anything undone which we possibly can do.

The least of these a serious care demands;
For though they're little, they are golden sands!

Who are the understanding persons? Let them show the wisdom from above by walking suitably to their character. If any account themselves stewards of the manifold gifts of God, let them see that all their thoughts, words, and works be agreeable to the post God has assigned them.

It is no small thing to lay out for God all which you have received from God. It requires all your wisdom, all your resolution, all your patience and constancy—far more than you ever had by nature, but not more than you may have by grace. For His grace is sufficient for you, and all things are possible to him that believeth.

By faith, then, "put on the Lord Jesus Christ." Put on the *whole armor* of God. Thus you shall be able to glorify Him in all your words and works. Indeed, to bring *every* thought into captivity to the obedience of Christ.

Sources of Readings, by Date

Individual readings are excerpts as noted from:

John Wesley, M.A., *Explanatory Notes Upon the New Testament*, (London: Epworth Press, 1976 ed).

Consecutive thematic readings are, in general, selected from sermons found in:

John Wesley, M.A., *Forty-Four Sermons*, (London: Epworth Press, 1958 ed).

A few selections are taken from:

The Works of John Wesley. (Salem, Ohio: Schmul Publishers, 1978). Vol. 5, 6, or 7, as indicated.

January 1–18: Sermon I: Salvation by Faith.

January 19: from *Explanatory Notes,* Matthew 3:2; 4:17, and 5:3.

January 20–23: from *Explanatory Notes,* on the Parable of the Sower.

January 24–February 7: Sermon VII: The Way to the Kingdom.

February 8–10: from *Explanatory Notes,* on the Parable of the Prodigal Son.

February 11–March 7: Sermon XII: The Means of Grace.

March 8: from *Explanatory Notes,* various verses on repentance.

March 9–21: Sermon XXVI: Sermon on the Mount, discourse xi: Enter by the Narrow Gate.

March 22–23: from *Explanatory Notes,* Matthew 16:24.

March 24–April 8: Sermon XXVIII: Sermon on the Mount, discourse xiii: Not everyone Who Says, "Lord, Lord. . ."

April 9: from *Explanatory Notes,* Romans 8:5–6.

April 10: from *Explanatory Notes,* 1 Corinthians 2:14–15.

April 11–21: Sermon II: The Almost Christian.

April 22: from *Explanatory Notes,* Matthew 18:3.

April 23–May 9: Sermon XXXIX: The New Birth.

May 10–22: Sermon X: The Witness of the Spirit.

May 23: from *Explanatory Notes,* various verses on New Testament grace.

May 24–25: from *Explanatory Notes,* 2 Peter 3:18.

May 26–30: from *Explanatory Notes,* Ephesians 6:10–18.

May 31–June 10: Sermon LXXXIX from *Works,* Vol. 7: The More Excellent Way.

June 11–25: Sermon XIV: The Marks of the New Birth.

June 26–27: from *Explanatory Notes,* 1 Thessalonians 5:16–19 and 23–24.

June 28: from *Explanatory Notes,* Colossians 3:5; Romans 8:13.

June 29–July 14: Sermon XIV from *Works,* Vol. 5: The Repentance of Believers.

July 15: from *Explanatory Notes,* Hebrews 9:14.

July 16: from *Explanatory Notes,* 2 Peter 1:2.

July 17–18: from *Explanatory Notes,* 2 Peter 1:5–8.

July 19–27: Sermon LXII, from *Works,* Vol. 6: The End of Christ's Coming.

July 28–August 9: Sermon XXXVII: Satan's Devices.

August 10–11: from *Explanatory Notes,* Luke 12:27–32; Matthew 6:25–31.

August 12–23: Sermon XV: The Great Privilege of Those That Are Born of God.

August 24: from *Explanatory Notes,* various verses on faith.

August 25–September 7: Sermon XXXI: The Law Established Through Faith.

September 8–13: Sermon XCIV from *Works,* Vol. 7: On Family Religion.

September 14–27: Sermon XLII: Self–Denial.

September 28–October 12: Sermon XIII: The Circumcision of the Heart.

October 13–25: Sermon XLIII: The Cure of Evil–Speaking.

October 26–November 4: Sermon XL: The Wilderness State.

November 5–18: Sermon XLI: Heaviness Through Manifold Temptations.

November 19–22: from *Explanatory Notes,* Matthew 6:7–13.

November 23–December 20: Sermon XXXV: Christian Perfection.

December 21–31: Sermon LI from *Works,* Vol. 6: The Good Steward.

Scripture Index